LINCOLN
EMPOWERED

Parent & Teacher Guide

This Parent and Teacher Guide is designed to help you support your student's learning. The information presented in this guide is based on the course content at the time of printing. Occasionally, the online version of your course may change slightly, but the tips in the Parent and Teacher Guide are designed to broadly cover the course's content.

This guide is arranged in lesson order. You will find everything you need for each day of the school year.

LINCOLN
LEARNING
SOLUTIONS

Course Introduction

Welcome to English Language Arts 4

Introduction

Welcome to English Language Arts 4, by Lincoln Empowered™. In this course, students will continue to expand their **reading**, **writing**, **spelling**, **speaking**, and **listening** skills. This year brings incredible developments in writing skills for fourth graders. Last year, students solidified their reading skills and began reading to learn. This year, students will solidify their writing skills, and their writing will take on new meaning as they develop the skills to express themselves in new and exciting ways. In addition to presenting ideas through writing, students will develop multimedia presentations and express their ideas orally with clarity and confidence.

The purpose of this Parent and Teacher Guide is to aid you as you help your student on the path to success. This guide contains an overview of the course content, an introduction to navigating the course online, course expectations, and useful teaching tips and suggestions.

Course at a Glance

Please guide your student to watch the brief welcome video for their course, which can be found just before the Lesson 1 folder. This engaging video is intended to excite your student and kickstart their learning. It will introduce your student to Ms. Grace, who will guide them on a quick journey through some major topics covered in the course. As your student progresses, Ms. Grace may return to provide encouragement or to simply add a personal touch.

Course Introduction

End of the Year Expectations for English Language Arts 4

By the end of the year, and in order to be fifth grade ready, your student will have mastered the following concepts:

Phonics and Word Recognition	The ability to use the knowledge of letter-sound correspondences, syllabification, patterns, and morphology to read unfamiliar multisyllable words accurately
Vocabulary	The ability to acquire and use a variety of grade-level appropriate words and phrases in conversation and in writing, including words that indicate precise actions, emotions, or states of being; the ability to use connecting words and phrases; the ability to use a variety of reading strategies to determine and clarify the meaning of words and phrases with unknown and multiple meanings, including figurative language in grade-level appropriate texts
Spelling	The ability to correctly spell grade-level appropriate words with the suffixes -ar, -ed, -er, -est, -ing, -al, -ly, -ful, -able, -ible, -al, -y, -ness, -ist, -less, and -or; words with the prefixes in- un-, re-, dis-, mis-, im-, pre-, and non-; words ending in ch and sh; words with Greek roots; homophones; possessives; compound words; words with silent letters; words with th, ph, wh, tch, dge, gh, gu, and eigh; contractions; words with soft c and soft g; words with double consonants; words with short and long vowel sounds; and irregular plural nouns
Reading	The ability to read, understand, and analyze grade-level appropriate texts, including literary fiction, nonfiction, and informational texts, independently with accuracy and ease, silently and aloud; the ability to read aloud at a natural pace, using expression and intonation appropriately; the ability to explain the importance of comprehension when reading and to use context clues and resources or to ask questions to understand a text
Interpretation of Texts	The ability to identify and state the main idea of a text, recount the key details, and explain how the key details support the main idea; the ability to interpret the cause and effect of events in texts; the ability to make inferences; the ability to identify the reasons and evidence speakers or authors give to support their points; the ability to identify, interpret, and compare similes, idioms, and metaphors
Story Elements	The ability to identify, describe, and analyze the following elements of a story or drama, citing specific details from the text to support their position: main idea, main character, minor character, supporting characters, protagonist, antagonist, plot, climax, resolution, setting, themes, and events; the ability to compare elements of plot (exposition, rising action, climax, falling action, resolution)
Compare and Contrast	The ability to compare and contrast the main ideas, points of view, characters, themes, and settings of two texts; the ability to compare and contrast an event or topic described from two different points of view; the ability to compare and contrast stories, myths, and traditional literature from different cultures by recognizing shared themes or topics and by analyzing similarities and differences in how these themes and topics are developed in each text
Genres of Literature	The ability to define the term genre and to identify and explain defining characteristics and differences between various genres of texts, including poetry, drama, fiction, nonfiction, and informational texts; the ability to read texts of various genres for understanding
Summarizing and Paraphrasing	The ability to paraphrase portions of a text after having heard the text read aloud; the ability to paraphrase text presented in many formats; the ability to summarize various types of texts clearly and succinctly
Computer Skills	The ability to use technology while doing research, to interact and collaborate with others, and to type and publish writing; the ability to type a minimum of one page in a single sitting; the ability to copy and paste images into an electronic document or presentation
Grammar and Punctuation	The ability to demonstrate grade-level appropriate command of English conventions and grammar with regard to quotations, relative pronouns, progressive verb tenses, modal auxiliaries, prepositional phrases, sentence fragments, run-on sentences, antecedents, coordinating conjunctions, compound sentences, capitalization, and punctuation; the ability to recognize verb tenses and use the correct tense

Speaking and Listening	The ability to participate in discussions about grade-level appropriate topics and texts, responding to the comments of others, building on what they said, and expressing their own opinions and ideas clearly in response; the ability to identify when a situation requires the use of formal English rather than informal English
Writing	The ability to write narrative, descriptive, opinion, persuasive, and informative pieces (introduction, body paragraphs, and conclusion), stating ideas, facts, and opinions clearly; the ability to use dialogue to develop characters and events in their writing; the ability to convey experiences and events with precision by using concrete descriptive words and phrases; the ability to write sentences in the present tense, past tense, and future tense; the ability to create an outline to organize their ideas in preparation for writing; the ability to make a plan for writing, to revise, to edit, and to improve a first draft of their writing using feedback from an adult; the ability to write for a variety of purposes and audiences; the ability to write pieces that require planning, research, and composition over an extended period of time (a week or more); the ability to write shorter pieces in a single sitting
Research Skills	The ability to conduct short research projects and summarize conclusions in writing; the ability to take notes while doing research and to organize the notes into categories for research; the ability to create a bibliography for a research project; the ability to gather information from print and electronic sources; the ability to gather information on the same topic from multiple texts and other sources, integrating the information to demonstrate understanding of the topic
Presentation Skills	The ability to report on a topic or text, tell a story, or retell an experience in an organized way, using relevant facts and details to support the main idea; the ability to speak clearly and audibly, with appropriate pacing and clear pronunciation; the ability to add audio recordings and visual displays to presentations to enhance the development of ideas; the ability to create a multimedia presentation to summarize a literary text
Reference Books	The ability to correctly use a dictionary, glossary, and thesaurus

Materials and Kits

An essential piece for your student's learning is found in the materials kit. The Lincoln Empowered™ materials kit provides many of the tools your student will need in order to succeed. Beyond the items in the kit, you will be asked to utilize common household objects. Your student should have pencil and paper or a notebook available for every lesson, so they will not be listed separately as required materials in the lesson content or this guide.

Assessments

There are two types of assessments in English Language Arts 4: Assess Its and Mastery Assess Its. Both are graded assessments. Assess Its are shorter assessments with a narrower scope of focus. The purpose of Assess Its is to gauge where your student is on the road to mastery of the targeted content. You can use the result of this formative assessment to reflect on the concepts and skills your student needs to revisit. Assess Its are often completed offline and then submitted for grading.

Mastery Assess Its are longer with a broader scope of focus. They serve as an opportunity for your student to demonstrate their level of mastery of a set of skills and concepts. Mastery Assess Its are typically completed and submitted online, within the course. All assessments in this course cover reading, writing, spelling, speaking, and listening.

English Language Arts Journal

Students should keep a journal throughout the course to use for written notes, vocabulary lists, activities, writing pieces, and questions. A three-ring binder or a primary composition book would be ideal. Regardless of the format you choose, it is important to teach your student to keep an organized journal. Here are some habits you and your student should practice until they become routine.

- Have the journal out and open for every lesson, along with a pencil for your student to use as a writing tool. (A pencil is preferable to a pen, as erasing and rewriting will often be necessary.)

- Remind your student to write the date at the top of a new page for every lesson. This is a great way to practice writing out dates in their full form and learning the appropriate placement of the comma between the date and year (e.g., May 1, 2017).

- Write neatly and clearly – check your student's notebook and give them feedback on their writing. Have them erase and rewrite if necessary.

- Teach your student to write down reactions, opinions, and questions in their reading journal while reading. Ask your student to read what they wrote aloud to you, and then discuss it.

- Prompt your student to write new words in their vocabulary list.

- Use your student's English Language Arts Journal to reinforce learning. Teach your student to look back at previously completed activities, notes, and words in order to solidify new learning by relating it to previously learned material.

Writing Portfolio

In order to keep a record of your student's growth as a writer and thinker, consider creating a writing portfolio with your student. A portfolio offers your student a way to share their learning with family members, which supports the development of their speaking and presentation skills, and it boosts their confidence. A half-inch, three-ring binder with clear document cover inserts would work well. Help your student to date every entry and put them in order.

Teach your student to keep all drafts of their writing, from a handwritten first draft to the typed and printed final draft. These drafts allow them to visualize the steps and results of the writing process. Have fun involving your student in the creation of their own portfolio, and be sure to ask them to share it with you at various points throughout the year.

Using the Internet

Some lessons will ask your student to use the Internet to search for information. There are a number of kid-friendly search engines available online, which strive to filter out inappropriate content. They include **Kiddle**, **KidRex**, **AskKids**, and **Kidzsearch**.

If it is necessary to sign up in order to gain access to a website, we advise students not to use their real name, but, instead, to make up a user name for online use. Remind your student to write this user name in their English Language Arts Journal and to share their password with you in case they forget it.

Instilling a Love for Language

In order for students to become good readers, writers, speakers, and listeners, they need to feel confident in their language abilities and find joy in reading, writing, and communicating. In addition to talking with your student to develop their listening and speaking skills, one of the most important things you can do is to foster a love of reading in a stress-free, enthusiastic environment. Research shows that the best way to improve reading skills is by reading. The only way students can do this is if the books and texts they are presented with are at their level.

Book Selection

In the Course Resources folder within the online course, you will find a recommended reading list for each grade level. If you find that your student is struggling with the texts in this course, try some of the third grade books. If you wish to supplement this course with additional books based on your student's interest, try some of the fourth grade selections. Finally, if the fourth grade texts are too easy for your student, try some of the fifth grade selections.

Reading Log

A reading log will be used throughout this course. The reading log is a chart provided for your student to use to record the books they read this year. It can be found in the Course Resources folder within the online course. Make the reading log a source of pride for your student. They should look back at their reading log and feel good about the reading they have done. Have fun with this assignment. And remember, students are never too old to read aloud to an audience or to be read to. Ask your student to read to you, or read to your student.

The Library

Now is a great time to introduce your student to using the library if you have not already done so. In addition to the excitement your student will find in being able to choose from such an abundance of books, audio books, and films, there are often scheduled events for children and families to enjoy, such as reading circles, author visits, and librarian-led activities. Using the library is also a way to practice caring for objects that are not personal possessions and being mindful of deadlines by returning books on or before the due date.

Understanding How People Learn

Helping Your Student

You play an important role in your student's learning, and being able to effectively support the learning process is key. This section will provide you with additional helpful hints, beyond the individual lesson pages, to bring learning to life inside and outside the classroom.

Did you know? The brain recognizes the five senses in five different areas. It is best for all learners to tap into as many of these areas as they can, simultaneously. This approach is called a multisensory experience for students.

Understanding Attention Span: A good rule of thumb in understanding your student's attention span is to consider their age. Students are generally able to actively concentrate for one minute per age year. Therefore, a fourth grader will only be able to focus on one thing, without a cognitive shift, for about nine to ten minutes. At that point, change the way you present an activity to keep your student engaged. For example, a simple change from reading to completing an activity will help your student to concentrate. You can also watch a video and pause it for a discussion. Alternating modes of learning will help your student stay engaged with the content.

Developmental Characteristics of Fourth Graders: Fourth grade is a challenging yet rewarding year. Fourth grade students are generally more sensitive and intense than they were in third grade. In an academic setting, their intensity translates to interest in learning many subjects, but their sensitivity means they are negatively affected by pressure and punishment. Being aware of these developmental tendencies of nine- and ten-year-old students can help you to be a better educational guide. Here are some tips to keep in mind this year to support your student.

- To help your student reach their potential and avoid defeat, create a low-pressure environment. Redirect your fourth grader with positive feedback and guidance as opposed to negative consequences.

- Watch out for the tendency of your student to be self-critical. Help them maintain a positive self-image and attitude toward learning by providing a great deal of encouragement.

- Create a schedule for your student, and involve them in designing a plan to complete their assignments. Goal setting and planning are skills most fourth graders have not yet developed.

Assess Prior Knowledge

It is always best to assess students' prior knowledge before they are introduced to a new topic. This simply means finding out what students already know (or think they know) about the topic. By knowing what your student knows, you are able to quickly review mastered content, uncover misunderstandings, and learn where you need to slow down and provide better support. Consider these tried and true staples of any educator's classroom.

1. **Ask a focus question:** Focus questions are written in a way that focuses the student's attention solely on the small task ahead and simply asks what they know.

2. **KWL Charts:** Work with your student to complete the chart to the right. K — list what the student knows; W — list what the student wants to know; L — list what the student has learned about a given topic.

3. **3-2-1:** Ask your student to share three things they know about the topic, two things they would like to know, and one question related to the topic.

Know what I *Know*	Wonder what I *Want* to know	Learn what I *Learned*

Language Development

Your student is constantly learning language through the words they hear around them in daily life. Encourage language development by reading books aloud, having conversations with your student, encouraging them to talk, and turning everyday talk into teachable moments. Here are a few points to help further support language learning:

Vocabulary and Grammar Building: There are many apps available to help your student learn and practice fourth grade vocabulary and grammar.

Using Context Clues: Teach your student to use contextual clues to read texts that contain new and unknown words. In order to support reading fluency and flow, help your student feel comfortable determining the meaning of an unknown word in the context rather than stopping to look up the meaning of every new word they encounter. To do this, refer to the pictures that accompany the text, talk about the big idea of the text, and ask your student what the surrounding words mean and whether they can provide clues to the meaning or connotation of the unknown word (e.g., positive or negative, past or present).

Letter and Grammar Cards: Help your student to practice learning new vocabulary and grammar by using flashcards. In addition to using paper index cards, there are a variety of websites and apps that allow users to create their own online flashcards with words of their choice. *Quizlet* is one example.

Word Walls: Dedicate a space for a word wall. Start with five words, and add around five words per week. Focus on high-frequency words and words that your student has encountered while reading. Start each English Language Arts lesson by reviewing at least one word on the word wall.

Living Language: Consider learning both inside and outside the classroom. Encourage games where your student can read or spell words that start with a certain letter while riding in the car or walking in the grocery store.

Audio Books: Consider incorporating audio books into your student's weekly reading activities. By increasing their exposure to good readers, your student will learn vocabulary, pronunciation, and inflection, and they will discover the importance of tone and expressive voice.

Vocabulary Lists: Have your student write the new words they are learning in a vocabulary list in their English Language Arts Journal. Your student can draw a picture or write a description for each definition. Make a point of using those words in conversation with your student, increasing their exposure to the words, and thereby helping them to internalize their meaning.

Independent Reading: Encourage reading. Set aside 20 to 30 minutes each day for independent reading. The more your student reads, the more vocabulary they will learn. Remind your student to record their accomplishments in their reading log when they finish a book.

Guided Reading

In addition to teaching students how to read, it is important to teach them how to comprehend what they read. Model reading strategies by posing and exploring questions with your student while reading.

Pre-Reading: Get your student wondering what the reading may be about and how it connects to their own experiences by asking and exploring some or all of these questions:

- What do you think this story/book/text is about?
- What do you think might happen? Why do you think this?
- What do you want to find out?
- Have you ever experienced anything like this?

During Reading: Ask your student questions to probe their understanding and clarify when needed. Ask questions to guide your student to make connections both within the story and to their own life. Encourage your student to revise their predictions about the story based on the information they have already read.

- Were your predictions correct?
- What have you found out so far?
- What do you think will happen next?
- What does this remind you of?

After Reading: Help your student summarize the story and form opinions about it. These are some questions to consider:

- Were your predictions correct?
- Did you like the ending?
- How do you feel about what the characters did?
- Would you have done anything differently?
- Did the text make you think of anything that has happened to you?
- What was your favorite part?

Tip: A Five *W*'s Chart can help your student organize information as they read and will, in turn, help them better organize the information in their mind. Ask your student to fill in the chart as they read or as soon as they finish.

The Five *W*'s	
Who? Who is the story/book/text about?	**What?** What does the main character do? What happens to the main character?
When? When does the story/book take place?	**Where?** Where does the story/book take place?
Why? Why do the characters do what they do? Why does the story end the way it does?	

Develop Metacognition

Metacognition is a complex word for something that is part of our daily lives. Simply explained, "meta" means after or beyond, and "cognition" means the process of acquiring knowledge. Therefore, metacognition is something we do after we gain knowledge. The process of metacognition is about self-monitoring, self-evaluating, and self-regulating all types of thought.

When students gain knowledge, it is up to teachers and parents to help them build on their knowledge. Helping your student to develop metacognitive skills is essential.

To help build metacognition, ask your student these questions:

- What are you thinking?
- What do you wonder?
- What did you notice?
- What questions do you have?
- What does this remind you of?
- What are you trying to figure out?
- What are you picturing in your head?
- How are you feeling?
- What do you find interesting?
- What other concept does this connect to?

The goal is to eventually move away from asking your student these questions to your student stating them without being prompted. Eventually, your student will say: "I'm thinking, I notice, I wonder…"

The Art of Questioning

To inquire about something is to ask questions about it, to examine or investigate it, or to probe and explore it. A good rule of thumb when guiding your student's learning is to tell less and ask more. While you don't want a student to hit their frustration point, grappling with content actually helps a student to more effectively master that content. To aid them in their learning, consider asking guided questions. This type of open-ended questioning requires more than a one-word answer. Lead your student through the content by posing good questions. A student will retain information longer if they discover the concepts themselves instead of being told.

Below are some questions for English Language Arts 4.

- What question would you ask about this text?
- What do you think this book is about? Why?
- Do you see any new words? What do you think they mean?
- Are there pictures or words that can help you figure out what ___ means?
- How does the illustration/picture relate to the text?
- Which words or passages describe the setting of the story?
- Can you summarize the main events of this story?
- What is the main idea of the text? Which passages in the text make you think this?
- Who does this character remind you of?

- How is this character's experience similar to another character's experience?
- How would you compare ___ to ___?
- How are ___ alike/different?
- How would you describe the author's point of view? What do you think they are trying to communicate through their writing? Which words or passages from the text make you think this?
- Why is ___ important?
- How would you describe ___?
- What facts from the text are important? Why?
- Which passages of the text express opinions? How can you tell these are opinions and not facts?
- Could the story have ended differently? How? Do you think it should have ended differently? Why?
- Can you summarize the text? Which details are the most important in retelling? Which details can be left out?
- What would happen if…?

Empowered™ Courses: What You Need to Know

LINCOLN
EMPOWERED

Lincoln Empowered™ is a unique kind of curriculum. Courses are composed of learning activities called learning objects. A number of learning objects are presented together as lessons. Learning objects are individual pages and activities that provide students with the content and practice they need to master specific learning objectives, or goals, for a course. Students are often asked to demonstrate mastery of learning objectives by completing assessments.

Engagement

Students are engaged through various activities, videos, and simulations. Students may be asked to complete a task on paper, or they may engage with a variety of online activities. TextPoppers, for example, are found within the content as blue, bold text. Students can hover over these words with a mouse or click on them to see definitions of key terms and phrases.

Learning Objects

Ten different types of learning objects exist within Lincoln Empowered courses:

 Read Its are the primary learning tools within a course. They contain all of the instructional information students need to demonstrate mastery of the granular learning objectives.

 **Practice Its** are interactive activities that can be accessed online or offline. They provide the opportunity for students to check their understanding of the learning objectives.

 Watch Its are learning tools that utilize videos to enhance the learning experience and bring abstract concepts to life for students.

 Play Its are content-focused, interactive games that support learning.

 Show Its are activities that provide the opportunity to show mastery of specific learning objectives.

 **Answer Keys** are available to the instructors for all Show Its and Apply Its. They provide correct answers and detailed feedback that can be shared with students.

 Assess Its are graded activities that allow students to demonstrate mastery of learning objectives and standards.

Reinforce Its are supplemental activities to assist students who may be struggling. They also offer a great review before taking assessments.

 Extend Its provide additional content to extend student knowledge.

 Apply Its are non-graded assessments that cover content from multiple lessons. Apply Its can be cumulative projects that allow students to demonstrate mastery of several learning objectives. Teachers can elect to make these gradable.

ENGLISH LANGUAGE ARTS 4
Course Introduction

Course Structure

Each Lincoln Empowered™ course is structured in a similar manner. When you and your student enter a course, you will find a number of topic folders. These topics reflect the key concepts that your student will learn in a specific grade and subject. Each topic folder contains a number of lessons.

Each lesson (e.g., Lesson 1, Lesson 2) represents one day of learning. Lesson folders contain the content, or the learning objects. A set of learning objects is presented to help a student master the content.

The Lincoln Empowered approach to instruction allows students multiple opportunities to learn and master objectives, which leads to mastery of the standards. It is not necessary for a student to complete every learning object. They were created to appeal to different modalities. You will notice that some content repeats, giving students additional exposure to a concept before an assessment. If your student has mastered the concept, move on to the next objective. Work the curriculum to meet your student's needs. There is flexibility in the "Its" that allows for student choice and greater differentiation, which puts you and your student in control of the learning.

Games and Videos

While games (Play Its) and videos (Watch Its) may appear after the content within the course, you may want to consider allowing your student to engage with these items first, especially when you need to grab their attention. This type of engagement builds excitement; it encourages the student to share prior knowledge or ask questions; and, it helps build knowledge for students who are lacking experience in a certain concept. Often, you will hear your student say, "They talked about that in the video," or other statements of excitement.

Course Resources

The first folder in your course is titled "Course Resources." It contains a set of useful resources that will help your student begin the course. Start by reviewing the Supply List and Pacing Guide. Then, view some of the materials you will need throughout the course.

Tips and Tricks

Documents & Handouts: Throughout the course, you will find many worksheets, stories, and texts provided as PDF files. In some cases, it is best to download these PDFs to your computer so that you can view them in a larger format, while in other situations it will be necessary to print these files.

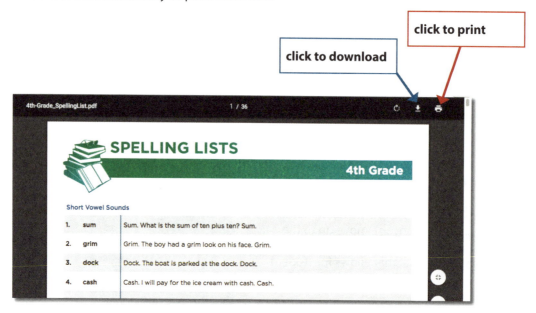

Optimizing Your View: Some PDFs, at first glance, do not seem ideal to read on the computer screen because of their large size. When you encounter these texts, if the content found in the PDF window is too large, click the "Fit to page" icon located at the bottom right of your PDF to adjust the zoom. This will auto adjust your view to your screen.

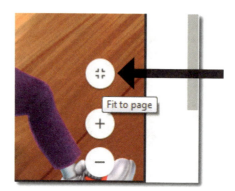

Time to Get Started

You now have all the information you need to have a successful year. So, what are you waiting for? Log in to your course and get started!

LESSON 1

Topic | **Fiction Elements**

Learning Objectives

The activities in this lesson will help your student meet the following objectives:

- describe the characters, setting, and events in a story
- explain a text you have read

Materials

- "Fingerprints" and "A Very Moody Wedding"
- highlighter
- teacher- or student-selected text
- "Blank Story Map" and "Weekly Reading Log" activity pages

Creating a Story Map

 Activate

1. Have your student hold up one hand, with their fingers spread out. Then, ask them to brainstorm the important parts of a story, one for each finger.
2. Your student may come up with the following parts:
   - characters, setting, problem, solution, and mood
   - characters, setting, beginning, middle, and end

 Engage

1. Begin by having your student read the content of the **Read It**.
2. Then, ask them, "How are story maps useful when studying literature?" (Answer: Story maps help a reader organize important elements of a story to better understand the text. They also encourage students to summarize specific parts of a story.)
3. Before having your student view the **Review: A Story and Its Parts - Watch It**, ask them to make the following circle map in their journal and to label the inside circle *Parts of a Story*.

Circle Map

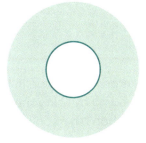

4. As your student watches the video, encourage them to write the various parts of a story in the outside circle.

Demonstrate

1. Now, direct your student to complete the **Show It** by reading the story, "A Very Moody Wedding," and creating a story map. Encourage your student to review the elements of a story map before they read the story so that they know exactly what to locate while reading.
2. Then, prompt them to compare their story map to the example provided in the **Show It AK**.
3. As an extension, have your student tell you a story about their day, perhaps at dinnertime. Then, have them identify the characters, setting, problem, and solution of that story.

Understanding

Activate

1. Provide your student with the following set of actions for a morning routine:
   a. Brush your teeth.
   b. Eat breakfast.
   c. Wake up.
   d. Get dressed.
2. Then, have your student repeat those actions verbally to you.
3. Next, ask your student to determine whether the order of this morning routine makes sense. Then, have them reorder the steps in the correct order.

Engage

1. Have your student read the content of the **Read It**.
2. Consider having your student create a bookmark of strategies used before reading, while reading, and after reading. This can serve as a quick reference for these strategies when your student is reading a variety of literature.
   a. Using a piece of paper, cut a larger rectangle out and divide it into three boxes. Label the sections *Before Reading*, *During Reading*, and *After Reading*.
   b. Then, prompt your student to place the specific strategies under each category.

Demonstrate

1. As your student is reading the "Fingerprints" passage in the **Show It**, encourage them to practice the strategies used before and during reading by using the following prompts:
   • Look at the picture. Make a prediction based on what you see.
   • What parts of the story can you relate your own experiences to?
   • How do you feel about the main character?
2. After they retell the story, instruct them to view the **Show It AK** to ensure they have included necessary details in their summary.
3. To reinforce learning, have your student ask a friend or a family member to tell them about their weekend. Then, have your student retell what they have heard and include four details.

LESSON 2

Topic	Fiction Elements

Learning Objectives

The activities in this lesson will help your student meet the following objectives:

- define the genre of narrative writing
- review nouns and pronouns

Materials

- "Special Sibling Discount"
- colored pencils
- dictionary
- index cards
- picture book with no words
- teacher- or student-selected texts

Define Narrative Writing

Activate

1. Prompt your student to open and view the **Narrative Writing - Watch It**.
2. After the video, ask your student to tell you the purpose of narrative writing. (Answer: to tell a story, whether fiction or nonfiction)

Engage

1. Start with the **Read It** and have your student work through the content.
2. Then, ask, "How would you describe the sequence of a narrative story?" (Possible answer: Narrative stories are told in chronological order from beginning, to middle, to end.)

Demonstrate

1. Next, have your student complete the activity in the **Show It**.
2. When they are finished, use the **Show It AK** with your student to check their responses.
3. For extra practice identifying examples of narrative writing, be sure to have your student complete the Application section of the **Show It**.
4. To extend learning, consider having your student create a narrative story using a picture book with no words. Your student will base the story on the illustrations in the picture book.

• • •

Parts of Speech Review I

 ## Activate

1. Write each of the following words on an index card.
   - *kitchen*
   - *president*
   - *disease*
   - *them*
   - *we*
   - *she*
2. Then, mix the cards up and ask them to sort the index cards into two categories, *nouns* and *pronouns*. (Answer: The nouns are *kitchen*, *president*, and *disease*; the pronouns are *them*, *we*, and *she*.)
3. Challenge your student to come up with two examples of nouns and two examples of pronouns.

 ## Engage

1. As your student reads the content of the **Read It**, have them create the following table in their journal to write down definitions of the terms *pronoun* and *noun* and examples of both.

	Noun	Pronoun
Definition		
Examples		

2. Next, have them complete the **Practice It** to further review pronouns and nouns.

 ## Demonstrate

1. Now, have your student complete the **Show It**.
2. When your student has finished, have them use the **Show It AK** to review sample sentences.
3. For the Application section of the **Show It**, have your student verbally identify nouns and pronouns in the paragraph they chose. You might suggest that your student copy and print the paragraph. They can then use blue and red colored pencils to identify nouns and pronouns just as they did in the first part of the **Show It**.

LESSON 3

Topic | Fiction Elements

Learning Objectives

The activities in this lesson will help your student meet the following objectives:

- retell the pivotal points of a story
- review adjectives and adverbs

Materials

- dictionary
- teacher- or student-selected text

Retelling Pivotal Scenes

Activate

1. Ask your student, "What are two jobs a reader has when reading?" Your student may mention that being able to pronounce, read, and understand the words is one job. Another job would be to understand and be able to retell what they read.
2. Then, ask them to define *retelling* in their own words. A possible reply may be "Retelling means to tell a story again in the order it happened".

Engage

1. Begin with the **Read It** and have your student work through the content.
2. As they read, discuss the meaning of a *pivotal part* of a story with your student. Ask them to define this phrase in their own words.

Demonstrate

1. Next, have your student move on to the **Show It**.
2. Prompt them to use the **Show It AK** to compare their work to a sample response.
3. For extra practice retelling a short story, be sure to have your student complete the Application section in the **Show It**.

• • •

Parts of Speech Review II

 **Activate**

1. Ask your student to define following parts of speech:
   - adjective (Answer: An adjective is a word or phrase that describes a noun.)
   - adverb (Answer: An adverb describes how a verb happens.)
2. Next, prompt them to write the following sentence in their journal and then identify the adjective and adverb:

   The man quickly walked to his silver truck after work. (Answers: *Quickly* is the adverb, and *silver* is the adjective.)

 **Engage**

1. As your student reads the content of the **Read It**, have them create the following table in their journal to write down definitions of the terms *adjective* and *adverb* and examples of both.

	Adjective	Adverb
Definition		
Examples		

2. Next, have them complete the **Practice It** activity to further review adjectives and adverbs.

 **Demonstrate**

1. Now, have your student complete the activity in the **Show It**.
2. When your student is finished, have them use the **Show It AK** to review sample sentences.
3. To address the Application section of the **Show It**, have your student scan a familiar text for adjectives and adverbs. Prompt them to identify the nouns and verbs that the adjectives and adverbs describe, too.
4. To extend learning, consider having your student create acrostic poems for the words *adjective* and *adverb*. Have them write each word vertically on a page in their journal. Then, have them brainstorm and write down adjectives and adverbs that begin with the letters from each word, as in the examples below.

Abundant   **A**bruptly
Dark   **D**elightfully
Jealous   **V**iolently
Elegant   **E**ndlessly
Cold   **R**andomly
Tasty   **B**eautifully
Irregular
Violet
Early

LESSON 4

Topic	Fiction Elements

Learning Objectives

The activities in this lesson will help your student meet the following objectives:

- identify the major events that occur in the plot of a story
- choose the appropriate articles to use with nouns in sentences

Materials

- "Parker's Promise"
- magazine
- timer

Action in a Plot

Activate

1. Direct your student to open and view the **Elements of Plot - Watch It**.
2. After the video, ask your student to draw a visual in their journal of plot structure. Encourage them to create a mountain-like image and include the following words and phrases: *exposition*, *rising action*, *climax*, *falling action*, and *resolution*.

Engage

1. Next, have your student complete the **Read It**.
2. Ask them to pause after they read the table describing rising action and falling action. Ask them, "What is the difference between the rising action and the falling action of a story?" A possible reply may be "The events in the story that lead up to the main event are the rising action, while the falling action happens after the climax and shows how the main event has affected the characters."

Demonstrate

1. Now, have your student complete the activities in the **Show It**.
2. When they are finished, use the **Show It AK** with your student to check their responses.
3. To reinforce learning, have your student open the **Plutarch's Library-Theo's Race - Play It** and play the game to apply reading comprehension skills.

• • •

Articles

Activate

1. Give your student a magazine and ask them to find the words *a*, *an*, and *the* in an article, advertisement, or column. Challenge them to find as many as they can in one minute.
2. Tell them that they are going to learn the rules for using these articles.

Engage

1. Start by having your student read through the content of the **Read It**.
2. Afterward, ask them to write in their journal the rules for using *a*, *an*, and *the*.
3. Then, prompt them to open the **Plutarch's Library-Articles, Nouns, Verbs - Play It** to review these parts of speech.

Demonstrate

1. Next, have your student complete the **Show It**.
2. When they are finished, work with your student to check their responses using the **Show It AK**.
3. For additional practice using the articles *a*, *an*, and *the*, direct your student to complete the Application section of the **Show It**.
4. To extend learning, consider having your student create a lost-and-found advertisement, challenging them to use the articles *a*, *an*, and *the* as well as adjectives and nouns in their descriptions. For example, they could choose to write a "lost pet" advertisement or an advertisement that describes a piece of jewelry found at a local park. Encourage them to be as descriptive as possible.

LESSON 5

Topic | Fiction Elements

Learning Objectives

The activities in this lesson will help your student meet the following objectives:

- write about the setting of a story
- create an illustration to depict one or more events from a story or drama

Materials

- "Blue Hole" and "My Not-So-Fun Trip to the Zoo"
- art supplies

Define Setting

Activate

1. Ask your student to describe their favorite room in their house or another place. Encourage them to use many details to describe what it looks like.
2. Use the following question prompts to promote thinking.
   - What is the environment like?
   - What objects are in the space?
   - What colors do you see?
   - How is it decorated?

Engage

1. Together with your student, read the content of the **Read It** aloud.
2. Afterward, ask them "How does a reader analyze the setting of a story?" They may mention that a reader looks at when and where the story takes place and observes how that atmosphere affects the plot and characters' feelings.
3. Next, prompt your student to open the **Exploring Setting - Watch It** and view the video to review the concept of setting.

Demonstrate

1. Move on to the **Show It** and have your student complete the activity.
2. Then, have your student use the **Show It AK** to review their response regarding the setting of the story.
3. To enrich learning, consider having your student draw a picture of themselves in four different settings. For example, they may select an island, a hospital, a farm, or a school. Then, ask your student to reflect on how each type of setting would affect how they feel and the actions they take.

Illustrating Key Events

Activate

1. Ask your student to explain the morning routine they complete before going to school. They may mention activities such as getting dressed, brushing their teeth, and eating breakfast. Remind your student to list these events in the order in which they happen.

Engage

1. Start by having your student read through the content of the **Read It**.
2. Encourage your student to take notes in their journal on time order words that represent sequential order, such as *first*, *next*, *then*, *finally*, and *last*.
3. Then, challenge your student to add to that list by brainstorming more time order words or phrases. *At the beginning*, *after that*, *at the end*, *later*, and *right after* are a few examples.

Demonstrate

1. Now, have your student complete the activity in the **Show It** using the text "The Coaster Challenge."
2. When they are finished, direct them to use the **Show It AK** to evaluate their responses.
3. To enrich learning, encourage your student to complete the Application section of the **Show It**.

LESSON 6

Topic	Fiction Elements

Learning Objectives

The activities in this lesson will help your student meet the following objectives:

- sequence key events in a story
- spell words with short vowel sounds

Materials

- "Front-Page News"
- art supplies
- dictionary
- poster board

Sequencing Key Events

Activate

1. Ask your student to tell you what happened, from beginning to end, in a movie they recently watched.
2. Afterward, tell your student that they have sequenced the movie's main events in order to retell the story in the order in which the events occurred.

Engage

1. Now, direct your student to read the content of the **Read It**.
2. Ask them, "How does ordering or sequencing events help readers?" (Answer: Sequencing helps a reader understand a story's events and also provides the ability to retell the events within a text in the order in which they occurred.)
3. Next, have your student open and view the **Review: Sequence of Story - Watch It** to review story elements and the importance of sequencing events. Instruct them to pause the video at 03:19 to engage in a discussion about how time order words and road signs serve a similar purpose.
4. Then, have them open and play the **Plutarch's Library-Sequence Events - Play It** to reinforce sequencing events from a story.
5. Now, have your student move on to the **Practice It** to complete the activity.

Demonstrate

1. Open the **Assess It** and have your student complete the activity. Help them to understand the expectations of the rubric before they create a poster to sequence the events from the story. When, they are finished, help them to review their work to make sure they have met the rubric expectations.
2. When they are finished, scan the document or take a photo of it and upload it to the Dropbox. For additional instructions on how to use the Dropbox, click on the paper clip icon in the upper-left corner of the **Assess It**.

● ● ●

Spelling Short Vowel Sounds

 **Activate**

1. Ask your student to tell you the short sounds of the vowels *a*, e, *i*, *o*, and *u*.

 **Engage**

1. Have your student read through the content of the **Read It**.
2. Assist them with defining the spelling words. Encourage them to use a dictionary for any unknown words.
3. Next, prompt your student to move on to the **Practice It**. Encourage them to play multiple rounds of the game in order to practice all the words. Spelling practice activities for this subtopic will span Lessons 6 through 8.

LESSON 7

Topic	Fiction Elements

Learning Objectives

The activities in this lesson will help your student meet the following objectives:

- identify the theme of a story
- distinguish between precise and general nouns
- spell words with short vowel sounds

Materials

- "Moses and His Lost Friends" and "The Tortoise and the Hare"
- news article
- thesaurus
- teacher- or student-selected text

Define Theme

Activate

1. Present an age-appropriate news article to your student. Read the article together.
2. Then, ask your student to determine the purpose of the article. Why was this article written?
3. For example, they may read an article about how a group of neighborhood locals cleaned up trash on a busy highway. The theme, or message of the story, may be responsibility, as the reader may learn the importance of doing the right thing and being a positive participant in their community.

Engage

1. Begin by prompting your student to open and view the **Themes in *The Wizard of Oz* - Watch It**. Ask them to make note of the username and password provided on the Discovery Education image. Be sure that they click the link for the video and enter the provided username and password to watch. Consider having them pause the video at 1:25 in order to make predictions about the themes they think are present in this story.
2. Then, have your student pay close attention to "The Tortoise and the Hare" as they complete the **Read It**. After they have read that passage, ask your student to think about how the characters changed and what they learned in connection with the theme of the story.

Demonstrate

1. Move on to the **Show It**. Allow your student to read the passage before they begin the assignment. As your student reads the passage, encourage them to circle any words, phrases, or sentences they think may be connected to the theme of the story.
2. Then, prompt them to use the **Show It AK** to compare their response with the theme provided.

● ● ●

Precise and General Nouns

Activate

1. Present the following descriptions to your student:
   - The fundraiser raised a lot of money.
   - The fundraiser raised $2,000 for the local animal shelter. The fundraiser also collected 40 pounds of pet supplies, including food, blankets, and cleaning supplies.
2. Then, ask them, "Which description is an example of sharing precise information, and which is an example of sharing only general information?" (Answer: The first description is general, and the second description is more precise.)

Engage

1. As your student reads the content of the **Read It**, have them take notes in their journal using the following table to write down definitions of the terms *precise noun* and *general noun* and examples of both.

	Precise Noun	General Noun
Definition		
Examples		

2. Discuss and review the use of a thesaurus to find synonyms.
3. Now, have your student complete the **Practice It** to apply what they have learned about precise and general nouns.

Demonstrate

1. Open the **Assess It** and have your student complete the activity. When they are finished, scan the document or take a photo of it and upload it to the Dropbox. For additional instructions on how to use the Dropbox, click on the paper clip icon in the upper-left corner of the **Assess It**.
2. As an extension to learning, have your student complete the Application section of the **Assess It**.

• • •

Spelling Short Vowel Sounds

Engage

1. Have your student complete the **Practice It** activity to review their spelling words. Spelling practice activities for this subtopic will span Lessons 6 through 8.

LESSON 8

Topic | Fiction Elements

Learning Objectives

The activities in this lesson will help your student meet the following objectives:

- describe the setting of a story
- choose more precise nouns in sentences
- spell words with short vowel sounds

Materials

- teacher- or student-selected text
- thesaurus
- variety of comic strips

Setting Description

 Activate

1. Ask your student to close their eyes and pretend that they are in a rain forest.
2. Give your student about 30 seconds, and then ask them to open their eyes and describe the setting.

 Engage

1. Begin by having your student open and view the **Setting - Watch It** to review what a setting is.
2. Then, have your student read the content of the **Read It**.
3. Have them pause at the image of the five senses. Ask, "How do you think the five senses—touch, sight, taste, smell, and hearing—allow a person to better describe a setting?" Your student may mention that the five senses help people to process information about their environment. Using the five senses to describe a setting helps a writer create a picture of where and when a story takes place.

 Demonstrate

1. Next, direct your student to complete the **Show It** activity.
2. Work with them to review their paragraph using the **Show It AK**.
3. To reinforce learning, consider having your student read a variety of comic strips and use the illustrations, dialogue, and character actions to determine the setting of each.

Precise Nouns

 **Activate**

1. Create the following matching activity in your student's journal:

dog	tiger
street	Great Dane
building	sandal
cat	Wolfe Lane
shoe	the Pentagon

2. Ask your student to draw a line to match the general noun to the precise noun. (Answers: *dog*: *Great Dane*; *street*: *Wolfe Lane*; *building*: *the Pentagon*; *cat*: *tiger*; *shoe*: *sandal*)

 **Engage**

1. Begin by having your student read through the content of the **Read It**, pausing to complete the activities.
2. Next, ask your student to use precise nouns to explain what they had for breakfast or lunch.
3. Then, prompt your student to complete the **Practice It** to apply their knowledge of precise nouns.

 **Demonstrate**

1. Now, have your student move on to the **Show It** and complete the activity.
2. Instruct your student to use the **Show It AK** to review a sample response.
3. Finally, encourage your student to complete the activity in the Application section of the **Show It**.

● ● ●

Spelling Short Vowel Sounds

 **Engage**

1. Have your student complete the activity in the **Practice It** in order to review their spelling words. They may play more than once if time allows. Spelling practice activities for this subtopic will span Lessons 6 through 8.

LESSON 9

Topic	Fiction Elements

Learning Objectives

The activities in this lesson will help your student meet the following objectives:

- determine the theme of a story from details in the text
- distinguish between precise and general verbs

Materials

- "Gum Now and Then"
- teacher- or student-selected text
- thesaurus

Theme Time

Activate

1. Provide the following theme concept to your student: courage.
2. Then, ask your student to pretend to be an author and create a title for a book with a theme of courage. For example, a possible book title could be *Brave Bernard*.
3. Next, ask them to provide a quick summary of what their book would be about. For example, "*Brave Bernard* is about a dog who gets lost in the wilderness and has to find his way home."

Engage

1. Have your student read the content of the **Read It**. Ask them to write the common examples of theme in their journal.
2. Discuss with your student the role supporting details play in understanding a story's theme.
3. Then, direct your student to view the **Examining Theme - Watch It**.
4. After the video, challenge your student to come up with an example of how people use theme beyond books. For example, artists use theme when creating pieces of artwork, and song writers use theme in the lyrics they write for songs.

Demonstrate

1. Now, instruct your student to complete the identifying theme activity in the **Show It**.
2. Help them to compare their response with the example in the **Show It AK**.
3. Prompt your student to complete the **Reinforce It** activity to review theme further.
4. To extend learning, consider having your student identify the themes of their favorite books, TV shows, or movies.

• • •

Precise and General Verbs

 Activate

1. Ask your student to act out five different verbs.
2. For example, they may select jumping, clapping, running, eating, and sleeping.
3. Then, ask them to use their own words to define the term *verb*. (Answer: A verb is a word used to describe an action.)

 **Engage**

1. As your student reads the content of the **Read It**, have them create the following table in their journal and use it to write down definitions of the terms *general verb* and *precise verb* and examples of both.

	General Verb	Precise Verb
Definition		
Examples		

2. Then, have your student refer to the list of verbs they acted out in the Activate section. Challenge them to replace each general verb with a precise verb.
3. Next, have them complete the **Practice It**. Prompt your student to check their work using the answer key.

 Demonstrate

1. Open the **Assess It** and have your student complete the activities. When they are finished, scan the document or take a photo of it and upload it to the Dropbox. For additional instructions on how to use the Dropbox, click on the paper clip icon in the upper-left corner of the **Assess It**.
2. Encourage your student to complete the Application section of the **Assess It** for an added challenge.

LESSON 10

| Topic | Fiction Elements |

Learning Objectives

The activities in this lesson will help your student meet the following objectives:

- create a main character for a narrative story
- explain the purpose of the minor characters in a story
- spell words with short vowel sounds

Materials

- "The Porcupine and the Firefly"
- play dough or modeling clay
- teacher- or student-selected text

Main Characters

Activate

1. Ask your student, "What makes a good story?" A possible reply may be "Characters and an interesting storyline can create a good story."
2. Then, ask them to use their own words to tell what a character in a story is. (Answer: Characters are the people, animals, or things in a story that are involved in the plot.)

Engage

1. Start by having your student read through the content of the **Read It**.
2. Afterward, ask them to think about character traits by brainstorming a quick list in their journal. For example, characters may be adventurous, clever, jealous, shy, and stubborn.
3. Then, direct them to open and play the **Plutarch's Library-The Porcupine and the Firefly - Play It** to practice their reading comprehension skills.

Demonstrate

1. Next, have your student move on to the **Show It** and complete the activity. Before they build their character, encourage your student to think about the character's physical traits (the traits you can see just by looking at the character). Things such as hair style and color, height, eye color, and shape are all things to consider.
2. Now, prompt them to use the **Show It AK** to review an example character and description. Encourage them to add details to their character description if needed.
3. Finally, move on to the Application section of the **Show It** and have your student identify a main character in a selected story or book.
4. To extend learning, consider having your student dress up as a character from a story and retell the tale by acting it out.

• • •

Minor Characters

 **Engage**

1. Beginning with the **Read It**, have your student work through the content.
2. When they are finished reading, ask them to state two differences between minor and main characters. (Answer: The minor characters of a story are not involved in the main plot, and their personalities are not developed like those of the main characters.)

 **Demonstrate**

1. Prompt your student to read the "The Porcupine and the Firefly" and to complete the activity in the **Show It**. Consider printing the story and encouraging your student to underline key parts of the text that describe the purpose of the minor characters as they read the narrative.
2. Then, have your student use the **Show It AK** to compare their sentences to the samples provided.
3. Finally, move on to the Application section of the **Show It** and have your student identify the minor characters in a selected story or book and then describe their purpose.

• • •

Spelling Short Vowel Sounds

 **Engage**

1. Encourage your student to review and practice their spelling words before they complete the **Assess It**.

 **Demonstrate**

1. Now move on to the **Assess It**. Have your student write, and correctly spell, the words they hear spoken in the assessment. This assessment covers the spelling words presented in Lessons 6 through 8.
2. When they are finished, scan the document or take a photo of it and upload it to the Dropbox. For additional instructions on how to use the Dropbox, click on the paper clip icon in the upper-left corner of the **Assess It**.

LESSON 11

| Topic | Fiction Elements |

Learning Objectives

The activities in this lesson will help your student meet the following objectives:

- compare and contrast the antagonist and protagonist in a story
- write a complete sentence about how the conflict is resolved in a story
- spell words with the long vowels *a* and *i*

Materials

- "Seymour and Stanley" and "The Sound Outside the Tent"
- art supplies
- dictionary
- fairy tales
- index cards
- poster board

Antagonists and Protagonists

Activate

1. Ask your student to brainstorm a list in their journal of four character traits that "good guys" and "bad guys" can have in a story.
2. The following are some possible character traits:
   - good guys: loyalty, generosity, responsibility, and trustworthiness
   - bad guys: argumentativeness, selfishness, dishonesty, and greed

Engage

1. First, have your student read the content of the **Read It**.
2. Afterward, ask them, "What do the terms *protagonist* and *antagonist* mean?" (Answer: *Protagonist* refers to the main character of a story; *antagonist* can refer to the villain of a story.)
3. Then, prompt your student to open and view the **Watch Its** titled **Protagonist and Antagonist** and **Antagonist and Protagonist**.
4. After they have viewed both videos, ask your student to think about the roles the protagonist and antagonist play in the conflict in a story. (Answer: The antagonist is usually causing or adding to the conflict, while the protagonist is trying to resolve the conflict and solve the problem.)

Demonstrate

1. Now, have your student move on to the **Show It**. Encourage them to find evidence in the text that supports their identification of the protagonist and antagonist in the "Lion and Tiger" passage. They should make two posters, one for the antagonist and one for the protagonist.
2. Next, have your student use the **Show It AK** to review their posters.
3. To reinforce learning, consider having your student read a variety of fairy tales and identify the protagonist and antagonist of each story. Encourage them to find textual evidence to prove their identifications.

Conflict Resolution

 **Activate**

1. Ask your student to share a time when they got into an argument with a friend, a sibling, or another family member.
2. Use the following question prompts to activate their thinking:
   - What was the argument about?
   - How did the argument begin?
   - Was the conflict resolved?

 **Engage**

1. Before they read the content of the **Read It**, have your student copy the table below into their journal. As they read the content, prompt them to take notes by describing each type of conflict in their own words.

Types of Conflict	
Character vs. Character	
Character vs. Nature	
Character vs. Society	
Character vs. Self	

 **Demonstrate**

1. Next, prompt your student to complete the activities in the **Show It**. Then, direct them to the **Show It AK** so that they can evaluate their responses.
2. To extend learning, consider having your student write an alternate ending to one of their favorite stories.

• • •

Spelling Long *a* and *i* Words

 **Activate**

1. Ask your student to tell you the sounds that long *a* and long *i* vowels make.

 **Engage**

1. Have your student begin with the **Read It**. Tell them to pay close attention to the Rules, Patterns, and Examples section.
2. Then, have your student read the list of spelling words. You may want them to write the words and their definitions on a sheet of paper or index cards.
3. Next, have your student complete the card sorting to practice the spelling words.
4. Last, move on to the **Practice It** for your student to complete the activity. Have them play the game multiple times so that they get an opportunity to practice all the words. Spelling practice activities for this subtopic will span Lessons 11 through 13.

LESSON 12

Topic | Fiction Elements

Learning Objectives

The activities in this lesson will help your student meet the following objectives:

- create a character map to describe the main character of a story
- explain how dialogue enhances a narrative story
- choose more precise verbs in sentences
- spell words with the long vowels *a* and *i*

Materials

- "We're Going to Have Some Fun Today"
- colored pencils
- teacher- or student-selected text
- thesaurus
- "Character Map" activity page

Main Character Description

Activate

1. Ask your student to brainstorm a list of five character traits they would use to describe themselves.
2. Then, begin a discussion of why they selected these traits.

Engage

1. Start by having your student read the content of the **Read It**.
2. Afterward, ask them, "How can you use inferring when reading to determine character traits?" (Answer: A reader can infer character traits of a main character by using the details, actions, events, and evidence provided in the story.)
3. Then, prompt your student to open and play the **Enlighten Maze-Story Elements Part One - Play It** to review characterization and other important story elements.

Demonstrate

1. Open the **Assess It** and have your student complete the activity. Ensure they review the expectations of the rubric before, during, and after they complete the activity.
2. When they are finished, scan the document or take a photo of it and upload it to the Dropbox. For additional instructions on how to use the Dropbox, click on the paper clip icon in the upper-left corner of the **Assess It**.
3. To enrich learning, have your student move on to the **Extend It** and write a short story using a completed character map. Prompt them to refer to the answer key at the bottom of the page to view a sample story.

• • •

Dialogue

Activate

1. Ask your student whether they know what the word *dialogue* means (Answer: Dialogue is a conversation between two or more people.)
2. Then, ask them when or where they think dialogue is used. (Answer: Dialogue is used when people talk to one another. It can be found, for example, in movies, books, and plays.)

Engage

1. As your student reads the content of the **Read It**, ask them to observe the punctuation used for the dialogue.
2. When they are finished, ask them, "Did you notice any specific punctuation being used for dialogue?" Tell them that quotation marks are used when writing dialogue to identify what is spoken.
3. Then, prompt your student to open the **Review: Understanding Quotes - Watch It** to learn about the importance of quotation marks in dialogue.
4. After the video, ask your student, "What role does a comma play in written dialogue?" (Answer: Commas are used to separate the dialogue from the rest of the sentence and encourage the reader to briefly pause when reading.)

Demonstrate

1. Next, have your student move on to complete the activity in the **Show It**.
2. Guide them to use the **Show It AK** to evaluate their answer.
3. Finally, move on to the Application section of the **Show It**. Have your student identify dialogue within a text and draw a picture to represent that dialogue.
4. To reinforce learning, consider having your student create their own comic strip and use speech bubbles to show the dialogue between the characters.

Precise Verbs

 Activate

1. Direct your student to list the verbs *run* and *sprint* in their journal.
2. Then, ask your student to identify the general verb and the precise verb. (Answer: *Run* is an example of a general verb, and *sprint* is an example of a precise verb.)

 Engage

1. Have your student read the content of the **Read It**.
2. Ask them to pause their reading after the Examples section. Challenge your student to come up with another precise verb for each example.
3. Have your student move on to the **Practice It** to apply their knowledge of precise verbs. Prompt them to check their work using the answer key at the bottom of the page.

 Demonstrate

1. Next, have your student complete the **Show It** activity.
2. Then, have them compare their precise verbs with the examples in the **Show It AK**.
3. Finally, move on to the Application section of the **Show It** and encourage your student to complete the activity for additional practice with precise verbs.

Spelling Long *a* and *i* Words

 **Engage**

1. Have your student complete the **Practice It** activity. Encourage them to play multiple rounds of the game in order to practice all the words. Spelling practice activities for this subtopic will span Lessons 11 through 13.

LESSON 13

Topic	Fiction Elements

Learning Objectives

The activities in this lesson will help your student meet the following objectives:

- create an illustration to describe a character from a story
- add adjectives to sentences to describe nouns
- spell words with the long vowels *a* and *i*

Materials

- art supplies
- teacher- or student-selected text

Illustrating Characters

Activate

1. Read the following scenario to your student.
   > Mary just started school at a new elementary school. She felt nervous and anxious about going to a new school. Mary walked into her classroom and sat down at her desk.
2. Have them complete a quick sketch showing what they think Mary looks like on her first day of school.

Engage

1. Start by having your student read the content of the **Read It**.
2. Then, ask your student why visualizing when reading a story helps a reader understand the text better. (Answer: Visualizing while reading helps a reader picture the story in their mind to better understand the characters, the setting, and the events in the plot of the story.)
3. Next, prompt your student to open and view the **Character Traits in Drama - Watch It**. After the video, ask them, "How do physical traits relate to the personal traits of a character?" (Answer: The way a person appears or dresses can indicate various personal traits. For example, if a person always smiles, they may be considered a happy person.)

Demonstrate

1. Now, have your student complete the activity in the **Show It**. Use the following question prompts to help your student visualize the character in the passage:
   - What does the character look like?
   - What are the character's feelings?
   - How are the events in the story affecting the character?
2. When they are finished, use the **Show It AK** with your student to check their response.
3. To reinforce learning, consider having your student draw a picture of a character from one of their favorite books.

• • •

Adjectives

Activate

1. Play a game of I Spy using adjectives. To do so, take turns with your student looking around the learning environment and using an adjective to describe an object (a noun). Then, the other person will try to guess the object being described. For example, your student may say "shiny," and you may guess a mirror.

Engage

1. As your student reads the content of the **Read It**, have them create the following table in their journal to write down the definition of the term *adjective* and examples of adjectives found in the **Read It**.

Adjectives		
Definition of Term	**Examples**	**Types**

2. Then, have your student open and view the **Watch Its** titled **Describe and Compare** and **Searching for Adjectives**.
3. While viewing, have your student refer to the table they created in their journal to complete the *Types* column. In this column, they should list the categories for adjectives, such as shape, color, size, and how many.
4. Next, have them open and play the **Plutarch's Library-Adjectives, Nouns, Verbs - Play It** to review what they have learned about adjectives.
5. Finally, have your student use the **Practice It** to add adjectives to various sentences.

Demonstrate

1. Now, have your student complete the **Show It** activity.
2. Work with them to check their answers using the examples in the **Show It AK**.
3. Finally, move on to the Application section of the **Show It** and have your student find adjectives in a selected book.
4. To extend learning, consider having your student point out nouns during their next car ride and generate adjectives to describe what they see.

• • •

Spelling Long *a* and *i* Words

Engage

1. Have your student complete the **Practice It** activity. Encourage them to play multiple rounds of the game in order to practice all the words. Spelling practice activities for this subtopic will span Lessons 11 through 13.

LESSON 14

Topic	Fiction Elements

Learning Objectives

The activities in this lesson will help your student meet the following objectives:

- write a narrative story using the main components of narrative writing
- distinguish between precise and general adjectives
- spell words with the long vowels *a* and *i*

Materials

- "Afraid of the Dark"
- teacher- or student-selected text
- thesaurus

Write a Narrative Story

 ## Activate

1. Begin by asking your student to explain what a narrative is in their own words. (Answer: A narrative is a story that describes events; it can be fiction or nonfiction.)
2. Then, ask them to provide examples of both fiction and nonfiction narratives. Fairy tales are examples of fictional narratives, while biographies of famous historical figures are examples of nonfiction narratives.

 ## Engage

1. Have your student pay close attention to the components of narrative writing as they read the content of the **Read It**.
2. Then, ask them to describe how these five elements of narrative writing work together to deliver a good story.
3. Next, have your student open and play the **Plutarch's Library-Narrative Elements - Play It** and encourage them to play more than once if time permits. This game will provide a review of the components of a narrative.

 ## Demonstrate

1. Open the **Assess It** and have your student complete the activity. Help them to understand the expectations of the rubric before they begin writing. When they are finished, help them to review their work to make sure they have met the rubric expectations.
2. When they are finished, scan the document or take a photo of it and upload it to the Dropbox. For additional instructions on how to use the Dropbox, click on the paper clip icon in the upper-left corner of the **Assess It**.
3. To extend learning, consider taking a trip to the local library and having your student find examples of narrative writing from a variety of genres.

• • •

Precise and General Adjectives

 **Activate**

1. Ask your student to state what an adjective is. (Answer: a word or phrase used to describe a noun)
2. Then, ask your student to provide adjectives to describe the nouns *constellation*, *song*, *island*, and *grass*.
3. To spark ideas, consider providing the following examples to your student: *illuminated constellation*, *loud song*, *deserted island*, and *prickly grass*. Then, allow them to come up with their own adjectives to describe the nouns.

 **Engage**

1. As your student reads the content of the **Read It**, have them create the following table in their journal to write down the definitions of *general adjective* and *precise adjective* and examples of both.

	General Adjective	Precise Adjective
Definition		
Examples		

2. Next, have your student use the **Practice It** to identify general adjectives and to generate precise adjectives to describe nouns. Prompt your student to check their work using the answer key at the bottom of the page.

 **Demonstrate**

1. Move on to the **Show It**. Allow your student to complete the review activity before they begin the assignment.
2. Then, prompt them to evaluate their T-chart using the **Show It AK**.
3. Finally, direct them to complete the Application section of the **Show It** by locating adjectives in a selected piece of literature.
4. To extend learning, consider having your student create a poem about themselves using adjectives.

● ● ●

Spelling Long *a* and *i* Words

 ## Engage

1. Encourage your student to review and practice their spelling words before they complete the **Assess It**.

 ## Demonstrate

1. Now move on to the **Assess It**. Have your student write, and correctly spell, the words they hear spoken in the assessment. This assessment covers the spelling words presented in Lessons 11 through 13.
2. When they are finished, scan the document or take a photo of it and upload it to the Dropbox. For additional instructions on how to use the Dropbox, click on the paper clip icon in the upper-left corner of the **Assess It**.
3. The next lesson is a **Mastery Assess It**. Encourage your student to review Lessons 1 through 14 in order to prepare for the assessment.

LESSON 15

Topic | **Fiction Elements**

Learning Objectives

The activities in this lesson will help your student meet the following objectives:

*   not applicable

Materials

*   none required

Mastery Assess It 1

1. **Mastery Assess It 1** will cover what your student has learned in Lessons 1 through 14.
2. Click on the **Mastery Assess It 1** icon to begin the online assessment.
3. Have your student read the instructions before they get started. Remind them to take their time and to do their best work.
4. When they are finished and ready for their assessment to be graded, have them click the **Submit** button.

LESSON 16

Topic	Analyzing Fiction

Learning Objectives

The activities in this lesson will help your student meet the following objectives:

- explain and illustrate how the use of descriptive words and phrases in a narrative text helps to create a clear image for readers
- spell words with the long vowels *e* and *o*

Materials

- "The Sorcerer's Apprentice"
- art supplies
- dictionary
- index cards

The Use of Descriptive Words

Activate

1. Ask your student to describe the current weather. If necessary, take a quick look outside to allow them to make an observation.
2. Discuss the importance of using descriptive words when providing information or telling a story.

Engage

1. Begin by having your student read the content of the **Read It**.
2. Encourage them to pause at the examples of the setting, character, and plot clues. Challenge your student to come up with a different example using descriptive words for each.

Demonstrate

1. Move on to the **Show It**. Prompt your student to read the directions carefully and create a brochure.
2. Then, instruct them to compare their brochure to the sample brochure in the **Show It AK**.
3. To extend learning, consider having your student write "Who am I?" and "What am I?" riddles using a variety of descriptive words. The following is an example of such a riddle:

    I am high in the sky. I provide light. Plants use my energy to create food. What am I? (Answer: the Sun)

• • •

Spelling Long *e* and *o* Words

Activate

1. Ask your student to make the long *e* and *o* sounds.
2. Then, ask them to say words with these sounds. Examples are *leaf* and *phone*.

Engage

1. As your student reads the **Read It**, have them pay close attention to the Rules, Patterns, and Examples section. Encourage them to print these tables out and fasten them into their journal for future reference.
2. Then, have your student read the list of spelling words. You may want them to write the words and their definitions on a sheet of paper or index cards.
3. Next, have your student complete the card sorting to practice the spelling words.
4. Finally, prompt your student to move on to the **Practice It** and play the game. Spelling practice activities for this subtopic will span Lessons 16 through 18.

LESSON 17

Topic | **Analyzing Fiction**

Learning Objectives

The activities in this lesson will help your student meet the following objectives:

- summarize a text
- summarize a fiction story
- spell words with the long vowels *e* and *o*

Materials

- "Charlotte's Web: A Lesson in Friendship," "A Different Goal," "K-K Gregory: Kid Inventor," and "Steven and the Turtles"
- teacher- or student-selected fictional text
- teacher- or student-selected text

Summarizing Text

Activate

1. Ask your student to share a story about an important event in their life.
2. Then, ask them to identify elements such as the main idea and important details of that story.

Engage

1. Prompt your student to read the content of the **Read It**.
2. Afterward, ask your student to identify the important parts of a summary. (Answer: main idea; supporting details; sequential order of events with beginning, middle, and end; and summarizing in your own words)
3. Then, direct your student to open and view the **Review for You: Summarizing - Watch It**. Consider having them pause the video at 3:34 to analyze the Five *W*'s and to explain how they help when summarizing a story (Answer: The Five *W*'s help a reader retelling a story to include all major story elements, such as characters, setting, and plot. They also help a reader organize what they have read in sequential order.)

Demonstrate

1. Next, have your student move on to the **Show It** activity. Encourage them to use the Five *W*'s to write their summary.
2. Prompt them to compare their summary with the example in the **Show It AK**.
3. For extra practice writing a summary, be sure to have your student complete the Application section of the **Show It**.
4. To extend learning, consider having your student draw five pictures with corresponding sentences to summarize their weekend.

• • •

Fiction Summary

 **Activate**

1. Ask your student to explain the difference between fiction and nonfiction. (Answer: Fiction is fake or created using imagination, while nonfiction is real and based on facts.)
2. Then, ask your student to give examples of fiction and nonfiction. A possible reply may be "A story about a talking lion would be an example of fiction, and a book about natural disasters is an example of a nonfiction text."

 **Engage**

1. Now, have your student read the content of the **Read It**, pausing at the important question words. Consider having your student create a quick visual device using their hand and fingers. Each finger would represent one of the Five *W*'s, the important question words for summarizing: *who, what, when, where,* and *why.*
2. To further explore summarization, prompt your student to open and view the **Summary - Watch It**. After the video, ask your student to summarize the story about Alice in their own words.

 **Demonstrate**

1. Open the **Assess It** and have your student complete the activity. When they are finished, scan the document or take a photo of it and upload it to the Dropbox. For additional instructions on how to use the Dropbox, click on the paper clip icon in the upper-left corner of the **Assess It**.
2. For an additional challenge, encourage your student to complete the task in the Application section of the **Assess It** by writing a summary of a selected fictional text.

● ● ●

Spelling Long *e* and *o* Words

 **Engage**

1. Have your student complete the **Practice It** activity. Encourage them to play multiple rounds of the game in order to practice all the words. Spelling practice activities for this subtopic will span Lessons 16 through 18.

LESSON 18

Topic | **Analyzing Fiction**

Learning Objectives

The activities in this lesson will help your student meet the following objectives:

- create original dialogue based on a situation in a fairy tale
- add adjective prepositional phrases to modify nouns in sentences
- spell words with the long vowels *e* and *o*

Materials

- "Cinderella: A Retelling"
- small object
- teacher- or student-selected texts
- two plastic cups

Dialogue in Situations

Activate

1. Ask your student to come up with two examples of the feelings a person can have when talking with another person. For example, a person may be angry when talking about how their car broke down on the side of the road. A person can also be excited, such as when talking about an upcoming vacation.

Engage

1. Have your student read through the content of the **Read It**.
2. Afterward, ask your student, "Why do writers use dialogue in a story?" (Answer: Writers use dialogue to allow the characters to express their feelings and share their thoughts about what is happening in the story.)

Demonstrate

1. Now, prompt your student to complete the activity in the **Show It**.
2. Encourage them to use the **Show It AK** to view a sample dialogue set.
3. Then, direct your student to complete the Application section in the **Show It** to further analyze the purpose of dialogue in a story.
4. To extend learning, ask your student to observe the dialogue that occurs during dinner. Ask them to observe the feelings of each person as they talk about their day.

● ● ●

Adjective Prepositional Phrases

 **Activate**

1. Present the following items to your student:
   - two plastic cups
   - a small object, such as an action figure
2. Then, ask your student to place the object in various locations relative to the cups using the following preposition words: *behind, beside, between, near, under, above,* and *after.*

 **Engage**

1. Begin by having your student open and view the **Airplanes and Clouds - Watch It**. As they are viewing the video, prompt them to create the following table in their journal and complete the *Preposition* and *Prepositional Phrase* columns.

	Preposition	Prepositional Phrase	Adjective Prepositional Phrase
Definition			
Examples			

2. Next, have your student read the **Read It**. As they read, have them finish the table in their journal by completing the *Adjective Prepositional Phrase* column.

 **Demonstrate**

1. Have your student move on to the **Show It** and complete the activity.
2. Then, use the **Show It AK** to work with them to review their sentences.
3. For extra practice identifying adjective prepositional phrases, be sure to have your student complete the Application section of the **Show It**.
4. To enrich learning, consider taking a walk around the neighborhood and observing the environment to create adjective prepositional phrases for what is observed.

• • •

Spelling Long *e* and *o* Words

 **Engage**

1. Have your student complete the activity in the **Practice It** to review and spell words with long *e* and long *o*. Encourage them to play multiple rounds of the game in order to practice all the words. Spelling practice activities for this subtopic will span Lessons 16 through 18.

LESSON 19

Topic | Analyzing Fiction

Learning Objectives

The activities in this lesson will help your student meet the following objectives:

- retell events from a fiction story in chronological order
- add adverbs to modify verbs in sentences

Materials

- "The Championship"
- colored pencils
- index cards
- teacher- or student-selected text

Fiction Events

Activate

1. Ask your student to provide examples they have seen of chronological order. For example, chronological order can be found in cookbooks with recipes, lists of events in history, calendars, and the grades students attend when going to school.

Engage

1. As your student reads the content of the **Read It**, have them pay careful attention to the important elements that should be included when retelling a story in chronological order.
2. Then, ask them why retelling a story in chronological order is important. (Answer: Chronological order is important because giving the exact order in which events occurred in a story helps a reader better understand the story elements.)
3. Next, have your student open and view the **Review: Story Comprehension - Watch It**. At the end of the video, ask your student to identify the strategies that were discussed that help a reader understand what they read. (Answer: Reading comprehension strategies include a Five W's chart and a beginning, middle, and end graphic organizer, which can be used for summarizing. Identifying both cause-and-effect relationships and the author's purpose also helps a reader comprehend a text.)

Demonstrate

1. Now, have your student complete the **Show It**. Encourage them to use a Five W's chart to help them retell the most important events from "The Championship."
2. When they are finished, have them read the example in the **Show It AK**, and prompt them to add to their summary if needed.
3. To extend learning, have your student select a process that happens in chronological order, such as planting a garden. Then, have them write step-by-step chronological instructions for the task.

• • •

Adverbs

 **Activate**

1. Write the following words in your student's journal: *slowly, yesterday, underground, almost, cheerfully, somewhere, often,* and *very.*
2. Then, ask your student to sort the words by whether they show how, when, where, or the extent of action.
   - How: *slowly, cheerfully*
   - When: *yesterday, often*
   - Where: *underground, somewhere*
   - Extent of Action: *almost, very*

 **Engage**

1. Next, have your student review adverbs by reading the content of the **Read It**. Challenge your student to come up with example adverbs to describe how, where, when and to what extent.
2. Then, prompt them to open and view the **Adverbs Are Awesome - Watch It**. Consider having them pause the video after each question/sentence and provide the answer before the answer is shared.
3. Next, have your student open and view **The Word on Adverb Alley - Watch It**. Consider having them pause at 3:41 to pay particular attention to relative adverbs. Encourage your student to write the term *relative adverb* in their journal and take note of its meaning and examples.
4. Now, prompt them to open and view the **Searching for Adverbs - Watch It** to explore the jungle to find adverbs. Challenge them to come up with a sentence about the jungle that uses a verb and an adverb.
5. Encourage them to use the **Play Its** titled **Plutarch's Library-Fun with Parts of Speech** and **Space Rox-Parts of Speech** to review adverbs as well as other parts of speech.

 **Demonstrate**

1. Move on to the **Show It** and have your student complete the activity by adding adverbs to the sentences provided.
2. Work with them to check their sentences using the examples in the **Show It AK**.
3. Finally, have your student complete the Application section of the **Show It** by identifying adverbs in a selected text.
4. To reinforce learning, consider playing a game of "Adverb Charades." Before playing the game, write 20 verbs on separate index cards. Taking turns, each person draws a card, thinks of an adverb for the verb drawn, and then acts out the pair to show the adverb and verb connection. The other person has to guess!

LESSON 20

Topic **Analyzing Fiction**

Learning Objectives

The activities in this lesson will help your student meet the following objectives:

- summarize a story after determining its theme
- distinguish between precise and general adverbs
- spell words with the long vowels *e* and *o*

Materials

- "The Girl with the Golden Teeth" and "Seymour and Stanley"
- magazine or newspaper
- teacher- or student-selected text
- thesaurus

Determine Theme and Summarize

Activate

1. Ask your student to define the word *theme* in their own words. A possible reply may be "*Theme* means the subject, topic, or central idea of something."
2. Then, ask your student to brainstorm a list of themes that stories could have. For example, freedom, friendship, bravery, and trust are all possible story themes.

Engage

1. Beginning with the **Read It**, prompt your student to read the content.
2. Then, ask them how a reader determines the theme of a story. (Answer: A reader gathers many details from the story and then makes a guess as to what the theme is.)
3. Next, direct your student to open and play the **Plutarch's Library-Letters from a Young Gold Miner - Play It** to employ their reading comprehension skills with a fictional text.

Demonstrate

1. Move on to the **Show It**. Consider printing out the "Seymour and Stanley" passage to allow your student to underline or circle four supporting details that provide clues about the theme of the story.
2. Then, have your student compare their work with the example in the **Show It AK**.
3. To extend learning, consider taking a trip to the local library to find fables, folktales, and fairy tales. Encourage your student to read a variety of these literature types to practice identifying the theme of a story.

● ● ●

Precise and General Adverbs

 **Activate**

1. Ask your student to define the term *adverb*. (Answer: An adverb is a word added to a sentence to modify a verb, an adjective, or another adverb. They describe how, to what extent, when, or where.)
2. Then, ask them to create a sentence using the verb swim that contains an adverb. For example: The shark can swim quickly in the ocean.

 **Engage**

1. Next, have your student review adverbs by reading the content of the **Read It**.
2. Encourage your student to create and complete the following table in their journal.

	General Adverb	Precise Adverb
Definition		
Examples		

3. Then, prompt your student to open and view the **Precise Adverbs - Watch It**. Consider having them pause the video at 2:13 and 2:35 to come up with their own precise adverb for each sentence.

Demonstrate

1. Now, have your student complete the **Show It** activity.
2. Guide them to compare their T-chart to the one provided in the **Show It AK**. Encourage them to revise their work if needed.
3. Finally, move on to the Application section of the **Show It** and have your student identify precise adverbs in a selected text.
4. As an extension, ask your student to observe a picture from a magazine, newspaper, or other form of text. Then, have them create a short story using precise adverbs.

● ● ●

Spelling Long *e* and *o* Words

Engage

1. Encourage your student to review and practice their spelling words before they complete the **Assess It**.

Demonstrate

1. Now move on to the **Assess It**. Have your student write, and correctly spell, the words they hear spoken in the assessment. This assessment covers the spelling words presented in Lessons 16 through 18.

2. When they are finished, scan the document or take a photo of it and upload it to the Dropbox. For additional instructions on how to use the Dropbox, click on the paper clip icon in the upper-left corner of the **Assess It**.

LESSON 21

Topic | **Analyzing Fiction**

Learning Objectives

The activities in this lesson will help your student meet the following objectives:

- write a dialogue for two characters who are trying to resolve a conflict
- create a multimedia presentation to summarize a literary text
- spell words with the long *u* sound

Materials

- "Afraid of the Dark" and "A Conflict on the Playground"
- dictionary
- index cards
- presentation software

Conflict in Dialogue

Activate

1. Ask your student to explain what dialogue is in their own words. They may mention that dialogue is a conversation between two or more people in a story. Dialogue is written with quotation marks to show what is being said.

Engage

1. Begin by having your student read the content of the **Read It**. Encourage them to pay particular attention to the examples of dialogue throughout the reading.
2. Then, ask them, "How does dialogue help the characters in a story solve problems or resolve conflicts?" (Answer: Dialogue allows characters to talk with one another, which helps when solving problems and resolving conflicts. Through dialogue, characters are able to express their feelings about the events of a story.)

Demonstrate

1. Open the **Assess It** and have your student complete the activity. Ensure they review the expectations of the rubric before, during, and after they complete the activity.
2. When they are finished, scan the document or take a photo of it and upload it to the Dropbox. For additional instructions on how to use the Dropbox, click on the paper clip icon in the upper-left corner of the **Assess It**.

• • •

Multimedia Summary

 ## Activate

1. Ask your student to think about various ways technology allows a person to present information. For example, they may mention things such as slide presentations, blogs, digital posters, web pages, or online videos.
2. Then, ask them to determine what the prefix *multi-* means (Answer: The prefix *multi-* means "many.")

 ## Engage

1. Have your student read the content of the **Read It**.
2. Then, ask them, "How is a slide show a useful way to present information?" A possible reply may be that a slide show allows a person to organize the information presented in many different slides using interactive components to keep the presentation interesting.

 ## Demonstrate

1. Next, prompt your student to carefully read the directions in the **Show It**. It may be useful for them to print out the story in the **Show It** and mark important events to include in their summary. Help guide your student to set up their slide show in the presentation software of their choice.
2. Use the **Show It AK** together to review a sample slide show setup.
3. To extend learning, consider having your student create a photo slide show of the progression of their life.

Spelling Long *u* Words

 ## Activate

1. Ask your student to tell you the sound that the long vowel *u* makes.
2. Then, ask them to tell you a few words that use this sound. Some examples include *unicorn*, *duty*, *proof*, *glue*, and *June*.

 ## Engage

1. Have your student begin with the **Read It**. Tell them to pay close attention to the Rules, Patterns, and Examples section.
2. Then, have your student read the list of spelling words. You may want them to write the words and their definitions on a sheet of paper or index cards.
3. Next, have your student complete the word searches to practice the spelling words.
4. Last, move on to the **Practice It** for your student to complete the activity. Have them play the game multiple times so that they get an opportunity to practice all the words. Spelling practice activities for this subtopic will span Lessons 21 through 23.

LESSON 22

Topic | Analyzing Fiction

Learning Objectives

The activities in this lesson will help your student meet the following objectives:

- describe a situation between two fairy tale characters
- add adverb prepositional phrases to modify verbs in sentences
- spell words with the long *u* sound

Materials

- highlighter
- newspaper
- small object

Describe a Situation

Activate

1. Ask your student to describe a gift they received. Perhaps they received this gift for their birthday or on a holiday.
2. Then, ask them to revisit the description they just provided to identify the descriptive words they used, as in the following example.

   For my **tenth** birthday, I got a **shiny**, **heart-shaped** locket on a **long** necklace. The necklace and locket were **silver**, and I put a **small** picture of my family on the inside of the locket.

Engage

1. Start by having your student read the content of the **Read It**. Prompt your student to work through the example regarding Maggie and the weather before checking the answer.
2. Then, ask, "How can the five senses help an author to write descriptively?" They may mention that the five senses allow a writer to fully interact with the environment or setting of a story to describe many elements.

Demonstrate

1. Now, have your student complete the activity in the **Show It**. Encouraging them to create a quick sketch of the fairy tale event they select prior to writing will help them visualize the details.
2. Direct them to use the **Show It AK** to view a sample response, paying special attention to the descriptive language used.
3. To extend learning, display an object from the learning environment. This could be a small statue, a trinket, or any available object. Then, have your student use descriptive writing to explain the item.

• • •

Adverb Prepositional Phrases

 **Activate**

1. Prompt your student to write the following sentence in their journal:

    In the beginning of the race, Margo ran quickly.

2. Then, ask your student to underline or highlight the prepositional phrase and the adverb.

    In the beginning of the race, Margo ran **quickly**.

    In the beginning is the prepositional phrase, and *quickly* is the adverb.

 **Engage**

1. Have your student read the content of the **Read It**.
2. Afterward, ask them to explain how an adverb prepositional phrase modifies a sentence. (Answer: It modifies an adverb, verb, or adjective to tell when, where, why, how, or to what extent.)
3. Next, have them complete the activity in the **Practice It**.

 Demonstrate

1. Open the **Assess It** and have your student complete the activity. Be sure that they review the expectations of the rubric before and after writing.
2. When they are finished, scan the document or take a photo of it and upload it to the Dropbox. For additional instructions on how to use the Dropbox, click on the paper clip icon in the upper-left corner of the **Assess It**.
3. To extend learning, encourage your student to read the news (in a newspaper or online) and challenge them to locate adverb prepositional phrases.

Spelling Long *u* Words

 **Engage**

1. Have your student complete the **Practice It** activity. Encourage them to play multiple rounds of the game in order to practice all the words. Spelling practice activities for this subtopic will span Lessons 21 through 23.

LESSON 23

Topic	Analyzing Fiction

Learning Objectives

The activities in this lesson will help your student meet the following objectives:

- support an explanation of an inference using evidence from a text
- add relative clauses to sentences to convey more precise meanings
- spell words with the long *u* sound

Materials

- "The Space Rocket"
- highlighter
- teacher- or student-selected text

Explaining Inferences

Activate

1. Tell your student that they are going to play a game of 20 Questions. If they have not played before, explain that the object of this game is to guess mystery objects by asking 20 questions. Here are the rules:
   - Player 1 selects an object, such as an animal, a vegetable, a mineral, or another item without telling Player 2.
   - Player 2 asks 20 questions to determine what the object is.
   - Player 1 uses the replies "yes" and "no" to answer each question.
   - Player 2 can guess the object at any point. Once the twentieth question has been asked, Player 1 can tell Player 2 the object if Player 2 has not guessed correctly.
   - Players switch roles and play again.
2. If your student is having difficulty formulating 20 questions, try using fewer questions. The general idea is to use clues in the answers to identify the object.

Engage

1. Begin by having your student open and view the **Making Inferences - Watch It**. After the video, ask your student to explain how context clues help readers make inferences. (Answer: Context clues are the hints an author gives in a story. A reader can take these context clues and what they already know about a story and make an inference.)
2. Then, prompt your student to read the content of the **Read It**.
3. Before they read the passages accompanying the bus and baseball images, ask them to analyze each picture and make an inference concerning what the passage will be about.

Demonstrate

1. Have your student move on to the **Show It** to complete the activity. Encourage them to print a copy of "The Space Rocket" and use a highlighter to identify any context clues that help them make their inference about the story.
2. Then, prompt your student to use the **Show It AK** to evaluate their response.
3. To extend learning, consider having your student create and respond to various riddles. Riddles are a great way to practice making inferences.

Relative Clauses

 ## Activate

1. Ask your student to take the following two sentences and combine them into one sentence: A bus goes into town. It runs every hour.
2. A possible combination may be the following: A bus that runs every hour goes into town.

 ## Engage

1. Ask your student to copy the table below into their journal before reading the content of the **Read It**. Then, as they read the content, prompt them to complete the table. Encourage them to describe what a relative clause is in the *Definition* column, add relative pronouns and relative adverbs in the *Key Words* column, and include sentences in the *Examples* column.

Relative Clauses		
Definition	**Key Words**	**Examples**

2. Next, have your student complete the activity in the **Practice It**. This will allow them to practice distinguishing between relative clauses and other sentence elements.

 ## Demonstrate

1. Now, have your student move on to complete the **Show It**.
2. Using the **Show It AK**, work with your student to compare their sentences to the examples provided.
3. Ensure your student completes the Application section of the **Show It** for extra practice identifying relative clauses.

Spelling Long *u* Words

 ## Engage

1. Have your student complete the **Practice It** activity. Encourage them to play multiple rounds of the game in order to practice all the words. Spelling practice activities for this subtopic will span Lessons 21 through 23.

LESSON 24

Topic	Analyzing Fiction

Learning Objectives

The activities in this lesson will help your student meet the following objectives:

- create an inference based on a text
- identify the past, present, and future progressive tenses of a verb

Materials

- envelopes
- teacher- or student-selected text

Let's Infer

Activate

1. Present the following set of clues to your student:

   I am round and can be oval in shape. I am green on the outside and pink on the inside. I have seeds. I am a fruit. What am I? (Answer: a watermelon)

2. Now, challenge your student to create a "What am I?" scenario. Then, make an inference using the clues your student provides.

Engage

1. Begin by having your student read the content of the **Read It**.
2. Then, ask them to think about examples of making inferences in everyday life. For example, if a person is wearing a business suit, carrying a briefcase, and heading to the airport, one can infer that they are a businessperson and most likely going on a business trip.
3. Next, prompt your student to use the **Plutarch's Library-Why Be Shy? - Play It** to practice various reading comprehension skills.

Demonstrate

1. Now, have your student complete the **Show It** activity. When they have finished, work with them to review the sample response in the **Show It AK**.
2. As an extension, consider playing a game of "Mystery Mail." Here are the rules:
   - Player 1 and Player 2 each must brainstorm a character.
   - Then, Player 1 and Player 2 each must write a short letter, excluding a signature, from this character. They also have to draw three objects that would describe the character writing the letter.
   - Next, each must place the letter and drawings in an envelope and seal it.
   - Then, they switch envelopes with the other player and open the letter received.
   - Each player has to make an inference about the identity of the character by using the letter and drawings as clues.

● ● ●

Progressive Verb Tenses

Activate

1. Ask your student to share what they ate for dinner yesterday, for breakfast this morning, and what they will eat for dinner tonight.
2. Then, ask them to think about what words they used in their descriptions that signify past, present, and future times.

Engage

1. Have your student start by reading the content of the **Read It**.
2. Then, ask them, "Why are progressive verb tenses important?" A possible reply may be "They tell when an action was happening in the past, is happening now, or will be happening in the future."
3. Next, have them complete the activities in the **Practice It** to apply what they have learned about progressive verb tenses. Prompt your student to check their work using the example answers at the bottom of the page.

Demonstrate

1. Finally, have your student complete the **Show It** activity and then use the **Show It AK** to review their answers.
2. For an added challenge, ensure they complete the Application section of the **Show It** by locating progressive verb tenses in a selected text.

| Topic | Analyzing Fiction |

Learning Objectives

The activities in this lesson will help your student meet the following objectives:

- write a narrative story that contains descriptive dialogue
- use verbs in the progressive tense correctly in writing
- spell words with the long *u* sound

Materials

- "Excerpt from 'The Queen of the Golden Heart'"
- magazine or another printed source
- teacher- or student-selected text

Write a Descriptive Dialogue

 Activate

1. Ask your student to share an interesting event that happened to them in the last few days. Encourage them to use as many details and descriptions as possible.

 Engage

1. Begin by having your student read the content of the **Read It**.
2. Afterward, ask your student to explain how dialogue and descriptive words make story elements such as characters, setting, plot, and mood more interesting. They may mention that dialogue and descriptive words help the reader to picture in their mind what is happening in the story.

 Demonstrate

1. Now, guide your student to complete the **Show It** activity. A helpful tip may be to have your student select a picture from a magazine or another printed source and use that image when writing their narrative story.
2. Then, help your student to check their work using the example in the **Show It AK**.
3. To extend learning, encourage your student to pay attention to dialogue at various times during the day in many environments, such as at libraries, during school, and at home. What types of descriptive words or phrases do they hear being used in conversations?

● ● ●

Write Progressive Tenses

Activate

1. Ask your student to use the verb *draw* in three sentences to show the past, present, and future progressive tenses. The following are examples:
   - I was drawing a picture yesterday.
   - She is drawing a picture.
   - He will be drawing a picture tomorrow in school.

Engage

1. Instruct your student to read the **Read It**.
2. Ask them, "What does the -*ing* ending on a verb represent?" (Answer: It is used to indicate an ongoing action.)

Demonstrate

1. Next, have your student complete the **Show It** activity.
2. Then, direct them to use the **Show It AK** to check their sentences with the examples provided.
3. For extra practice, prompt your student to complete the Application section of the **Show It** by identifying verbs in a selected text and turning those verbs into progressive tense verbs.

Spelling Long *u* Words

Engage

1. Encourage your student to review and practice their spelling words before they complete the **Assess It**.

Demonstrate

1. Now move on to the **Assess It**. Have your student write, and correctly spell, the words they hear spoken in the assessment. This assessment covers the spelling words presented in Lessons 21 through 23.
2. When they are finished, scan the document or take a photo of it and upload it to the Dropbox. For additional instructions on how to use the Dropbox, click on the paper clip icon in the upper-left corner of the **Assess It**.

LESSON 26

Topic	Analyzing Fiction

Learning Objectives

The activities in this lesson will help your student meet the following objectives:

- explain how to use transitional words in writing
- describe how characters in a story successfully resolve a conflict
- spell irregular plural nouns

Materials

- "Marissa and the Mess" and "Snow-White"
- colored pencils
- dictionary
- index cards
- teacher- or student-selected text
- "Transitional Words Concept Map" activity page

Transitional Words

Activate

1. Ask your student to write the following words and phrases in their journal: *then*, *next*, *in conclusion*, *first*, *after that*, and *third*.
2. Then, ask them, "When would you see these words and phrases in a sentence?" (Answer: They are used to link ideas together to show a sequential order of events.)

Engage

1. Begin by having your student read the content of the **Read It**.
2. Afterward, ask them to think about what it would be like to read a story or paragraph that did not use transitions. A possible reply may be "If a story was not told using transitions, it would be difficult to understand the sequence of events."

Demonstrate

1. Next, have your student complete the **Show It**.
2. When your student has finished, work with them to compare their concept map with the examples provided in the **Show It AK**.
3. As an extension, consider having your student create a storyboard to describe an event or activity they attended. Encourage them to draw a picture in each box and include transition words when writing sentences to describe what happened.

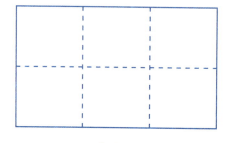

Successful Conflict Resolution

 Activate

1. Ask your student to share a time when they solved a problem that they faced. For example, they may have broken their glasses in half and solved this problem by using some tape to wrap the middle of the glasses until they got a new pair.

 Engage

1. Start by having your student view the **Fiction: A Made-Up Story - Watch It**.
2. Prompt your student to pause the video at 3:29, and ask them to state the conflict of the story and how it was resolved. (Answer: Ed's problem was that he really felt unsure about his place in his new family as he struggled to fit in. The solution to this problem happened when Ed's step-dad showed him that he accepted him just the way he was.)
3. Then, instruct your student to read the content of the **Read It**.
4. Afterward, ask them to suggest another way to solve the conflict in "Marissa and the Mess."

 Demonstrate

1. Next, have your student complete the activity in the **Show It**.
2. Finally, direct them to evaluate their response using the **Show It AK**.
3. For additional practice identifying conflict and resolution in a text, ensure your student completes the Application section of the **Show It**.

Spelling Irregular Plural Nouns

 Activate

1. Ask your student to tell you what a noun is and what the word *plural* means. (Answer: A noun is a person, place, thing, or idea. *Plural* means "more than one.")

 Engage

1. Have your student begin with the **Read It**, telling them to pay close attention to the Rules, Patterns, and Examples section.
2. Then, have your student read the list of spelling words. You may want them to write the words and their definitions on a sheet of paper or index cards.
3. Next, have them complete the word search activities to practice the spelling words.
4. Last, move on to the **Practice It** for your student to complete the activity. Have them play the game multiple times so that they get an opportunity to practice all the words. Spelling practice activities for this subtopic will span Lessons 26 through 28.

LESSON 27

Topic	Analyzing Fiction

Learning Objectives

The activities in this lesson will help your student meet the following objectives:

- infer what comes next in a paragraph
- identify examples of transitional words in a narrative text
- spell irregular plural nouns

Materials

- "Ollie's Outing"
- art supplies
- highlighter
- picture with no words from a magazine

Text Inferences

Activate

1. Provide your student with a picture with no words from a magazine.
2. Then, ask them to infer what is taking place in the photo by using the clues from the image.

Engage

1. After your student has read the content of the **Read It**, have them describe the similarities between an inference and a prediction. (Answer: Both refer to a conclusion made based on observations and facts.)
2. Then, have them open and view the **Inference and Drawing Conclusions - Watch It**. Ask them to make note of the username and password provided on the Discovery Education image. Be sure that they click the link for the video and enter the provided username and password to watch. Consider having them pause the video at 3:50, 4:08, and 4:49 to make inferences about the character Gulliver in *Gulliver's Travels*.

Demonstrate

1. Next, have your student move on to the **Show It** to make an inference and predictions based on the prompt provided.
2. Finally, instruct your student to use the **Show It AK** to check their answers.
3. To extend learning, consider having your student create a travel itinerary for a specific place by only providing clues and not giving the precise location. Then, encourage them to give this travel itinerary to someone else and ask that person to make an inference and guess the location.

• • •

Use of Transitional Words

 ## Activate

1. Ask your student to generate a list of five transitional words or phrases. Examples include *in the beginning*, *next*, *finally*, *after that*, and *second*.

 ## Engage

1. Begin by prompting your student to read the content of the **Read It**.
2. Encourage them to copy the table of example transition words and phrases in their journal.
3. As an added challenge, prompt your student to replace the transition words or phrases provided with different transitional cues while reading "The Mangled Mirror Tragedy."
4. Then, have them open and view the **Transitions and Connections - Watch It**. Encourage your student to complete the activity at the end of the video by writing sentences about tunnels using transitional tags.

 ## Demonstrate

1. Now, have your student move on to the **Show It** activity. Consider printing "Ollie's Outing" so that your student can highlight the transitional words and phrases as they read the text.
2. Help them to use the **Show It AK** to review their work.
3. To reinforce learning, consider having your student create a schedule for their day using transitional words.

Spelling Irregular Plural Nouns

 ## Engage

1. Have your student complete the **Practice It** activity. Encourage them to play multiple rounds of the game in order to practice all the words. Spelling practice activities for this subtopic will span Lessons 26 through 28.

LESSON 28

Topic | **Analyzing Fiction**

Learning Objectives

The activities in this lesson will help your student meet the following objectives:

- predict what will happen next in a story
- select appropriate transitional words to complete a story
- write sentences using verbs in the past, present, and future progressive tenses
- spell irregular plural nouns

Materials

- scissors
- teacher- or student-selected text
- "Transitional Words Cloze Exercise" activity page

What Happens Next

Activate

1. Show your student a weekly weather forecast for their town.
2. Then, ask them to make predictions about the weather based on their observations.

Engage

1. Now, have your student read through the content of the **Read It**.
2. Afterward, ask them to think about various predictions people make in their everyday lives. For example, people may guess what will happen in school, guess what will be served for dinner, and guess what their favorite TV show will be about. Challenge your student to supply their own example of when predictions are made throughout the day.

Demonstrate

1. Open the **Assess It** and have your student complete the activity. When they are finished, scan the document or take a photo of it and upload it to the Dropbox. For additional instructions on how to use the Dropbox, click on the paper clip icon in the upper-left corner of the **Assess It**.

● ● ●

Transitional Cloze Exercise

 ## Activate

1. Ask your student to come up with a sentence using the transition word *suddenly*. For example: Suddenly, the sky became dark and lightning lit up the sky.

 ## Engage

1. As your student reads the content of the **Read It**, engage in a discussion about how transition words help the organization of a paragraph. (Answer: Transition words are used in a paragraph to help the content flow smoothly. They also provide clues about the sequence of events in a story.)

 ## Demonstrate

1. Next, have your student complete the **Show It** using the "Transitional Words Cloze Exercise" activity page.
2. Consider printing out the activity page and cutting out the transitional words and phrases in the word bank. Then, your student will be able to move the words and phrases in and out of the blanks to see what makes sense.
3. Finally, direct your student to evaluate their answers using the **Show It AK**.

Changing Verb Tense

 ## Engage

1. Begin by having your student read the content of the **Read It**.
2. When they are finished, ask them, "What role do helping verbs play in determining the verb tense being used?" A possible reply may be, "Helping verbs are added before the verb ending in *-ing* to tell a reader if the action was happening in the past, is happening in the present, or will be happening in the future."

 ## Demonstrate

1. Next, have your student complete the **Show It** activity. Encourage them to rewrite the sentences in their journal.
2. Then, prompt them to compare their sentences to the examples provided in the **Show It AK**.
3. For extra practice with progressive verb tenses, ensure your student completes the Application section of the **Show It**.

Spelling Irregular Plural Nouns

 **Engage**

1. Have your student complete the **Practice It** activity. Encourage them to play multiple rounds of the game in order to practice all the words. Spelling practice activities for this subtopic will span Lessons 26 through 28.

LESSON 29

Topic | Analyzing Fiction

Learning Objectives

The activities in this lesson will help your student meet the following objectives:

- support a conclusion by identifying the *who, what, when, where, why,* and *how* of a text
- sort adjectives into categories based on type
- spell irregular plural nouns

Materials

- "George Washington Carver: Scholar, Scientist, Inventor" and "It's Party Time!"
- teacher- or student-selected text

Conclusion Diagram

Activate

1. Ask your student to think about a time when they recently had to draw conclusions about something. For example, maybe they were reading an advertisement for a new toy and had to use the clues in the image and details about the toy to understand how it worked. Discuss their experience.

Engage

1. Have your student read the content of the **Read It**. Guide them to pause their reading and recreate the conclusion diagram in their journal.
2. Then ask them, "Why do readers need to draw conclusions when they read?" A possible reply may be "Often, authors do not clearly state information in a story. Readers need to use their background knowledge to draw conclusions to understand what is happening."
3. Prompt your student to read "George Washington Carver: Scholar, Scientist, Inventor" in the **Practice It** and answer the questions to practice drawing conclusions.

Demonstrate

1. Open the **Assess It** and have your student complete the activity. Ensure they review the expectations of the rubric before, during, and after they complete the activity.
2. When they are finished, scan the document or take a photo of it and upload it to the Dropbox. For additional instructions on how to use the Dropbox, click on the paper clip icon in the upper-left corner of the **Assess It**.

• • •

Adjective Categories

 **Activate**

1. Ask your student to look outside and provide a description of what they see using adjectives.

 **Engage**

1. Begin by having your student read the content of the **Read It**.
2. Then, have them complete the following table in their journal to identify adjective categories by writing down examples for each:

Adjective Categories							
Opinion	Size	Age	Shape	Color	Origin	Material	Purpose

3. For additional practice identifying adjective categories, prompt your student to complete the sorting activities in the **Practice It**.

 **Demonstrate**

1. Open the **Assess It** and have your student complete the activity. When they are finished, scan the document or take a photo of it and upload it to the Dropbox. For additional instructions on how to use the Dropbox, click on the paper clip icon in the upper-left corner of the **Assess It**.
2. For an additional challenge, ensure your student completes the Application section of the **Assess It** by identifying adjectives and their categories in a selected text.

● ● ●

Spelling Irregular Plural Nouns

 **Engage**

1. Encourage your student to review and practice their spelling words before they complete the **Assess It**.

 **Demonstrate**

1. Now move on to the **Assess It**. Have your student write, and correctly spell, the words they hear spoken in the assessment. This assessment covers the spelling words presented in Lessons 26 through 28.
2. When they are finished, scan the document or take a photo of it and upload it to the Dropbox. For additional instructions on how to use the Dropbox, click on the paper clip icon in the upper-left corner of the **Assess It**.
3. The next lesson is a **Mastery Assess It**. Encourage your student to review Lessons 16 through 29 in order to prepare for the assessment.

LESSON 30

Topic	Analyzing Fiction

Learning Objectives

The activities in this lesson will help your student meet the following objectives:

- not applicable

Materials

- none required

Mastery Assess It 2

1. **Mastery Assess It 2** will cover what your student has learned in Lessons 16 through 29.
2. Click on the **Mastery Assess It 2** icon to begin the online assessment.
3. Have your student read the instructions before they get started. Remind them to take their time and to do their best work.
4. When they are finished and ready for their assessment to be graded, have them click the **Submit** button.

LESSON 31

| Topic | Fiction Point of View |

Learning Objectives

The activities in this lesson will help your student meet the following objectives:

- determine the point of view of a story
- write a narrative that includes transitional words and phrases
- spell words with prefixes

Materials

- "The Porcupine and the Firefly"
- dictionary
- index cards
- picture from a magazine, newspaper, or book with no words
- recipe
- teacher- or student-selected text
- "Weekly Reading Log" activity page

Determine Point of View

 Activate

1. To activate background knowledge, have your student open and view the **Exploring Points of View - Watch It**.
2. After the video, ask your student to explain the difference between first-person and third-person point of view. (Answer: First-person point of view is written from the perspective of a character, while third-person point of view is written from the perspective of a narrator.)
3. Then, ask them, "Why do authors choose different points of view when writing a story?" A possible reply may be "Authors use different points of view to convey the meaning and message of a story. Different points of view allow the reader to understand a story from different perspectives."

 Engage

1. Have your student read the content of the **Read It** and copy the point of view chart into their journal.
2. Ask them, "Which point of view do you prefer to read, first person or third person? Why?" Answers will vary, but a possible reply may be "I like reading stories written in first-person point of view because I can imagine being the character in the story and visualize the events that are happening."

 Demonstrate

1. Now, have your student move on to the **Show It** to determine the point of view in "The Porcupine and the Firefly." As they read, encourage them to look for pronouns that provide clues about the point of view that is being used.
2. Prompt them to compare their answer with the example in the **Show It AK**.
3. To extend learning, provide your student with a picture from a newspaper, magazine, or book that has no words. Then, have them write two short stories for the picture that express a first-person point of view and a third-person point of view. The storyline should remain the same so that your student can see how the different points of view change the way a story is written and read.

Transitional Words Narrative

 Activate

1. Give your student a written recipe.
2. Ask them to locate and identify any transitional words or phrases used in the recipe, such as *first*, *second*, *next*, *then*, and *last*.

 Engage

1. Begin by having your student read the content of the **Read It**.
2. Then, ask them to explain why the use of transition words in a narrative is important. (Answer: Transition words help readers to know when the story is moving from one event to the next.)

 Demonstrate

1. Open the **Assess It** and have your student complete the activity. Help them to understand the expectations of the rubric before they begin writing. Help them to review their work when they are done to make sure they have met the rubric expectations.
2. When they are finished, scan the document or take a photo of it and upload it to the Dropbox. For additional instructions on how to use the Dropbox, click on the paper clip icon in the upper-left corner of the **Assess It**.

Spelling Words with Prefixes

 Activate

1. Ask your student to tell you what a prefix is. (Answer: Prefixes are added to the beginning of root or base words to change their meaning.)
2. Then, challenge your student to list four words that have prefixes. *Repay*, *dislike*, *precook*, and *unlucky* are a few examples.

 Engage

1. Have your student begin with the **Read It**, telling them to pay close attention to the Rules, Patterns, and Examples section.
2. Then, have your student read the list of spelling words. You may want them to write the words and their definitions on a sheet of paper or index cards. As they write, instruct them to underline the prefix and explain how the prefix changes the word. For example, the word *obey* means to follow the guidance of someone. If they add the prefix *dis-*, the word thus formed means to not follow the guidance of someone.
3. Next, have your student complete the card sorting activities to practice the spelling words.
4. Last, move on to the **Practice It** for your student to complete the activity. Have them play the game multiple times so that they get an opportunity to practice all the words. Spelling practice activities for this subtopic will span Lessons 31 through 33.

LESSON 32

Topic	Fiction Point of View

Learning Objectives

The activities in this lesson will help your student meet the following objectives:

- describe the five senses
- write sentences that contain adjectives from various categories written in the proper order
- spell words with prefixes

Materials

- "A Walk Along the Ocean"
- small object
- teacher- or student-selected text

The Five Senses

 ## Activate

1. Ask your student to name the five senses. (Answer: taste, sight, touch, smell, and hearing)
2. Then, ask them to identify the senses that they use to observe things in their learning environment. For example, a piece of food can be tasted, they can look out the window, typing on a keyboard uses touch, they can smell lunch cooking, and they can hear music on a radio.

 ## Engage

1. Begin by having your student read the content of the **Read It**. As they read "A Walk Along the Ocean," instruct them to point out details that appeal to the five senses.
2. Then, ask them to provide one reason why using the five senses when writing creates a more detailed, engaging story. A possible reply is "Using the five senses helps readers to imagine the events in a story."

 ## Demonstrate

1. Now, prompt your student to complete the activity in the **Show It**.
2. Guide them to compare their sentences with the examples in the **Show It AK**.
3. As an extension, have your student select one object from their learning environment and write a "What am I?" riddle about it using the sentence starters below. They need not cover all the senses. At the end, they should write "What am I?" When they are finished, have your student read their riddle to a peer or adult to see whether they can guess the object.
   - I look like…
   - I smell like…
   - I taste like…
   - I feel like…
   - I sound like…

• • •

Ordering Adjective Sentences

 ## Activate

1. Begin by asking your student to describe the clothes they are wearing.
2. Then, ask them what descriptive words are called. (Answer: adjectives)

 ## Engage

1. As your student reads the content of the **Read It**, consider having them pause the reading to create their own silly sentence to help them remember the order of adjectives in a sentence.
2. Also, remind them to pay close attention to the grammar rules for listing two or more adjectives in a sentence. They should copy these rules into their journal.

 ## Demonstrate

1. Next, prompt your student to complete the **Show It**. Encourage them to refer to the rules for listing adjectives in a sentence they copied into their journal from the **Read It**.
2. Then, have your student compare their sentences to the examples in the **Show It AK** to ensure they listed adjectives in the correct order.
3. For extra practice, have your student complete the Application section of the **Show It**.
4. To extend learning, the next time your student is in the car or taking a walk, have them create sentences using more than one adjective to describe what they observe.

Spelling Words with Prefixes

 ## Engage

1. Have your student complete the **Practice It** activity. Encourage them to play multiple rounds of the game in order to practice all the words. Spelling practice activities for this subtopic will span Lessons 31 through 33.

LESSON 33

| Topic | Fiction Point of View |

Learning Objectives

The activities in this lesson will help your student meet the following objectives:

- compare and contrast first-person and third-person narration
- spell words with prefixes

Materials

- white paper plates

First and Third Person

Activate

1. Present the following short stories to your student:
   - Mary woke up early on Saturday morning. She had to get ready to help her grandmother plant a garden in their backyard. She was so excited about helping her grandmother, she had trouble sleeping that night.
   - I was feeling anxious. I had tryouts for my high school basketball team. I practiced all week long. I really hope I make the team!
2. Then, ask them to identify which short story is written in first-person point of view and which story is written in third-person point of view (Answer: The story about Mary is written in third-person point of view and the story about basketball tryouts is written in first-person point of view.)
3. Finally, ask them how they reached their conclusions. They should mention the pronouns *she* and *her* and *I* and *my*.

Engage

1. Begin by having your student view the **Fox & Crow: What's the Point? - Watch It**. Encourage them to pause the video at 1:05, 1:24, and 1:38 to locate pronouns in the story that would provide clues to whether the story was written in first- or third-person point of view.
2. After the video, ask them to explain the difference between third-person omniscient and third-person limited point of view. (Answer: Third-person omniscient is when the narrator knows all the thoughts and feelings of all characters in a story. Third-person limited is when the narrator only knows the thoughts and feelings of one character.)
3. As they read the content of the **Read It**, ask them to state the pronouns used in first-person point of view (*I, me, mine, myself, we, us, ours, ourselves*) and third-person point of view (*he, she, it, him, her, his, hers, they, them*).

Demonstrate

1. Next, have your student move on to create a Venn diagram to compare and contrast first-person and third-person point of view in the **Show It**.
2. Consider creating an interactive Venn diagram using white paper plates to make this activity more engaging. Instruct your student to fasten two plates together. Have them trace where the plates intersect to create the middle of the Venn diagram.
3. Instruct them to use the **Show It AK** to check their work. Encourage them to add additional information to their Venn diagram if necessary.
4. As an extension, challenge your student to turn a first-person point of view text into one written using a third-person point of view. Engage them in a discussion about how the different perspective changes the story.

● ● ●

Spelling Words with Prefixes

Engage

1. Have your student complete the **Practice It** activity. Encourage them to play multiple rounds of the game in order to practice all the words. Spelling practice activities for this subtopic will span Lessons 31 through 33.

LESSON 34

| Topic | Fiction Point of View |

Learning Objectives

The activities in this lesson will help your student meet the following objectives:

- compare and contrast the points of view in two stories
- identify sensory words and phrases in a narrative text
- spell words with prefixes

Materials

- "Afraid of the Dark" and "You Never Forget How to Ride a Bike"
- highlighter
- teacher- or student-selected text

Compare Points of View

 Activate

1. Ask your student to compare and contrast two living types of animals, such as bats and eagles.
2. Ask them to state three differences and three similarities when comparing and contrasting.
3. Here is an example response:
   - Bats are mammals, are nocturnal, and have fur.
   - Eagles hatch from eggs, raise their young in nests, and have feathers.
   - Both have wings, fly, and have feet.

 Engage

1. Begin by prompting your student to read the content of the **Read It**.
2. As they read the passages, encourage them to create a Venn diagram in their journal to jot down notes about how the passages differ or are the same.

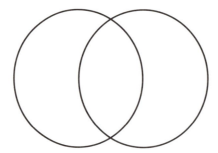

3. After they have read the passages, have them compare their diagram to the completed diagram in the **Read It**.
4. Next, prompt them to open the **Plutarch's Library-Point of View - Play It** to identify sentences showing first- and third-person point of view. If time permits, allow them to play more than once to get extra practice.

Demonstrate

1. Open the **Assess It** and have your student complete the activity. Ensure they review the expectations of the rubric before, during, and after they complete the activity.
2. When they are finished, scan the document or take a photo of it and upload it to the Dropbox. For additional instructions on how to use the Dropbox, click on the paper clip icon in the upper-left corner of the **Assess It**.
3. For extra practice identifying points of view, ensure your student completes the Application section of the **Assess It**.

● ● ●

Sensory Words and Phrases

Activate

1. Ask your student to describe a place they would like to go on vacation.
2. Then, ask them to identify all the words or phrases they used to describe the place.

Engage

1. As your student reads the content of the **Read It**, engage them in a discussion about how a reader uses the sensory details of a story. Possible discussion points include how sensory details help a reader to imagine the setting and characters and how appealing to the five senses allows a reader to fully immerse themselves in the story.
2. Next, have them view the **Sensory Words and Phrases - Watch It**. Have them pause the video at each sentence and story example, and challenge them to identify the sensory words or phrases before the answers are provided.

Demonstrate

1. Encourage your student to print out "You Never Forget How to Ride a Bike" from the **Show It** before completing the task. This will allow them to use a highlighter to locate sensory words or phrases within the text.
2. When they are done, direct your student to use the **Show It AK** to see example sensory words and phrases from the story.
3. As an extension, consider having your student narrate their day or weekend using as many sensory words and phrases as they can in their story.

● ● ●

Spelling Words with Prefixes

Engage

1. Encourage your student to review and practice their spelling words before they complete the **Assess It**.

Demonstrate

1. Now move on to the **Assess It**. Have your student write, and correctly spell, the words they hear spoken in the assessment. This assessment covers the spelling words presented in Lessons 31 through 33.

2. When they are finished, scan the document or take a photo of it and upload it to the Dropbox. For additional instructions on how to use the Dropbox, click on the paper clip icon in the upper-left corner of the **Assess It**.

LESSON 35

Topic **Fiction Point of View**

Learning Objectives

The activities in this lesson will help your student meet the following objectives:

- create two versions of the same story in different points of view
- identify prepositions in sentences
- spell words with suffixes

Materials

- "Margaret and Gert" and "Waynesboro to Washington"
- colored pencils
- dictionary
- "Find Prepositions" activity page

Describing Point of View

Activate

1. Review the first verse of the nursery rhyme "Mary Had a Little Lamb" with your student.

   > Mary had a little lamb,
   > Its fleece as white as snow.
   > And everywhere that Mary went,
   > The lamb was sure to go.

2. Then ask them, "From whose point of view is the song?" It is written in the third person about Mary and her lamb.
3. Next, challenge them to change the lyrics so it is written from a first-person point of view, as if Mary were speaking. For example, it could begin "I had a little lamb...."

Engage

1. As your student reads the content of the **Read It**, have them choose a first-person and third-person pronoun and verbally create their own sentence for each pronoun.
2. Then, as your student reads "Waynesboro to Washington" and "Margaret and Gert," encourage them to identify sentences that indicate the story's point of view.
3. After reading each text, help them follow the four steps for determining point of view in the Tips section before answering the comprehension questions.

Demonstrate

1. Now, direct them to complete the **Show It** activity. Remind them that both versions of the story need to be about the woman on stage.
2. Finally, work with them to compare their stories with the examples in the **Show It AK**.

• • •

Prepositions

 **Engage**

1. While your student reads the **Read It**, instruct them to choose three of the sample prepositions to note in their journal. Tell them to include an illustration and sentence for each preposition.
2. Next, direct them to open the **Plutarch's Library-Prepositions - Play It** to play the game.

 **Demonstrate**

1. Have your student move on to the activity page in the **Show It**.
2. Then, help them use the **Show It AK** to check their answers.

• • •

Spelling Words with Suffixes

 **Activate**

1. Start by having your student open the **Prefixes and Suffixes - Watch It** to view the video to learn about affixes.
2. Then, prompt them to explain the difference between prefixes and suffixes. (Answer: A prefix is a letter or group of letters added to the beginning of a root word, and a suffix is added to the end of a word.)

 **Engage**

1. Have your student read the content of the **Read It**. Instruct them to note the rules for adding suffixes to root words in their journal. Particularly emphasize when the silent letter e at the end of a word is dropped.
2. Next, guide them to practice adding suffixes to root words in the **Plutarch's Library-Word Endings - Play It**.
3. Finally, direct them to complete the activity in the **Practice It**. Spelling practice activities for this subtopic will span Lessons 35 through 37.

LESSON 36

Topic | **Fiction Point of View**

Learning Objectives

The activities in this lesson will help your student meet the following objectives:

- identify descriptive words and phrases that relate to the five senses
- identify prepositional phrases in sentences
- spell words with suffixes

Materials

- teacher- or student-selected text
- thesaurus
- "Prepositions and Prepositional Phrases" and "Using Descriptive Words" activity pages

Descriptive Words Chart

Activate

1. Begin by having your student step outside and close their eyes. Ask them to use their senses of smell and hearing to make observations of their environment.
2. Then, direct them to open their eyes and use their senses of sight and touch to make more observations. Discuss how using their sense of taste may be challenging if there is nothing available to eat safely.

Engage

1. As your student reads the **Read It**, discuss how a thesaurus is a great tool to help describe objects. If they are unfamiliar with a thesaurus, help them look up a synonym for one of the descriptive words in the text in a print or online version.

Demonstrate

1. Now, instruct your student to complete the "Using Descriptive Words" activity page in the **Show It**.
2. Next, assist them in evaluating their responses using the **Show It AK**.
3. To extend learning, remind them to use their senses while writing descriptions for other assignments.

● ● ●

Prepositional Phrases

 **Activate**

1. Guide your student to open the **Get Prepped for Prepositions - Watch It** to review information about prepositions.
2. Have them pause the video at 3:50 to identify the preposition and prepositional phrase. Continue the video to check their response.
3. As each new sentence is presented, have your student pause the video and identify the preposition and prepositional phrase.

 **Engage**

1. Have your student read the contents of the **Read It**.
2. Play a game with your student. Call out different prepositional phrases and have your student act out each phrase. For example, if you call out "under the table," your student should move quickly under a table while indicating the preposition (*under*). Continue calling out prepositional phrases for a few minutes.
3. Next, guide your student to complete the activity in the **Practice It**.

 **Demonstrate**

1. Now, instruct your student to move on to the "Prepositions and Prepositional Phrases" activity page in the **Show It**.
2. When they are finished, work with them to check their answers using the **Show It AK**.
3. For extra practice, have them complete the Application section of the **Show It** using a selected text.

• • •

Spelling Words with Suffixes

 **Engage**

1. Direct your student to complete the activity in the **Practice It** to study the spelling words. Spelling practice activities for this subtopic will span Lessons 35 through 37.

LESSON 37

Topic | **Fiction Point of View**

Learning Objectives

The activities in this lesson will help your student meet the following objectives:

- construct a poster with examples and illustrations of the conventional adjective categories
- use sensory details when writing about a personal experience
- spell words with suffixes

Materials

- "The Air Is Different Up There"
- art supplies
- glue
- highlighter
- magazine
- poster board
- scissors
- thesaurus

Ordering Adjectives Poster

 ## Activate

1. Start by instructing your student to cut five adjectives out of a magazine. Ask them whether any of the adjectives can be grouped together in some way, such as by color, size, or shape.
2. Then, tell them to glue the adjectives on a piece of paper. Guide them to glue the adjectives in their groups, if possible.

 ## Engage

1. As your student reads the **Read It**, have them write the list of adjective categories in order in their journal.

   - opinion
   - size
   - age
   - shape
   - color
   - origin
   - material
   - purpose

2. Challenge them to write a long sentence that contains at least five of the eight categories of adjectives. Be sure they follow the comma rules provided in the **Read It**.

Demonstrate

1. Now, direct your student to make the poster in the **Show It**. They can either start a new poster or add to the paper they started in the Activate. Encourage them to use a thesaurus to add interesting adjectives to their poster. Ensure they review the rubric before they begin.
2. Help your student to evaluate their poster using the rubric. Allow them to refer to the **Show It AK** to view a sample poster.
3. To extend learning, have your student give a presentation and share their poster with peers or family members.

•••

Using Sensory Details

 **Engage**

1. As your student reads the **Read It**, consider having them print the text, "The Air Is Different Up There," and mark the sensory details with a highlighter. Encourage them to read the entire text and then reread it searching for the sensory details.

 **Demonstrate**

1. Next, instruct your student to complete the **Show It** activity. Encourage them to use the following chart to brainstorm sensory details for each sense before they begin to write.

Hearing	
Touch	
Sight	
Smell	
Taste	

2. Then, have them view the writing sample in the **Show It AK**.

• • •

Spelling Words with Suffixes

 **Engage**

1. Have your student complete the activity in the **Practice It**. Spelling practice activities for this subtopic will span Lessons 35 through 37.

LESSON 38

Topic	**Fiction Point of View**

Learning Objectives

The activities in this lesson will help your student meet the following objectives:

- describe how a text would be different if it was written from a different point of view
- construct sentences that contain prepositional phrases
- spell words with suffixes

Materials

- flower
- tape

Changing Point of View

Activate

1. Place a flower between you and your student so that you are both seeing different parts of the flower. Describe the flower from your perspective.
2. Next, ask your student to describe the flower from their perspective.
3. Last, discuss the differences between your descriptions. Lead your student to understand that your different positions caused you to have different views of the flower, but neither was wrong.

Engage

1. As your student reads the contents of the **Read It**, emphasize the advantages and disadvantages of first- and third-person stories.

Demonstrate

1. Now instruct your student to complete the **Show It** activity.
2. When they are finished, help them to evaluate their letter using the **Show It AK**.
3. To extend learning, have your student write the story from the first-person perspective or from the point of view of one of the judges or another person waiting to audition.

● ● ●

Write Prepositional Phrases

 **Activate**

1. Begin by having your student open the **Exploring Prepositional Phrases - Watch It**. Ask them to make note of the username and password provided on the Discovery Education image. Be sure that they click the link for the video and enter the provided username and password to watch.
2. Have them pause the video at 3:55 to identify the prepositional phrase and again at 4:46 to add a prepositional phrase to the sentence.

 **Engage**

1. While your student reads the content of the **Read It**, have them use the prepositional phrases from the flip-book in sentences.
2. Encourage your student to print out the chart of common prepositions and fasten it in their journal for future reference. Alternatively, they can copy the chart by hand.

 **Demonstrate**

1. Next, have your student complete the activity in the **Show It**.
2. Help them check that each sentence has a preposition followed by a noun or pronoun. They can refer to the **Show It AK** for a sample sentence.

• • •

Spelling Words with Suffixes

 **Engage**

1. Encourage your student to review the list of spelling words from Lesson 35 before they complete the **Assess It**.

 **Demonstrate**

1. Now move on to the **Assess It**. Have your student write, and correctly spell, the words they hear spoken in the assessment. This assessment covers the spelling words presented in Lessons 35 through 37.
2. When they are finished, scan the document or take a photo of it and upload it to the Dropbox. For additional instructions on how to use the Dropbox, click on the paper clip icon in the upper-left corner of the **Assess It**.
3. The next lesson is a **Mastery Assess It**. Encourage your student to review Lessons 31 through 38 in order to prepare for the assessment.

LESSON 39

Topic | **Fiction Point of View**

Learning Objectives

The activities in this lesson will help your student meet the following objectives:

- not applicable

Materials

- none required

Mastery Assess It 3

1. **Mastery Assess It 3** will cover what your student has learned in Lessons 31 through 38.
2. Click on the **Mastery Assess It 3** icon to begin the online assessment.
3. Have your student read the instructions before they get started. Remind them to take their time and to do their best work.
4. When they are finished and ready for their assessment to be graded, have them click the **Submit** button.

LESSON 40

| Topic | Making Comparisons |

Learning Objectives

The activities in this lesson will help your student meet the following objectives:

- compare a written text with visual images from that text
- write about an event using descriptive words and phrases
- spell words with Greek and Latin parts

Materials

- "Blue Hole" and "Easily Scared"
- colored pencils
- dictionary
- index cards
- magazine
- teacher- or student-selected text

Visuals

 ## Activate

1. Tell your student they are going to play the game "Picture Dictation."
   a. Select a picture of a setting from a magazine, such as a house with a garden, a person walking a dog in a park, etc. Do not let your student view the picture!
   b. As you describe the picture to your student, instruct them to draw what they hear. Be specific. For example, say there is a flower garden in the lower left-hand corner, the front door is in the center of the house, etc.
   c. After your student draws their picture, compare it to the magazine image. Discuss how what they visualize from a verbal description may differ from an actual picture.
2. Now, explain to your student that they will be learning how pictures can help a reader comprehend and make predictions about a reading.

 ## Engage

1. Begin with the **Read It**. Have your student read all the content.
2. Ask them to pause to review the questions to ask when comparing a visual and the text. Then, ask your student why it is important to use visuals to make predictions about a story.

 ## Demonstrate

1. Next, have your student complete the **Show It** activity. Suggest that they use a Venn diagram graphic organizer to complete the assignment in their journal.

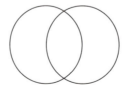

2. Use the examples in the **Show It AK** to review your student's answers together.
3. To extend learning, have your student predict what a story will be about by looking at the picture on the front cover of a book before they begin reading.

• • •

Descriptive Words Paragraphs

 **Engage**

1. Start by having your student read the content of the **Read It**.
2. Discuss with your student how descriptive words can make characters come to life for a reader.
3. Next, have your student view the **Descriptive Writing - Watch It**. Ask the following questions about the video:
    *   What are the four main characteristics of descriptive writing? (Answer: vivid sensory details, figurative language, precise language, and organization)
    *   What are several different types of figurative language that can be used in descriptive writing? (Answer: analogies, similes, or metaphors)
    *   What is the significance of action verbs in descriptive writing? (Answer: Action verbs hold the reader's attention, evoke powerful emotions, and demonstrate action instead of describing it.)

 Demonstrate

1. Open the **Assess It** and have your student complete the activity. When they are finished, scan the document or take a photo of it and upload it to the Dropbox. For additional instructions on how to use the Dropbox, click on the paper clip icon in the upper-left corner of the **Assess It**.
2. To extend learning, have your student read the paragraph about the beach in the **Read It** and draw an illustration to accompany the text.

Spelling with Greek Parts

 **Engage**

1. Begin with the **Read It** and have your student read the content. Consider having them copy into their journal the chart that lists common roots and their meanings.
2. Direct your student to read the list of spelling words. You may want them to write each word and its definition in their journal or on an index card.
3. Then, have your student complete the crossword activities to practice using the spelling words.
4. Next, have them view the **Greek Roots - Watch It**. This video discusses three roots—*chrono*, *dem*, and *path*—and the English words that are derived from them.
5. Move on to the **Greek and Latin Affixes and Roots - Practice It** so that your student can complete the activity identifying the meanings of words by using common Greek and Latin affixes and roots as clues.
6. As an opportunity for your student to review their spelling words, have them complete the **Spelling with Greek Parts A - Practice It** activity. Have them play multiple rounds of the game for a chance to practice spelling all the words. Spelling practice activities for this subtopic will span Lessons 40 through 42.

LESSON 41

Topic	Making Comparisons

Learning Objectives

The activities in this lesson will help your student meet the following objectives:

- compare two or more texts
- explain how a relative pronoun is used in a sentence
- spell words with Greek and Latin parts

Materials

- "Break a Leg," "The Flip," "Myth of the Seasons," and "Pandora's Box"
- colored pencils
- dry erase board and marker

Text to Text

Activate

1. Ask your student to compare the fairy tales *Sleeping Beauty* and *Cinderella* by completing a Venn diagram graphic organizer of the similarities and differences on a dry erase board.
2. Explain to them that they will be exploring how making connections between texts helps comprehension.

Engage

1. As your student reads the content of the **Read It**, engage them in a discussion regarding the questions the reader should ask to determine what information in a text is important.
2. Before they read the two texts, have them copy the following table into their journal.

	"Break a Leg"	"The Flip"
Characters		
Character Traits		
Setting		
Events		
Ending		
My Feelings		

3. Then, have them complete the table as they read both texts.
4. Finally, ask your student to compare their completed table with the one in the **Read It**.

Demonstrate

1. Now, have your student move on to the **Show It** and complete the activity. Suggest that they use a graphic organizer to organize the information before beginning their paragraph.
2. Finally, allow your student to check their response using the **Show It AK**.

• • •

Recognizing Relative Pronouns

Engage

1. Have your student read the content of the **Read It**.
2. Suggest that your student identify the relative pronouns in each sentence in the book first. Then, read on to check their responses and see how the relative pronouns are used.
3. Direct your student to open the **Recognizing Relative Pronouns - Watch It**. Have them pause the video and identify the relative pronouns in each sentence before the narrator shares the answer.

Demonstrate

1. Move on to the **Show It** and have your student complete the sorting activity to review the differences between nouns and relative pronouns.
2. Then, have them complete the writing activity. Have your student refer to the reading or video if necessary. Remind your student to consult the Student Response Checklist when they have completed their paragraph. They may add an illustration to accompany their writing.
3. Finally, using the **Show It AK**, work with your student to compare their paragraph to the example provided.

● ● ●

Spelling with Greek Parts

Engage

1. Have your student complete the **Practice It** activity. Encourage them to play multiple rounds of the game in order to practice all the words. Spelling practice activities for this subtopic will span Lessons 40 through 42.

LESSON 42

Topic | Making Comparisons

Learning Objectives

The activities in this lesson will help your student meet the following objectives:

- explain how the values and beliefs of different cultures are expressed through traditional literature
- identify the method used to end a narrative text
- spell words with Greek and Latin parts

Materials

- "How an Inheritance Was Divided," "Myth of the Seasons," "The Tortoise and the Hare," and "The Two Villages"
- teacher- or student-selected narrative text

Cultural Values and Beliefs

Activate

1. Ask your student whether they have ever read a story that teaches a moral, or lesson. Explain to them this type of literature is called a fable.
2. Tell them they will be learning about three types of traditional literature.

Engage

1. Start by having your student create the following chart in their journal.

Fables	Folktales	Myths

2. As your student reads each section of the **Read It**, prompt them to fill in the details for each type of traditional literature.
3. Next, have your student view the **Watch Its** titled **Mythology: Pandora** and **Mythology: King Midas**. Instruct them to add any additional details that they learn about myths to their chart.

Demonstrate

1. Now, direct your student to complete the **Show It** activity.
2. Using the example in the **Show It AK**, work with your student to review their list.
3. To extend learning, have your student read additional fables, folktales, and myths. Perhaps they can find a reading buddy to share the stories with and explain the morals and lessons of the stories. Then, suggest that they put on a performance and act out the stories.

• • •

Ending Narrative Text

 **Engage**

1. Have your student create a circle map in their journal like the one below, labeling the inner circle *Ways to End a Narrative*.

Circle Map

2. Next, have your student read the content of the **Read It**. As they read, ask them to complete the outside circle with details about the different ways to end, or conclude, a narrative.

 **Demonstrate**

1. Now, instruct your student to complete the activity in the **Show It**.
2. Using the **Show It AK**, work with your student to check their answer.
3. To extend learning, when your student is reading stories for pleasure, have them refer to the circle map and determine the kind of conclusion the author uses.

● ● ●

Spelling with Greek Parts

 **Engage**

1. Guide your student to complete the spelling activity in the **Practice It**. Encourage them to repeat it multiple times, if necessary. Spelling practice activities for this subtopic will span Lessons 40 through 42.

LESSON 43

Topic **Making Comparisons**

Learning Objectives

The activities in this lesson will help your student meet the following objectives:

- justify the use of relative pronouns in context
- brainstorm ideas for ending a narrative

Materials

- "Examples of Different Book Endings"
- scissors
- tape

Relative Pronouns in Context

 ### Activate

1. Ask your student to name several of their relatives. They may mention their mom, dad, brother, sister, grandparent, aunt, uncle, etc.
2. Then, ask them to share what a relative is. (Answer: a person whom one is related to)
3. Tell them that they will be learning about relative pronouns, words that relate, or connect, nouns or noun phrases to their descriptions.

 ### Engage

1. As your student reads the **Read It**, have them pause at the Using Relative Pronouns section. Ask them to verbally share one sentence for each relative pronoun relating to the picture. Then, have them read on to see other examples.

 ### Demonstrate

1. Now, have your student move on to the **Show It** and identify the relative pronouns in the word search. Have them complete the activity by explaining the purpose of the relative pronoun in each sentence.
2. Finally, allow your student to check their responses with the **Show It AK**. Instruct them to circle any incorrect response and write the correct answer next to it.

• • •

Brainstorm Conclusion Ideas

 ## Activate

1. Ask your student to share the ending of their favorite book, movie, or television show.
2. Then, ask them to explain why the ending is good.
3. Tell them they will be learning about the various types of endings, or conclusions.

 ## Engage

1. Starting with the **Read It**, have your student read through the content.
2. Consider printing a copy of the chart in the **Read It** that lists the ways to end a narrative and what each one means. Cut the types of conclusions and their meanings and have your student sort them together for practice. When they have matched them all correctly, print out a second copy of the chart that your student can secure in their journal for reference.

 ## Demonstrate

1. Next, have your student complete the **Show It**. Let your student refer to the reading or their notes if necessary.
2. Finally, have your student compare their work to the examples in the **Show It AK**.
3. To extend learning, challenge your student to come up with alternative endings for some of the stories they have read or some movies or television episodes they have watched.

LESSON 44

Topic | **Making Comparisons**

Learning Objectives

The activities in this lesson will help your student meet the following objectives:

- compare the themes in fables from different cultures
- describe how a conflict could be resolved to effectively conclude a narrative
- spell words with Greek and Latin parts

Materials

- "Book Conclusion Summaries," "The Dog and His Reflection: An Aesop Fable," "The Lion and the Mouse: An Aesop's Fable," and "Spider and the Honey Tree: An African Fable"

Comparing Themes

Activate

1. Ask your student whether they have ever had a birthday party that was planned around something specific. Was it a superhero party or a princess party? Tell them this is referred to as the theme of the party.
2. Explain to your student that stories also have themes.

Engage

1. Begin by having your student read the content of the **Read It**. Ask them to note in their journal the way to remember what a theme is.
2. Next, engage in a conversation about how the thoughts, speech, and actions of the characters can communicate the theme of a story.
3. Then, direct your student to write the questions to consider when comparing two stories in their journal for future reference.

Demonstrate

1. Now, have your student complete the **Show It** activity. Suggest that they use a Venn Diagram graphic organizer to complete the assignment in their journal.

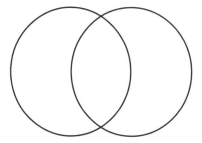

2. Use the **Show It AK** to review your student's answers with the examples provided.

Conflict in a Conclusion

Activate

1. Ask your student to share a time when they had a conflict with someone. How did they resolve the issue?
2. Tell your student that stories also contain conflicts that need to be resolved.

Engage

1. As your student reads the content of the **Read It**, instruct them to draw and label the plot diagram in their journal. Tell them to add details to each part.
2. Discuss ways that conflicts can be resolved in narratives. Ask your student to share examples of stories they have read that incorporated these resolutions.
3. Then, ask your student to identify the conflict and resolution in each of the three summaries of conclusions.

Demonstrate

1. Next, have your student move on to the **Show It** and complete the activity.
2. Using the example paragraph in the **Show It AK** as a reference, work with your student to review their paragraph.
3. To extend learning, play "Alternative Endings." Name a story your student has read, or a movie or television show they have watched, and have them share an alternative ending.

Spelling with Greek Parts

Engage

1. Encourage your student to review and practice their spelling words before they complete the **Assess It**.

Demonstrate

1. Have your student complete the **Assess It**. Have them write, and correctly spell, the words they hear spoken in the assessment. This assessment covers the spelling words presented in Lessons 40 through 42.
2. When they are finished, scan the document or take a photo of it and upload it to the Dropbox. For additional instructions on how to use the Dropbox, click on the paper clip icon in the upper-left corner of the **Assess It**.

LESSON 45

Topic | **Making Comparisons**

Learning Objectives

The activities in this lesson will help your student meet the following objectives:

- compare the patterns of events in myths
- write a new ending for a familiar fairy tale
- construct sentences containing relative pronouns
- spell words that are homophones

Materials

- "The Fearful Knight," "Izanagi and Izanami," "Orpheus and Eurydice," and "Pandora's Box"
- dictionary
- highlighter
- index cards

Comparing Patterns of Events

Activate

1. Ask your student to share their routine for getting up in the morning. Do they tend to do the same thing in the same order each morning? In other words, is there a pattern they follow?
2. Tell your student that patterns of events are also found in traditional literature, such as myths.

Engage

1. Begin with the **Read It** and have your student read the content.
2. Then, ask them to explain what a pattern of events is. (Answer: A pattern of events comprises the details or storyline of a story.)
3. Consider printing out "Pandora's Box" and having your student highlight the events in the story as they read.
4. Then, have them compare what they highlighted with the events of the timeline in the **Read It**. Encourage your student to pay close attention to the order of events.

Demonstrate

1. Next, move on to the **Show It** and have your student complete the timeline activity.
2. When they are finished, have them use the **Show It AK** to check their answers.
3. To extend learning, have your student compare the patterns of events in two of their favorite movies. Are they both the same genre?

• • •

Write a New Ending

Activate

1. Ask your student to share some ways to end a narrative. Do they have a favorite?

Engage

1. Now, direct your student to work through the content of the **Read It**. Have them explain the elements of a good story.
2. Before your student reads the summary of "Goldilocks and the Three Bears," ask them to share an alternative ending to the story. How does their conclusion differ from the alternative ending offered in the **Read It**? How are they similar?
3. Then, have your student open and view the **Write a New Ending - Watch It**. Challenge your student to create an alternative ending for "Jack and the Beanstalk."

Demonstrate

1. Next, have your student complete the **Show It**. Encourage them to choose the story for which they would most enjoy creating an ending.
2. Using the example in the **Show It AK**, work with your student to review their work.
3. To extend learning, challenge your student to create an alternative ending to their favorite story.

● ● ●

Writing Relative Pronouns

 **Activate**

1. Ask your student to describe a relative pronoun to review its meaning. (Answer: A relative pronoun is a word that connects a noun or noun phrase to its description.)

 **Engage**

1. Now, direct your student to read the content of the **Read It**. Have them note the examples of how specific relative pronouns refer to things, people, or both.
2. Challenge your student to read the sentence in the left-hand column of the chart and explain why that specific relative pronoun is used in the sentence. Then, have them read the middle column to check their explanation.
3. Next, have your student view the **Substitute, Please! - Watch It** to review the differences among subject, object, and relative pronouns.

 **Demonstrate**

1. Open the **Assess It** and have your student complete the activity. Be sure that they review the expectations of the rubric before and after writing.
2. When they are finished, scan the document or take a photo of it and upload it to the Dropbox. For additional instructions on how to use the Dropbox, click on the paper clip icon in the upper-left corner of the **Assess It**.

• • •

Spelling Homophones

 **Activate**

1. Have your student view the **Homophones and Homographs - Watch It** to review homonyms, homophones, and homographs.
2. Explain to your student that they will be focusing on homophones. These are words that sound the same but have different meanings and spellings.

 **Engage**

1. Next, have your student read through the content of the **Read It**. Review the Rules, Patterns, and Examples section listing common homophones.
2. Then, have your student read the list of spelling words. You may want them to write the words and their definitions on a sheet of paper or index cards. Discuss the meanings of each homophone pair.
3. Challenge your student to verbally share sentences using both homophones.
4. Now, have your student complete the matching game to practice the spelling words.
5. Last, move on to the **Practice It** for your student to complete the activity. Have them play multiple rounds to get an opportunity to practice all the words. Spelling practice activities for this subtopic will span Lessons 45 through 47.

LESSON 46

Topic	Making Comparisons

Learning Objectives

The activities in this lesson will help your student meet the following objectives:

- use prior knowledge to determine the meanings of words that allude to mythology
- identify relative adverbs in context
- spell words that are homophones

Materials

- none required

Words Alluding to Mythology

Activate

1. Ask your student whether they have ever heard the term *nemesis*. What does it mean?
2. Tell them that often an enemy is described as a nemesis; for example, Batman's nemesis could be the Riddler. Explain that words often derive from another language or other sources—in this case, Greek mythology. Nemesis was a goddess who brought retribution to those that deserved it.
3. Tell your student that they will be learning about other words that derive from myths.

Engage

1. Have your student read the content of the **Read It**.
2. As they read, ask them to list the five common terms derived from mythology in their journal. Ask them to circle any that they have heard before.
3. Next, have your student play the game in the **Plutarch's Library-Daedalus and Icarus - Play It** to reinforce reading comprehension.

Demonstrate

1. Then, direct your student to complete the **Show It** activity reviewing words and phrases derived from Greek mythology.
2. Using the **Show It AK**, work together with your student to check their answers.

• • •

Relative Adverbs

 **Activate**

1. Ask your student what adverbs are. (Answer: words that describe verbs or adjectives)

 **Engage**

1. While your student reads the **Read It**, have them write the three relative adverbs in their journal.
2. Discuss the *which* tip to apply when identifying relative adverbs. Have them make note of this tip in their journal as well. Then, have them reread the first set of sentences testing this tip.
3. Direct your student to open the **Relative Adverbs - Watch It**. Have them pause the video at 3:05 and determine the relative adverb that best completes each sentence.
4. Next, have your student complete the **Practice It** activity by saying the relative adverb in each sentence.

 **Demonstrate**

1. Move on to the **Show It**. Allow your student to complete the review activity before they begin the assignment.
2. As an alternative, have them number in their journal from 1 to 10 and simply write the relative adverb for each sentence.
3. Then, prompt your student to check their responses using the **Show It AK**. Have them explain why any answers are incorrect.
4. Finally, ask your student to complete the **Extend It** for additional practice.

• • •

Spelling Homophones

 **Engage**

1. Guide your student to complete the spelling activity in the **Practice It**. Encourage them to repeat it multiple times, if necessary. Spelling practice activities for this subtopic will span Lessons 45 through 47.

LESSON 47

Topic	**Making Comparisons**

Learning Objectives

The activities in this lesson will help your student meet the following objectives:

- write a short narrative with an effective conclusion
- construct sentences that contain relative adverbs
- spell words that are homophones

Materials

- "The Climb" and "Unusual Day: Journal Entry"
- highlighter

Write an Effective Conclusion

 Activate

1. Ask your student to share their favorite ending of a book or movie and explain why it is their favorite.
2. Tell them they will be exploring how to write an effective conclusion.

 Engage

1. Begin with the **Read It** and have your student read the content, reviewing the five components of a narrative.
2. If possible, have them share examples of each of the techniques for crafting a conclusion in a narrative.

 Demonstrate

1. Now, have your student complete the **Show It**. Encourage them to choose the topic for which they would most enjoy creating a story.
2. Consider having your student read the example in the **Show It AK** before they begin to gain an understanding of the expectations of the assignment.

• • •

Writing Relative Adverbs

 ## Activate

1. Ask your student to share the three relative adverbs that they learned about in Lesson 46. (Answer: *where*, *when*, and *why*)

 ## Engage

1. As your student reads the **Read It**, have them take additional notes in their journal identifying when each relative adverb is used.
2. Consider printing out "Unusual Day: Journal Entry" and having your student highlight the relative adverbs.

 ## Demonstrate

1. Next, move on to the **Show It** and have your student complete the activity.
2. Finally, have your student use the **Show It AK** to view examples of sentences using relative adverbs.
3. Suggest to your student that they check their work using the *which* tip. Have them read each sentence but replace the relative adverb with a preposition and the word *which*.

● ● ●

Spelling Homophones

 ## Engage

1. Guide your student to complete the spelling activity in the **Practice It**. Encourage them to repeat it multiple times, if necessary. Spelling practice activities for this subtopic will span Lessons 45 through 47.

LESSON 48

Topic | **Making Comparisons**

Learning Objectives

The activities in this lesson will help your student meet the following objectives:

- write a narrative story about a personal experience
- compare the elements of plot in folktales from different cultures
- revise sentences to include relative adverbs
- spell words that are homophones

Materials

- "The Air Is Different Up There," "Little Red Cap: A German Folktale," and "The Wolf and the Goat: A Persian Folktale"
- tape
- teacher- or student-selected text

Write a Personal Narrative

 ## Activate

1. Ask your student to share what they know about narrative stories. They may mention that they tell a story.
2. Tell your student that they will be learning more about personal narratives.

 ## Engage

1. While your student reads the **Read It**, have them take notes in their journal on the characteristics of a good personal narrative.
2. Discuss what it means to use a first-person point of view. Ask your student why it is important to write a narrative in the past tense. (Answer: because the event has already happened)
3. Review the five components of a narrative: setting, characters, plot, climax, and resolution. Remind your student that all components need to be included when they write their own personal narrative in the **Show It** later.
4. Have your student open the **Can't Get Enough of That Zoo - Watch It**.
   a. Pause the video at 0:45 to review the elements of a personal narrative.
   b. Pause the video at 2:00 and have your student copy the Five *W*'s graphic organizer into their journal.
   c. Instruct them to copy the time-ordered sequence chart that is shared at 2:50 into their journal as well.
5. Discuss with your student the benefits of using graphic organizers when writing a personal narrative.

 ## Demonstrate

1. Now, have your student complete the **Show It**. Encourage them to choose a topic they would enjoy writing about. They can select one of the suggested topics or come up with one of their own.
2. You can have your student read the example **Show It AK** before they begin to gain an understanding of the expectations of the assignment. As a suggestion, have your student evaluate the sample story by having them identify the following:
   - the five components of a narrative
   - the elements of a personal narrative discussed in the **Watch It**
   - the first-person point of view

Comparing Elements of Plot

 **Engage**

1. Have your student pay close attention to the parts of the plot as they complete the **Read It**.
2. If your student has not already done so in a previous lesson, encourage them to draw the plot diagram in their journal, or print it out and secure it there, as a visual reference tool. They may also include notes on each part below the diagram.
3. Suggest to your student that they search the Internet for different versions of "The Three Little Pigs" and compare them using a plot diagram.
4. Then, have your student view the **Comparing Elements of Plot - Watch It** to see how the elements of plot in folktales can be identified and compared.

 **Demonstrate**

1. Open the **Assess It** and have your student complete the activity. Help them to understand the expectations of the rubric before they begin writing. When they are finished, help them to review their work to make sure they have met the rubric expectations.
2. When they are finished, scan the document or take a photo of it and upload it to the Dropbox. For additional instructions on how to use the Dropbox, click on the paper clip icon in the upper-left corner of the **Assess It**.

● ● ●

Relative Adverbs in Context

 **Engage**

1. Have your student review the relative adverbs by reading the content in the **Read It**. Have them identify the relative adverbs in the sentences in the flip-book before they read on to see the answers.

 **Demonstrate**

1. Now, have your student complete the **Show It** activity.
2. Then, have them compare their answers to the examples in the **Show It AK**.
3. Finally, move on to the Application section of the **Show It** and have your student identify the relative adverbs in a story of their choice.

● ● ●

Spelling Homophones

 **Engage**

1. Encourage your student to review and practice their spelling words before they complete the **Assess It**.

 Demonstrate

1. Have your student complete the **Assess It**. Have them write, and correctly spell, the words they hear spoken in the assessment. This assessment covers the spelling words presented in Lessons 45 through 47.
2. When they are finished, scan the document or take a photo of it and upload it to the Dropbox. For additional instructions on how to use the Dropbox, click on the paper clip icon in the upper-left corner of the **Assess It**.

LESSON 49

| Topic | Making Comparisons |

Learning Objectives

The activities in this lesson will help your student meet the following objectives:

- compare characters in stories from different cultures
- identify the structure of an explanatory text

Materials

- "The Dangers of Smoking," "Letters from a Young Gold Miner," and "Summer Camp Letter"
- teacher- or student-selected text

Comparing Characters

Activate

1. Ask your student to name and describe their favorite character from their favorite book. What qualities does this character have that they admire?
2. Tell them they will be looking at characters in different stories and their traits.

Engage

1. Begin with the **Read It**. Have your student read all the content, pausing to answer the questions.
2. Discuss with your student how the setting can enhance a character in a story. How do cultural details impact a character as well?

Demonstrate

1. Now, have your student complete the activity in the **Show It**.
2. Although responses will differ based on the reader, guide your student to use the **Show It AK** to review possible answers.

• • •

Structure of Explanatory Text

 Engage

1. As your student reads the content of the **Read It**, instruct them to write the five common explanatory text structures in their journal.
2. Then, ask them to add details such as cue words as they read further.

Demonstrate

1. Next, have your student complete the **Show It** using the explanatory essay "The Dangers of Smoking."
2. Work together to check their answers using the **Show It AK**.
3. Finally, move on to the Application section of the **Show It** and have your student identify the structure of a selected explanatory text.
4. The next lesson is a **Mastery Assess It**. Encourage your student to review Lessons 40 through 49 in order to prepare for the assessment.

Topic	**Making Comparisons**

Learning Objectives

The activities in this lesson will help your student meet the following objectives:

- not applicable

Materials

- none required

Mastery Assess It 4

1. **Mastery Assess It 4** will cover what your student has learned in Lessons 40 through 49.
2. Click on the **Mastery Assess It 4** icon to begin the online assessment.
3. Have your student read the instructions before they get started. Remind them to take their time and to do their best work.
4. When they are finished and ready for their assessment to be graded, have them click the **Submit** button.

LESSON 51

Topic | **Informational Text Structure**

Learning Objectives

The activities in this lesson will help your student meet the following objectives:

- recognize cause and effect relationships in a text
- choose the correct modal auxiliaries to complete sentences
- spell VCV words

Materials

- dictionary
- dominoes
- small object
- teacher- or student-selected text

Cause and Effect

Activate

1. Start by having your student stand up dominoes in a line and place a small object, such as an animal figurine, at the end. Tell them their objective is to knock the object over using the dominoes.
2. Then ask them, "What caused the object to fall over?" Tipping the first domino in line caused the rest of the dominoes to fall, eventually knocking the object over.

Engage

1. As your student reads through the **Read It**, direct them to choose one of the following transitions to use in a sentence: *as a result*, *because*, *consequently*. Have them write the sentence in their journal.
2. Then, after they read the example story, have them determine the cause and effect situations before they read the answers at the bottom.
3. Next, instruct them to read about common informational text structures in the **Practice It**. Have them focus particularly on the fifth page, which covers cause and effect.

Demonstrate

1. Now, guide your student to complete the activity in the **Show It**. Encourage them to use a graphic organizer, such as the one below, in their journal to take notes before they write.

Cause	Effect

2. Last, use the **Show It AK** to help your student check their responses.

● ● ●

Choosing Modal Auxiliaries

 **Activate**

1. Prompt your student to use the word *could* in a sentence. For example: I wish I could go to the mall.

 **Engage**

1. While your student reads the content of the **Read It**, instruct them to write the list of modal auxiliary words in their journal.
2. Challenge them to verbally use three of the words in their own sentences.
3. Then, have your student complete the sorting activity in the **Practice It**.

 **Demonstrate**

1. Next, have your student move on to complete the activities in the **Show It**.
2. Work with them to check their answers using the **Show It AK**.
3. For the Application section of the **Show It**, help them identify modal auxiliary words in a selected text.

Spelling VCV Words

 **Activate**

1. Ask your student to name the vowels in the word *paper*. (Answer: *a* and *e*)
2. Then, ask them whether they are long or short vowels. (Answer: *A* is long, and *e* is short.)
3. Next, ask them, "What type of letter is between the two vowels?" (Answer: a consonant)

 **Engage**

1. Begin with the **Read It** and have your student read the content. Discuss how to determine the syllable break. Point out that it falls after the first vowel in each word.
2. Then, have your student write the list of spelling words in their journal for reference.
3. Last, prompt them to play the game in the **Practice It**. Spelling practice activities for this subtopic will span Lessons 51 through 53.

LESSON 52

Topic | **Informational Text Structure**

Learning Objectives

The activities in this lesson will help your student meet the following objectives:

- recall the chronological order of events in an informational text
- generate ideas or details using a brainstorming technique
- spell VCV words

Materials

- "California Gold Rush" and "An Excerpt from *The Hunted*"
- black construction paper
- glue
- paper strips
- recipe
- timer

Chronological Order

Activate

1. Before you begin, cut the instructional steps of a recipe into pieces and omit the numbers if present.
2. Give your student the strips and instruct them to read all the steps first.
3. Then, have them put the steps in order from beginning to end.

Engage

1. Start by having your student read the content of the **Read It**.
2. Have them read "California Gold Rush" in its entirety first.
3. Then, consider printing the text for your student to annotate the sequence of events by writing numbers next to the lines that describe the events.
4. Last, have them compare their notes with the list of chronological events that follows the text.

Demonstrate

1. Now, direct your student to complete the ordering activity in the **Show It** using "An Excerpt from *The Hunted*." Allow them to write the ten events on paper strips and then glue them onto a piece of black construction paper.
2. Work with them to check their order of events using the example in the **Show It AK**.

Brainstorming Topic Ideas

 **Engage**

1. As your student reads the **Read It**, ask them which brainstorming technique they like most. Why?
2. Discuss how some techniques might be better for some people while others may like a different style. Explain that it is good to try different approaches, but also to find one that works well for them.

 **Demonstrate**

1. Next, instruct your student to complete the **Show It** activity. If necessary, assist them in thinking of a topic to brainstorm. Examples include animals, shelters, and occupations.
2. Finally, help them compare the results of their brainstorming with the example in the **Show It AK**.

● ● ●

Spelling VCV Words

 **Engage**

1. Now, have your student complete the activity in the **Practice It**. Encourage them to play multiple times, if needed. Spelling practice activities for this subtopic will span Lessons 51 through 53.

LESSON 53

Topic | **Informational Text Structure**

Learning Objectives

The activities in this lesson will help your student meet the following objectives:

- revise sentences to include the correct modal auxiliaries
- develop a topic with supporting details
- spell VCV words

Materials

- "How Bees Carry Pollen"

Can, *May*, and *Must*

Activate

1. Prompt your student to verbally use the words *can*, *may*, and *must* in three different sentences.

Engage

1. As your student reads the content of the **Read It**, have them explain the difference between the auxiliary words can and may. *Can* is used to show ability, and *may* is used to show permission.

Demonstrate

1. Now, have your student complete the **Show It** activity.
2. After they are finished, help them to check their answers using the **Show It AK**.

• • •

Details to Develop a Topic

 **Activate**

1. Start by having your student open the **Central Idea of Inf. Text - Watch It** to learn how to determine the main idea of a text.
2. Have them pause the video at 1:45 to identify the central idea. Discuss what all the details have in common. All three details highlight the damage on the playground equipment.

 **Engage**

1. As your student reads the **Read It**, prompt them to take note of the topic triangle in their journal.
2. Then, after they read "How Bees Carry Pollen," have them make a topic triangle for the text.
   - Topic: How Bees Carry Pollen
   - Subtopic: Bees pollinate flowers while they collect pollen for food.
   - Supporting Details:
     - collect pollen
     - mix pollen with nectar
     - put mixture in pollen basket
     - transfer pollen from basket

 Demonstrate

1. Now, instruct your student to write an explanatory paragraph for the **Show It**. Prompt them to use a kid-friendly website such as Kiddle to research the topic. While they are taking notes, encourage them to use a topic triangle graphic organizer in their journal. They may also refer to the Student Response Checklist in the **Show It** to guide their work.
2. Help them to compare their paragraph with the sample in the **Show It AK**.

● ● ●

Spelling VCV Words

 **Engage**

1. Direct your student to complete the spelling activity in the **Practice It**. Spelling practice activities for this subtopic will span Lessons 51 through 53.

LESSON 54

Topic Informational Text Structure

Learning Objectives

The activities in this lesson will help your student meet the following objectives:

- order main events from a text in a logical sequence
- write a paragraph that includes modal auxiliaries
- explain the main ideas of an informational text

Materials

- "The Assassination of Abraham Lincoln" and "Landing on the Moon"
- highlighter
- paper strips
- teacher- or student-selected text
- "Order Events Outline" activity page

Ordering Main Events

Activate

1. Start by writing the following four sentences on strips of paper.
   a. A tooth becomes loose.
   b. The tooth falls out.
   c. The tooth is placed under a pillow.
   d. The tooth fairy leaves a surprise and takes the tooth.
2. Mix up the strips.
3. Then, ask your student to order the events. Prompt them to explain their thinking.

Engage

1. Have your student read the content of the **Read It**.
2. After they have read the passage about Martin Luther King, Jr., ask them, "Why is the first sentence not in the best place for it in the paragraph?" They should respond by saying that his death is the end of his life, so the writer should begin by giving some background information first.
3. Discuss how reading the information in chronological order makes it easier to understand.

Demonstrate

1. Now, instruct your student to complete the "Order Events Outline" activity page in the **Show It**. Explain that some of the lines may not be needed.
2. Then, help them to check their work using the **Show It AK**. Encourage them to make any necessary changes so that the events are in chronological order.

Using Modal Auxiliaries

 **Engage**

1. As your student reads the content of the **Read It**, guide them to pay special attention to the modal auxiliary word *must*, because this word can be tricky for some students. Ask them how it is used. *Must* is used to show necessity.
2. Then, prompt them to verbally create their own sentences for the words *can*, *may*, and *must*.

 Demonstrate

1. Next, direct your student to complete the activity in the **Show It**. Encourage them to underline the modal auxiliary words in their sentences.
2. When they are finished, work with them to compare their paragraph with the sample in the **Show It AK**.

The Five *W*s

 Activate

1. Begin by having your student open the **Read All About It - Watch It** to learn about informational texts.
2. Have them pause the video at 3:40 and identify the five *W*'s from the circus article. They may not remember all the details, but they can review them in the remainder of the video.

 **Engage**

1. While your student reads the content of the **Read It**, print the text "Landing on the Moon." Allow them to highlight the five *W*'s in the article.

 Demonstrate

1. Now, direct your student to complete the **Show It** activity. Encourage them to make a chart in their journal to organize their responses.

Who?	
What?	
When?	
Where?	
Why?	

2. Work with your student to check their responses using the **Show It AK**.
3. Finally, direct your student to complete the activity in the Application section of the **Show It**.

LESSON 55

Topic   Informational Text Structure

Learning Objectives

The activities in this lesson will help your student meet the following objectives:

- write an organized explanatory essay with an introduction, a body, and a conclusion
- identify the nouns and verbs in sentences
- spell VCV words

Materials

- "The Common Crutch: Caffeine" and "Outline for 'The Common Crutch: Caffeine'"
- teacher- or student-selected text

Write an Explanatory Essay

Activate

1. Start by having your student hold up their hand and use it to name the parts of an essay. For example, the thumb could be the introduction, the three middle fingers body paragraphs, and the pinkie the conclusion.

Engage

1. As your student reads the content of the **Read It**, challenge them to describe the contents of the essay based on the "Outline for 'The Common Crutch: Caffeine.'"

Demonstrate

1. Open the **Assess It** and have your student complete the activity. Ensure they review the expectations of the rubric before, during, and after they complete the activity.
2. When they are finished, scan the document or take a photo of it and upload it to the Dropbox. For additional instructions on how to use the Dropbox, click on the paper clip icon in the upper-left corner of the **Assess It**.

● ● ●

Complete Sentences

 **Activate**

1. Start by having your student open and view the **Name That Sentence Part - Watch It** to learn about sentence structure.
2. Have them pause the video at 1:49 and explain the two main parts of a sentence. They should say that the two parts are a subject and a predicate.
3. Have them pause again at 2:04 to identify the subject and predicate in the sentence. Continue watching to hear the answer.

 **Engage**

1. While your student reads the **Read It**, discuss the differences between the examples of complete sentences and fragments.
2. Your student may play the game in the **Space Rox-Parts of Speech - Play It** and complete the **Practice It** as needed.

 Demonstrate

1. Next, instruct your student to complete the activity in the **Show It**.
2. Help them to check their answers using the **Show It AK**.
3. For the Application section of the **Show It**, assist them in identifying the subject and predicate in the sentences from a selected text.

• • •

Spelling VCV Words

 **Engage**

1. Encourage your student to review and practice their spelling words before they complete the **Assess It**.

 Demonstrate

1. Now move on to the **Assess It**. Have your student write, and correctly spell, the words they hear spoken in the assessment. This assessment covers the spelling words presented in Lessons 51 through 53.
2. When they are finished, scan the document or take a photo of it and upload it to the Dropbox. For additional instructions on how to use the Dropbox, click on the paper clip icon in the upper-left corner of the **Assess It**.

LESSON 56

Topic **Informational Text Structure**

Learning Objectives

The activities in this lesson will help your student meet the following objectives:

- explain how the author of a text develops the main idea
- construct simple sentences
- spell words with the VCCV pattern

Materials

- "The Legend of the Men Who Visited the Sun"
- dictionary
- dry erase board and marker
- index cards
- newspaper or online news
- teacher- or student-selected text

How Authors Develop Main Ideas

 ## Activate

1. Direct your student to read the heading of a newspaper or online news article.
2. Then ask them, "What is the main idea of the article?" They should be able to get a good idea of the main idea from the heading.

 ## Engage

1. Begin by having your student read through the content of the **Read It**. Prompt them to verbally explain the main idea of the excerpt from *The Moon-Spinners*. The main idea of the text is the phases of the Moon. It is described through a tale of girls who spin the light from the Moon.

 ## Demonstrate

1. Open the **Assess It** and have your student complete the activity. Be sure that they review the expectations of the rubric before and after writing.
2. When they are finished, scan the document or take a photo of it and upload it to the Dropbox. For additional instructions on how to use the Dropbox, click on the paper clip icon in the upper-left corner of the **Assess It**.

● ● ●

Creating Simple Sentences

 **Activate**

1. Start by having your student open the **Exploring Subjects and Predicates - Watch It** to learn about parts of sentences.
2. Then, have them explain the difference between simple and complete subjects and predicates. The simple subject is the noun that tells who or what the sentence is about, and the simple predicate is the verb showing the action in which the subject is participating. Complete subjects and predicates tell more about this noun and verb.

 **Engage**

1. As your student reads the content of **Read It**, discuss how the sentences in the flip-book only have simple subjects and predicates, as there are no adjectives, adverbs, or other elements providing more information about the noun and the verb.
2. Then, instruct your student to open the **Sentence Subjects & Predicates - Watch It**. Have them pause the video at 2:10 to identify the subject. They should continue to pause from time to time to identify the subjects and predicates in the other sentences that are presented.
3. Next, guide your student to complete the **Practice It**. Prompt your student to check their work using the answer key at the bottom of the page.
4. Your student may use the **Beaker's Big Buzz-Punctuation - Play It** to practice their skills in sentence structure and punctuation.

 **Demonstrate**

1. Now, have your student move on to the **Show It** activity.
2. When they are finished, help them to compare their sentences to the examples in the **Show It AK**.

• • •

Spelling VCCV Words

 ## Activate

1. Write the phrase *summer blossom* on a dry erase board.
2. Then, ask your student, "Can you find a vowel-consonant-consonant-vowel (VCCV) pattern in each word?"
3. Tell them to underline the letters in the pattern for each word.

 ## Engage

1. As your student reads through the content of the **Read It**, ask them how they know where the syllable break falls in each word. The syllable break is between the double consonants in the middle of each word.
2. Then, instruct them to write the words on index cards and look up any unknown words in the dictionary. Let them know they will use these flashcards later.
3. Last, have them play the game in the **Practice It**. Spelling practice activities for this subtopic will span Lessons 56 through 58.

LESSON 57

Topic	**Informational Text Structure**

Learning Objectives

The activities in this lesson will help your student meet the following objectives:

- create images to illustrate a topic
- identify the subjects and predicates in sentences you have written
- spell words with the VCCV pattern

Materials

- art supplies
- magazine
- previously written simple sentences
- spelling flashcards
- teacher- or student-selected text

Illustrate to Understand

Activate

1. Begin by having your student select an image from a magazine and share at least three observations about the image.
2. Then, discuss how the image helps them understand more about the topic.

Engage

1. As your student reads the content of the **Read It**, prompt them to describe three details of each image in the flip-book.
2. Then, ask them to discuss how pictures help a reader to better understand what they are reading. They may mention that pictures bring the words to life and help the reader to clarify their thinking.

Demonstrate

1. Now, instruct your student to complete the **Show It** activity. Allow them time to draw or search for pictures.
2. When they are finished, help them to check their images using the **Show It AK**.

• • •

Reading Simple Sentences

 Activate

1. Have your student open and view the **Review: Subjects and Predicates - Watch It**.
2. Have them pause the video at 1:34 to identify the subject and predicate.

 Engage

1. As your student reads the **Read It**, have them pay special attention to the prepositional phrases added to the simple sentences.

 Demonstrate

1. Next, direct your student to complete the activity in the **Show It**. They can use a writing draft if they have not specifically written a list of sentences.
2. Refer to the **Show It AK** for sample sentences.
3. For the Application section of the **Show It**, assist your student in choosing a character to describe from a selected text.

Spelling VCCV Words

 **Engage**

1. Prompt your student to review the spelling flashcards they made in Lesson 56. Encourage them to repeat the spelling of the words they are struggling with most. Remind them that all the words have double consonants in the middle of the word.
2. Then, have them complete the activity in the **Practice It**. Spelling practice activities for this subtopic will span Lessons 56 through 58.

LESSON 58

Topic | **Informational Text Structure**

Learning Objectives

The activities in this lesson will help your student meet the following objectives:

- develop a topic of interest by writing factual sentences
- clarify details in an explanatory text by adding relevant quotations
- spell words with the VCCV pattern

Materials

- art supplies
- encyclopedia
- highlighter
- index cards
- spelling flashcards

Develop a Topic with Facts

 ### Activate

1. Instruct your student to open an encyclopedia and read a random fact. If they do not have a physical encyclopedia book, they may use an online source such as *Kiddle Encyclopedia*. Tell them to click on a topic of interest from the contents list and then click on a secondary link to read a fact.

 ### Engage

1. As your student reads the **Read It**, ask them whether any of the facts presented in the example are new information for them.
2. Then, ask your student why facts are important when writing an explanatory text. They should mention that explanatory writing is meant to provide information, and facts are needed to do so.

 ### Demonstrate

1. Next, guide your student to complete the research activity in the **Show It**. Allow them to use index cards to write their facts.
2. Finally, help them compare their facts with the samples in the **Show It AK**.

• • •

Using Relevant Quotations

 **Engage**

1. While your student reads the content of the **Read It**, have them read the examples with and without quotations aloud so they hear the full effect of adding quotations.
2. Ask your student what adding quotations from others can do for their writing. (Answer: Adding quotations makes writing more credible and can also add interest.)
3. Discuss the importance of finding a balance, because having too many quotations can make it hard to understand a piece of writing.

 **Demonstrate**

1. Now, direct your student to move on to the **Show It** activity. Encourage them to read their revised paragraph aloud when they are done.
2. Then, work with them to evaluate their paragraph using the **Show It AK**.

● ● ●

Spelling VCCV Words

 **Engage**

1. Prompt your student to clap the syllables for each of the words on their spelling flashcards from Lesson 56.
2. Then, have them complete the spelling activity in the **Practice It**. Spelling practice activities for this subtopic will span Lessons 56 through 58.

LESSON 59

Topic | **Informational Text Structure**

Learning Objectives

The activities in this lesson will help your student meet the following objectives:

- identify supporting details in an informational text
- clarify technical or uncommon terms

Materials

- highlighter
- thesaurus
- "'The Moon'" and "Vocabulary Development Sheet" activity pages

Supporting Details

Activate

1. Begin by asking your student, "What details can you give about a trip to the zoo?" For example, visitors can see animals from all over the world. Encourage them to share at least three details. If they have never visited a zoo, have them view an online virtual zoo tour.

Engage

1. As your student reads through the content of the **Read It**, have them take note in their journal of the various types of details that can be used in an informational text.
2. Then, direct them to open and play the **Enlighten Maze-Story Elements Part Two - Play It** as a review.

Demonstrate

1. Now, instruct your student to move on to the **Show It** and complete the activity page. Tell them to identify the type of detail next to each underlined or highlighted detail.
2. When they are finished, assist them in checking their answers using the **Show It AK**.

Technical or Uncommon Terms

Engage

1. While your student reads the **Read It**, emphasize the use of synonyms to help clarify terms. Have them choose one of the terms to look up in a thesaurus.

Demonstrate

1. Next, have your student complete the "Vocabulary Development Sheet" activity page in the **Show It**.
2. Then, help them compare their answers to the chart in the **Show It AK**.
3. To extend learning, encourage your student to use the chart from the **Show It** while reading technical texts to better understand challenging terms.

LESSON 60

Topic | **Informational Text Structure**

Learning Objectives

The activities in this lesson will help your student meet the following objectives:

- define the term *inference*
- revise sentence fragments by making them complete sentences
- spell words with the VCCV pattern

Materials

- spelling flashcards
- teacher- or student-selected text

Inference

Activate

1. Begin by reading the following set of clues to your student and asking them to solve the riddle.
   All shiny and silver
   With a beautiful face
   You look into me
   And find this place.
   (Answer: mirror)
2. Ask them to name the details that can help them solve the riddle. (Answers: *shiny, silver, face, look into*)
3. Then, discuss how they can make inferences based on what they know about objects matching these terms to arrive at the solution.

Engage

1. As your student reads the content of the **Read It**, prompt them to make the inferences for the examples before reading the answers.
2. Then, direct them to write the definition of the term *inference* in their journal.

Demonstrate

1. Now instruct your student to complete the definition activity in the **Show It**.
2. When they are finished, help them to check their response with the **Show It AK**.
3. For the Application section of the **Show It**, help your student to make an inference from a selected text.

• • •

Correcting Sentence Fragments

 ## Activate

1. Have your student open the **Review for You: Sentences - Watch It**.
2. As they watch, have them pause the video at 1:08 to explain what a sentence fragment is. A sentence fragment is missing either the subject or the predicate.

 ## Engage

1. While your student reads the **Read It**, encourage them to identify the missing parts in the sentence fragments.

 ## Demonstrate

1. Open the **Assess It** and have your student complete the activity. When they are finished, scan the document or take a photo of it and upload it to the Dropbox. For additional instructions on how to use the Dropbox, click on the paper clip icon in the upper-left corner of the **Assess It**.

Spelling VCCV Words

 ## Engage

1. Encourage your student to review their flashcards from Lesson 56 before they complete the **Assess It**.

 ## Demonstrate

1. Now move on to the **Assess It**. Have your student write, and correctly spell, the words they hear spoken in the assessment. This assessment covers the spelling words presented in Lessons 56 through 58.
2. When they are finished, scan the document or take a photo of it and upload it to the Dropbox. For additional instructions on how to use the Dropbox, click on the paper clip icon in the upper-left corner of the **Assess It**.

LESSON 61

Topic	Informational Text Structure

Learning Objectives

The activities in this lesson will help your student meet the following objectives:

- write an inference that includes details to support it
- revise run-on sentences
- spell words that are possessives

Materials

- "Becoming a Doctor"
- teacher- or student-selected text
- "Weekly Reading Log" activity page

Details Supporting Inferences

Activate

1. Share the following scenario with your student and ask them what they think happened: Maria returned home and noticed the gate was open. She looked everywhere but could not find her dog Muffy.
2. Your student should respond that Muffy escaped through the opened gate.

Engage

1. After your student reads the example in the **Read It**, have them verbally share their inference before they answer the question.

Demonstrate

1. Open the **Assess It** and have your student complete the activity. Help them to understand the expectations of the rubric before and after writing.
2. When they are finished, scan the document or take a photo of it and upload it to the Dropbox. For additional instructions on how to use the Dropbox, click on the paper clip icon in the upper-left corner of the **Assess It**.

• • •

Correcting Run-On Sentences

 **Activate**

1. Have your student view the **Can You Fix It? - Watch It** to learn about run-on sentences.
2. After viewing, ask them to explain the meaning of a run-on sentence in their own words. They may mention that it is when two complete thoughts are in the same sentence but need to be separated by a period or comma and conjunction.

 **Engage**

1. While your student reads the **Read It**, prompt them to explain the difference between a simple and compound sentence. (Answer: A simple sentence is one thought that includes a subject and predicate, whereas a compound sentence has two complete thoughts joined by a conjunction.)

 **Demonstrate**

1. Open the **Assess It** and have your student complete the activity. When they are finished, scan the document or take a photo of it and upload it to the Dropbox. For additional instructions on how to use the Dropbox, click on the paper clip icon in the upper-left corner of the **Assess It**.

● ● ●

Spelling Possessives

 Activate

1. Start by having your student view the **Review: Possessive Pronouns - Watch It**.
2. Next, prompt them to explain the meaning of the term *possessive pronoun*. (Answer: A possessive pronoun is a word that replaces a noun and shows ownership of something. Examples of possessive pronouns include *his*, *hers*, *theirs*, and *my*.)

 **Engage**

1. Now, direct your student to read the content of the **Read It**. Discuss the difference between singular and plural possessive pronouns. (Answer: Singular is for one person, such as *my*; plural is for more than one person, such as *theirs*.)
2. Afterward, instruct them to write the list of spelling words in their journal.
3. Finally, guide them to play the game in the **Practice It**. Spelling practice activities for this subtopic will span Lessons 61 through 63.

LESSON 62

Topic	**Informational Text Structure**

Learning Objectives

The activities in this lesson will help your student meet the following objectives:

- use context clues to confirm words you do not recognize
- explain the rules of capitalization
- spell words that are possessives

Materials

- "Liftoff"
- highlighter

Context

Activate

1. Start by having your student open the **Context Clues - Watch It** to view the video.
2. Tell your student to pause the video at 1:30 to guess the meaning of the unknown word based on the context.
3. Have them continue watching the video to clarify the meaning of the unknown word.

Engage

1. As your student reads the content of the **Read It**, instruct them to take notes about the types of context clues in their journal. Encourage them to include examples for reference.
2. Next, instruct them to open the **Plutarch's Library-Flight - Play It** to complete the game.

Demonstrate

1. Now, prompt your student to complete the **Show It** activity. Instruct them to print the text and use a highlighter to mark and label the clues that help define the words in bold.
2. Afterward, remind them to check their answers in the **Show It AK**.

• • •

Capitalization Rules

Activate

1. Have your student open the **Capitalize This - Watch It** and ask them to make note of the username and password provided on the Discovery Education image. Be sure that they click the link for the video and enter the provided username and password to watch.
2. Next, prompt them to share a few examples of capitalization rules presented in the video. They may mention that you should capitalize proper nouns of specific names of people or places.

Engage

1. While your student reads the **Read It**, instruct them to make a list of capitalization rules with examples in their journal.
2. Your student may use the **Play Its** titled **Plutarch's Library-Correct Capitalization** and **Plutarch's Library-Rules for Capitalization**, as well as the **Practice It**, as needed.

Demonstrate

1. Now, direct your student to move on to the chart activity in the **Show It**.
2. When they have finished, tell them to compare their answers to the examples in the **Show It AK**.
3. To extend learning, encourage your student to revisit their notes when they complete writing assignments.

• • •

Possessive Pronouns

Engage

1. Start by having your student verbally use five words from the spelling list in sentences.
2. Finish by directing them to play the game in the **Practice It** to review the spelling words. Spelling practice activities for this subtopic will span Lessons 61 through 63.

LESSON 63

Topic **Informational Text Structure**

Learning Objectives

The activities in this lesson will help your student meet the following objectives:

- develop an idea within a particular category
- write an explanatory paragraph using definitions, details, and quotations
- spell words that are possessives

Materials

- dry erase board and marker
- "Blank Paragraph Outline" activity page

Develop an Idea

Activate

1. Write *Summer Break* in the middle of a dry erase board and circle it.
2. Now, prompt your student to brainstorm as many ideas as they can that are related to the topic. Tell them to write their ideas on the board under the topic.
3. Which three ideas are the most connected? Discuss how this may help narrow down a topic for writing.

Engage

1. As your student reads the **Read It**, prompt them to explain how the example narrows down the topic of mythology. (Answer: The example focuses specifically on one character in mythology.)

Demonstrate

1. Continue to the chart activity in the **Show It**. Your student may need to do some research to find specific details.
2. When they are finished, direct them to compare their response to the example in the **Show It AK**.

• • •

Write an Explanatory Paragraph

 **Activate**

1. Have your student view the **Fact/Definition/Detail/Quote - Watch It** to learn how to add supporting details for a writing topic.
2. While viewing, instruct them to pause the video at 4:00 and make a checklist in their journal of the four main types of supporting details they can use in their writing.

 **Engage**

1. After your student reads the content of the **Read It**, ask them if they would add any other details to the example paragraph.

 **Demonstrate**

1. Open the **Assess It** and have your student complete the activity. Be sure they review the expectations of the rubric before, during, and after they complete the activity.
2. When they are finished, scan the document or take a photo of it and upload it to the Dropbox. For additional instructions on how to use the Dropbox, click on the paper clip icon in the upper-left corner of the **Assess It**.

● ● ●

Spelling Possessives

 **Engage**

1. Begin by having your student explain the meaning of the term *possessive pronoun*. (Answer: A possessive pronoun is a word that replaces a noun and shows ownership of something. Examples of possessive pronouns include *his*, *her*, *theirs*, and *my*.)
2. Finally, prompt them to complete the exercise in the **Practice It**. Allow them to repeat the activity for extra practice. Spelling practice activities for this subtopic span Lessons 61 through 63.

LESSON 64

Topic: Informational Text Structure

Learning Objectives

The activities in this lesson will help your student meet the following objectives:

- describe different ways to structure an informational text
- rewrite sentences with capitalization errors correctly

Materials

- "Ruby Bridges: A Brave Girl Who Changed History"
- art supplies
- highlighter
- poster board
- teacher- or student-selected text

Overall Structure of Text

Activate

1. Start by having your student view the **Informational Text Structures - Watch It**.
2. When your student is finished watching, ask them to name the five main types of informational texts. (Answer: description, chronology, compare and contrast, cause and effect, and problem and solution)

Engage

1. While your student reads the **Read It**, instruct them to take notes about the five types of informational text structures.
2. Next, have them print the text about Ruby Bridges. Tell them to read the entire text before determining its structure. Encourage them to go back and use a highlighter to mark the details that support their claim.

Demonstrate

1. Open the **Assess It** and have your student complete the activity. When they are finished, scan the document or take a photo of it and upload it to the Dropbox. For additional instructions on how to use the Dropbox, click on the paper clip icon in the upper-left corner of the **Assess It**.
2. Now, help them determine the type of text structure for the Application section.

● ● ●

Capitalization Mistakes

Engage

1. After your student reads the **Read It**, guide them to create a rhyme or song about the rules of capitalization. Help them find a song online for inspiration.
2. For additional practice identifying and revising capitalization mistakes, have your student play the **Plutarch's Library-Capitalization - Play It**.

Demonstrate

1. Move on and instruct your student to complete the sentence correction in the **Show It**.
2. When they have finished, have them check their answers in the **Show It AK**.
3. To extend learning, challenge them to reread their writing assignments and edit any capitalization errors.

LESSON 65

Topic | **Informational Text Structure**

Learning Objectives

The activities in this lesson will help your student meet the following objectives:

- explain how the author of a text develops the main idea in a logical sequence
- use the cloze technique to complete a paragraph with linking words
- spell words that are possessives

Materials

- "Building Character by the Way of Fish"

Transition Words and Phrases

Activate

1. Begin by having your student open and view the **Transition Words and Phrases - Watch It**.
2. Tell them to pause the video at 3:53 and focus on the "sequence or time" section. Ask them if they can think of any other sequence words such as *first*, *second*, or *last*.

Engage

1. While your student reads the content of the **Read It**, instruct them to take notes about the transitional examples and their meanings in their journal. They can reference this list when they are writing.

Demonstrate

1. Open the **Assess It** and have your student complete the activity. Be sure that they review the expectations of the rubric before and after writing.
2. When they are finished, scan the document or take a photo of it and upload it to the Dropbox. For additional instructions on how to use the Dropbox, click on the paper clip icon in the upper-left corner of the **Assess It**.

• • •

Linking Words and Phrases

 **Engage**

1. As your student reads the **Read It**, have them verbally use three of the connector words in sentences.

 **Demonstrate**

1. Now, go to the **Show It** and have your student complete the activity. Allow them to print the content so they can fill in the blanks.
2. Next, prompt them to check their answers in the **Show It AK**.

Spelling Possessives

 **Engage**

1. Encourage your student to review the list of spelling words before they complete the **Assess It**.

 **Demonstrate**

1. Now move on to the **Assess It**. Have your student write, and correctly spell, the words they hear spoken in the assessment. This assessment covers the spelling words presented in Lessons 61 through 63.
2. When they are finished, scan the document or take a photo of it and upload it to the Dropbox. For additional instructions on how to use the Dropbox, click on the paper clip icon in the upper-left corner of the **Assess It**.
3. The next lesson is a **Mastery Assess It**. Encourage your student to review Lessons 51 through 65 in order to prepare for the assessment.

LESSON 66

Topic | **Informational Text Structure**

Learning Objectives

The activities in this lesson will help your student meet the following objectives:

- not applicable

Materials

- none required

Mastery Assess It 5

1. **Mastery Assess It 5** will cover what your student has learned in Lessons 51 through 65.
2. Click on the **Mastery Assess It 5** icon to begin the online assessment.
3. Have your student read the instructions before they get started. Remind them to take their time and to do their best work.
4. When they are finished and ready for their assessment to be graded, have them click the **Submit** button.

LESSON 67

Topic	Analyzing Nonfiction

Learning Objectives

The activities in this lesson will help your student meet the following objectives:

- summarize a text
- construct sentences using appropriate capitalization
- spell compound words

Materials

- "The Arctic"
- dictionary
- dry erase board and marker
- teacher- or student-selected text

Summarizing Content

Activate

1. Ask your student to tell you about a television show or movie that they recently saw.
2. When they are finished, ask them if they told you every single thing that happened.
3. Remind them that summaries do not contain every detail, just those that are the most important.

Engage

1. Beginning with the **Read It**, encourage your student to answer any in-text questions aloud before reading the answers.
2. Pause to allow your student time to complete the question at the end of the content.
3. Now, ask your student why it is important to include any proper names in their summaries. (Answer: so they know what is being discussed)

Demonstrate

1. Move on to the **Show It** and have your student use "The Arctic" to complete the activity.
2. Using the **Show It AK**, work with your student to review their summary.
3. Afterward, have your student complete the Application section of the **Show It** using their selected text.
4. To extend learning, encourage your student to read articles about current events and summarize what they have read.

• • •

Capitalization Sentences

 ## Activate

1. Write the following on the dry erase board: arnold and i are going on vacation to arizona.
2. Next, ask your student what is wrong with the sentence. (Answer: Proper nouns are not capitalized.)

 ## Engage

1. Direct your student to read the content of the **Read It**. Pause after reading the Capitalization Is Important section so they can write the five rules in their journal.
2. After reading the Movies and Book Titles and Proper Adjectives sections, give your student time to add the two new rules of capitalization to the list in their journal.
3. Now, instruct your student complete the **Plutarch's Library-Editing for Capitalization - Play It** to review the capitalization rules.

 ## Demonstrate

1. Continue to the **Show It** and have your student complete the activity.
2. Go to the **Show It AK** and have them compare their sentences to the examples provided.
3. As an added challenge, instruct your student to name the rule that applies to each example sentence.

 • • •

Spelling Compound Words

 ## Activate

1. Draw a picture of a sun and a pair of glasses on the dry erase board. Encourage your student to guess the word that is suggested by the pictures. (Answer: *sunglasses*)
2. Now, switch roles and have them draw pictures for two words that make up one word while you guess it.
3. Explain that these are called compound words.

 ## Engage

1. As your student works through the **Read It**, have them look up any unfamiliar words in the dictionary. Encourage them to draw quick pictures to illustrate each compound word after completing the activity in the text.
2. Next, have your student move on to the **Practice It** for another activity that incorporates their spelling words. Spelling practice activities for this subtopic will span Lessons 67 through 69.

LESSON 68

Topic | **Analyzing Nonfiction**

Learning Objectives

The activities in this lesson will help your student meet the following objectives:

- recognize connecting words and phrases common to the informative writing genre
- use pauses and voice inflection to indicate punctuation in sentences read aloud
- spell compound words

Materials

- "Marissa and the Mess"
- highlighter
- "Patterns of Organization" activity page

Patterns of Organization

Activate

1. Ask your student to think about or look at their closet. How is it organized? Is it organized by color or type of clothing?
2. Explain that an informational text can have different patterns of organization, just like a closet.

Engage

1. After reading the content of the **Read It**, have your student print and place the Patterns of Organization in Writing chart in their journal for future reference.

Demonstrate

1. Next, prompt your student to complete the "Patterns of Organization" activity page in the **Show It**.
2. Now, tell your student to use the **Show It AK** to ensure they highlighted examples of connecting words and phrases.
3. To reinforce learning, encourage your student to point out patterns of organizations as they read.

● ● ●

Reading Direct Quotations

 **Engage**

1. As your student reads the **Read It**, allow them to practice reading quotations aloud using "Marissa and the Mess."
2. For extra practice using quotations correctly, have your student open the **Plutarch's Library-Quotations - Play It**.

 Demonstrate

1. Move on to the **Show It** and have your student complete the activity. They may read to an adult, a peer, or themselves (in the mirror).
2. Now, tell them to use the **Show It AK** to ensure they have met the criteria for the activity.

Spelling Compound Words

 Activate

1. Ask your student to define *compound words*. (Answer: two words that are joined together to create a new word with a new meaning)

 **Engage**

1. Now, instruct your student to practice their spelling words by completing the activity in the **Practice It**. They may play the game more than once if time allows. Spelling practice activities for this subtopic will span Lessons 67 through 69.

LESSON 69

| Topic | Analyzing Nonfiction |

Learning Objectives

The activities in this lesson will help your student meet the following objectives:

- write factual sentences to develop an idea
- explain a scientific concept
- spell compound words

Materials

- "Synthesizing Food"
- art supplies
- socks

Develop a Category

Activate

1. Instruct your student to organize the socks in their sock drawer or their art supplies. How did they organize them? Is there another way to organize them?
2. Now, encourage your student to organize their socks or art supplies in at least two different ways. They may organize them by color, style, size, or purpose.
3. Explain that just as socks and art supplies can be categorized, so can topics in writing.

Engage

1. Starting with the **Read It**, have your student work through the content.
2. After reading, ask them if they can think of anything to add to the flip-book about a garter snake's appearance.

Demonstrate

1. Next, instruct your student to complete the activity in the **Show It**. They may copy the chart into their journal or organize the information in some other way.
2. Encourage them to use words from the Patterns of Organization in Writing chart they added to their journal from Lesson 68.
3. When they are finished, remind them to use the **Show It AK** to compare their response to the example provided.

• • •

Explaining Scientific Concepts

 Engage

1. As your student reads the content of the **Read It**, encourage them to paraphrase the text aloud before reading the answers.
2. Encourage them to write a definition of *paraphrase* in their journal. (Answer: to restate a text using your own words; should include the most important facts and details)

 **Demonstrate**

1. Next, instruct your student to use "Synthesizing Food" to complete the **Show It**.
2. Now, go to the **Show It AK** so your student can compare their sentences to the examples provided.
3. To extend learning, challenge your student to read a nonfiction article in a print or an online newspaper written for kids. Then, have them paraphrase aloud what they have read.

● ● ●

Spelling Compound Words

 Engage

1. Finally, prompt your student to complete the activity in the **Practice It** in order to review their spelling words. They may play the game more than once if time allows. Spelling practice activities for this subtopic span Lessons 67 through 69.

LESSON 70

Topic	Analyzing Nonfiction

Learning Objectives

The activities in this lesson will help your student meet the following objectives:

- identify the author's intent in an informational text
- spell compound words

Materials

- "Graphic Organizer" activity page

Using a Graphic Organizer

Activate

1. Ask your student if they have ever needed to organize their thoughts or notes.
2. Explain that they could use a graphic organizer to do so.

Engage

1. While completing the **Read It**, prompt your student to state the author's intent before viewing the answers.
2. Next, have your student open and view the **Author's Purpose Types - Watch It**. Pause the video at 2:22 to allow them to write down the questions for determining the author's purpose.
3. Afterward, ask your student what strategy they can use to determine the author's purpose. (Answer: Look at the titles of a text.)

Demonstrate

1. Continue to the **Show It** and direct your student to complete the "Graphic Organizer" activity page.
2. When your student is finished, have them use the examples in the **Show It AK** to evaluate their work.

● ● ●

Spelling Compound Words

 **Engage**

1. Instruct your student to review and practice the spelling words a few times before they complete the **Assess It**.

 Demonstrate

1. Now move on to the **Assess It**. Have your student write, and correctly spell, the words they hear spoken in the assessment. This assessment covers the spelling words presented in Lessons 67 through 69.
2. When they are finished, scan the document or take a photo of it and upload it to the Dropbox. For additional instructions on how to use the Dropbox, click on the paper clip icon in the upper-left corner of the **Assess It**.

LESSON 71

| Topic | Analyzing Nonfiction |

Learning Objectives

The activities in this lesson will help your student meet the following objectives:

- write an explanatory paragraph using a graphic organizer and linking words
- demonstrate how to punctuate direct quotations in sentences
- spell words with inflected endings

Materials

- art supplies
- dictionary
- index cards
- teacher- or student-selected text
- "Blank Graphic Organizer" activity page

Organized Paragraph

Activate

1. Ask your student why it is important to be organized in writing. (Answer: Organized writing gets the point across and is easier to understand.)

Engage

1. Beginning with the **Read It**, have your student work through the content.
2. While reading the flip-book, instruct them to pay close attention to the different parts of an explanatory paragraph.
3. Now, tell them to verbalize the answers to any questions before checking to see if they are right.

Demonstrate

1. Next, direct your student to complete the **Show It** using the "Blank Graphic Organizer" activity page. Encourage them to make a flip-book after they have completed the graphic organizer.
2. Afterward, have them use the example in the **Show It AK** to evaluate their response.

• • •

Transposing Direct Quotations

 ## Activate

1. Ask your student when they should use quotation marks. (Answer: to identify a speaker's exact words or a quotation from a text)

 ## Engage

1. After your student reads the **Read It**, instruct them to write the six rules of using quotation marks in their journal. They may want to include an example of each rule as well.

 ## Demonstrate

1. Now, prompt your student to complete the activity in the **Show It**.
2. Continue to the **Show It AK** and have your student review their answers.
3. When they have finished, have your student complete the Application section of the **Show It** using their selected text.

Spelling Inflected Endings

 ## Engage

1. As your student reads the **Read It**, have them copy the chart under the heading Rules, Patterns, and Examples into their journal.
2. Next, prompt them to read the list of spelling words. Have them write the words and their definitions on index cards or a sheet of paper.
3. Now, encourage your student to complete the sorting activity to practice the spelling words.
4. Finally, move on to the **Practice It** for your student to complete the activity. Encourage them to play multiple rounds of the game if time allows. Spelling practice activities for this subtopic will span Lessons 71 through 73.

LESSON 72

Topic	Analyzing Nonfiction

Learning Objectives

The activities in this lesson will help your student meet the following objectives:

- analyze an experiment by using the scientific method
- identify direct quotes in sentences
- spell words with inflected endings

Materials

- "An Experiment with Air Pressure"
- highlighter

Scientific Method

 ## Activate

1. Ask your student if they have ever conducted an experiment. Maybe they tried to see which ice cream flavor melts the quickest or how many marshmallows they could put in their mouth at one time.
2. Tell them that they were probably using the scientific method when they conducted their experiment.

 ## Engage

1. Begin by having your student copy the following chart into their journal.

Question	
Hypothesis	
Procedure	
Observations	
Conclusion	

2. As they read the content of the **Read It**, instruct your student to take notes about each part of the scientific method.
3. Next, have your student open and view the **Scientific Method - Watch It**. As they watch the video, encourage them to add any new information to their notes.

 ## Demonstrate

1. Using "An Experiment with Air Pressure," instruct your student to complete the activity in the **Show It**.
2. When they are finished, have them use the **Show It AK** to check their work.
3. To extend learning, challenge your student to develop their own experiment. As they conduct their experiment, they should fill in the information about each step of the scientific method.

• • •

Identifying Direct Quotations

 **Engage**

1. Starting with the **Read It**, have your student work through the content.
2. Continue by prompting them to view the **Review: Quotation Marks - Watch It**.
3. Afterward, answer any questions they may have about the **Read It** or **Watch It**.

 **Demonstrate**

1. Next, go to the **Show It** and have your student complete the activity.
2. Encourage them to print the activity and place it in their journal before highlighting the quotations.
3. Now, instruct them to use the **Show It AK** to review their answers.

● ● ●

Spelling Inflected Endings

 **Engage**

1. Finally, prompt your student to complete the activity in the **Practice It** to review their spelling words. If time permits, allow them to play the game more than once. Spelling practice activities for this subtopic will span Lessons 71 through 73.

LESSON 73

Topic	Analyzing Nonfiction

Learning Objectives

The activities in this lesson will help your student meet the following objectives:

- gather information from a scientific text
- identify the appropriate places for commas and quotation marks in sentences
- spell words with inflected endings

Materials

- "Archimedes and Density" and "The Fundamental States of Matter"

Scientific Text

Activate

1. Ask your student what areas of science interest them. They may mention animals, the ocean, landforms, and outer space.
2. Next, tell them that they will read scientific texts.

Engage

1. Now, go to the **Read It** and have your student work through the content.
2. Ask your student to explain the purpose of a scientific text. (Answer: It provides information about scientific topics.)
3. After reading "Archimedes and Density," prompt your student to describe what they learned from reading this scientific text.

Demonstrate

1. Move on to the **Show It** and instruct your student to complete the activity using "The Fundamental States of Matter."
2. Instruct them to check their work using the example in the **Show It AK**.
3. To extend learning, encourage your student to read a book about an area of science that interests them. After reading, ask them to explain what they learned.

● ● ●

Adding Direct Quotations

 ## Activate

1. Ask your student why they might include a direct quotation in their writing. (Answer: to show a speaker's words or to quote another text)

 ## Engage

1. While reading the **Read It**, prompt your student to complete the question in the content.
2. Next, have your student open and view the **Who Said What? - Watch It**.
3. Afterward, ask your student to tell you two things that they learned from the reading and the video.
4. For extra practice, have your student open the **Plutarch's Library-Quotations - Play It**.

 ## Demonstrate

1. Open the **Assess It** and have your student complete the activity. Be sure they review the expectations of the rubric before and after they complete the activity.
2. When they are finished, scan the document or take a photo of it and upload it to the Dropbox. For additional instructions on how to use the Dropbox, click on the paper clip icon in the upper-left corner of the **Assess It**.

Spelling Inflected Endings

 ## Engage

1. Now, have your student complete the activity in the **Practice It** to review their spelling words. If time permits, allow them to play the game more than once. Spelling practice activities for this subtopic span Lessons 71 through 73.

Topic	Analyzing Nonfiction

Learning Objectives

The activities in this lesson will help your student meet the following objectives:

- recognize subject-specific vocabulary used in an informational text
- illustrate domain-specific vocabulary after reading a text

Materials

- "Literary Devices in Poetry" and "Classification of Triangles"
- dictionary
- dry erase board and marker

Subject-Specific Words

 Activate

1. Write the following words on the dry erase board: *tempo*, *duet*, *harmony*, and *chords*.
2. Ask your student to which subject those words belong. (Answer: music)

 Engage

1. Next, instruct your student to read the content of the **Read It**.
2. Ask them to brainstorm at least two more subject-specific words for each of the four subjects: science, social studies, mathematics, and English.
3. Allow your student time to read "Literary Devices in Poetry" before answering the question in the content.

 Demonstrate

1. Continue to the **Show It** and have your student complete the activity.
2. Now, go to the **Show It AK** and have them review their work.
3. To extend learning, challenge your student to point out subject-specific words as they read.

• • •

Domain-Specific Vocabulary

 **Engage**

1. As your student reads the **Read It**, encourage them to find the remaining domain-specific word definitions in a print or online dictionary.

 **Demonstrate**

1. Next, direct your student to complete the activity in the **Show It** using "Classification of Triangles."
2. Finally, have them use the **Show It AK** to evaluate their work.
3. To reinforce learning, have your student call out domain-specific words they see on billboards or advertisements.

Topic	Analyzing Nonfiction

Learning Objectives

The activities in this lesson will help your student meet the following objectives:

- restate the main ideas of a technical text
- use domain-specific terms to write about a topic
- spell words with inflected endings

Materials

- "How to Build a House of Interlocking Bricks"
- a recipe

Technical Information

Activate

1. Ask your student if they have ever read an instruction manual or a recipe.
2. Tell them that these are examples of technical texts.

Engage

1. Beginning with the **Read It**, encourage your student to write the types of technical texts in their journal.
2. Next, instruct your student to open and view the **Technical Information - Watch It**. While watching, tell them to pay close attention to each step. Pause the video at 2:33, 2:46, and 3:00 to allow them to simplify the steps. Continue playing the video to see if they have simplified correctly.
3. Afterward, ask your student to name a strategy for understanding a technical text. (Answer: Restate the main idea of each step.)

Demonstrate

1. Now, prompt your student to complete the **Show It** using "How to Build a House of Interlocking Bricks."
2. When they are finished, have them evaluate their response using the example in the **Show It AK**.
3. To reinforce learning, have your student read a recipe and summarize the main idea of each step. Cook the dish together.

• • •

Using Domain-Specific Terms

Engage

1. As your student reads the **Read It**, encourage them to look up the definitions of any domain-specific terms with which they are unfamiliar.

Demonstrate

1. Open the **Assess It** and have your student complete the activity. Ensure they review the expectations of the rubric before, during, and after they complete the activity.
2. When they are finished, scan the document or take a photo of it and upload it to the Dropbox. For additional instructions on how to use the Dropbox, click on the paper clip icon in the upper-left corner of the **Assess It**.

• • •

Spelling Inflected Endings

Engage

1. Instruct your student to review and practice the spelling words a few times before they complete the **Assess It**.

Demonstrate

1. Now move on to the **Assess It**. Have your student write, and correctly spell, the words they hear spoken in the assessment. This assessment covers the spelling words presented in Lessons 71 through 73.
2. When they are finished, scan the document or take a photo of it and upload it to the Dropbox. For additional instructions on how to use the Dropbox, click on the paper clip icon in the upper-left corner of the **Assess It**.

LESSON 76

Topic	Analyzing Nonfiction

Learning Objectives

The activities in this lesson will help your student meet the following objectives:

- recall facts from a historical text
- write an informative paragraph using domain-specific vocabulary
- spell words with inflected endings that change *y* to *i*

Materials

- "The Boston Massacre" and "Frederick Douglass: Abolitionist"
- dictionary
- index cards
- "Blank Graphic Organizer" activity page

Recalling Historical Facts

Activate

1. Ask your student to tell you about a historical event that they have recently learned about in social studies.
2. Now, ask them if it was easy or difficult to remember everything they had learned.

Engage

1. Begin by having your student complete the **Read It**. Prompt them to take notes about "Frederick Douglass: Abolitionist."
2. Next, tell them to compare their notes to those in the **Read It**. If they took too many notes, help them locate the important facts. If they took too few, have them go back and read again, this time focusing on each stage of Frederick Douglass's life.
3. For extra practice, have your student open the **Plutarch's Library-Clara Barton - Play It**.

Demonstrate

1. Continue to the **Show It** and direct your student to use "The Boston Massacre" to complete the activity.
2. When they are finished, have them compare their notes to the examples provided in the **Show It AK**.
3. To extend learning, encourage your student to take notes as they read about historical events in social studies. This will help them to better recall the information.

• • •

Write an Informative Paragraph

 ## Activate

1. Ask your student to define *domain-specific terms*. (Answer: words that are specific to a particular field of study or subject area; words that are used to teach, learn, and discuss subject-specific concepts)

 ## Engage

1. As your student reads the content of the **Read It**, have them look up any domain-specific words with which they are unfamiliar.
2. Afterward, allow them time to complete the crossword puzzle.

 ## Demonstrate

1. Now, instruct your student to complete the **Show It** using the "Blank Graphic Organizer" activity page.
2. When they are finished, have them evaluate their response using the example in the **Show It AK**.

 • • •

Spelling Inflected *y* Words

 ## Engage

1. While reading the **Read It**, have your student copy the chart under the heading Rules, Patterns, and Examples into their journal.
2. Next, prompt your student to read the list of spelling words, writing them on index cards or a sheet of paper.
3. Have your student complete the word searches to practice the spelling words.
4. Move on to the **Practice It** for your student to complete the activity. Spelling practice activities for this subtopic will span Lessons 76 through 78.

LESSON 77

Topic | Analyzing Nonfiction

Learning Objectives

The activities in this lesson will help your student meet the following objectives:

- integrate information from different sources to write about a topic
- write the simple sentences that are combined with a coordinating conjunction in a compound sentence
- spell words with inflected endings that change *y* to *i*

Materials

- none required

Integrating Information

Activate

1. Ask your student if they think they can learn all there is to learn about outer space from just one book.
2. Explain that while researching, it is important to get information from multiple sources.

Engage

1. Starting with the **Read It**, encourage your student to write or print and place the checklist for determining appropriate sources into their journal.
2. Challenge your student to name sources that would be useful when researching space travel. Examples include NASA's website, books about spaceships, a newspaper article about the first successful trip to the Moon, or a magazine article featuring astronauts.

Demonstrate

1. Next, go to the **Show It** and prompt your student to complete the activity. It may be helpful to have your student write down the facts from each of their sources before composing their journal entry.
2. Using the example in the **Show It AK**, have your student review their journal entry.

● ● ●

Identifying Simple Sentences

Activate

1. Challenge your student to come up with a sentence containing only three words. Examples of three-word sentences include the following:
   - I like running.
   - She eats pancakes.
   - We love movies.
2. Next, challenge them to come up with a sentence containing only two words. Examples of two-word sentences include the following:
   - They sleep.
   - We shop.
   - He jumps.

Engage

1. Continue to the **Read It** and have your student work through the content.
2. After reading, ask them to explain the parts of a simple sentence. (Answer: A simple sentence has one subject and one predicate. The subject is the person, place, or thing the sentence is about, while the predicate is the subject's action or state of being.)
3. Now, ask your student to explain the purpose of conjunctions. (Answer: Conjunctions help join words or phrases. Coordinating conjunctions join sentences.)
4. Encourage your student to write the list of conjunctions in their journal.

Demonstrate

1. Move on to the **Show It** and have your student complete the activity.
2. Afterward, remind them to check their answers using the **Show It AK**.
3. To reinforce learning, encourage your student to write a song to help them remember the coordinating conjunctions. They may search the Internet to see example videos for inspiration.

Spelling Inflected *y* Words

Engage

1. Now, have your student complete the activity in the **Practice It** to review their spelling words. If time permits, allow them to play the game more than once. Spelling practice activities for this subtopic will span Lessons 76 through 78.

LESSON 78

Topic | **Analyzing Nonfiction**

Learning Objectives

The activities in this lesson will help your student meet the following objectives:

- explain the purpose of a concluding sentence
- use appropriate conjunctions to complete compound sentences
- spell words with inflected endings that change *y* to *i*

Materials

- teacher- or student-selected text

Concluding Sentence

Activate

1. Ask your student what the end of a writing piece is called. (Answer: conclusion)

Engage

1. After reading the **Read It**, ask your student how each concluding sentence in the content reiterates the information in the introductory sentence.
2. Next, have your student view the **Concluding Statements - Watch It**.
3. When your student is finished watching the video, discuss why it is not a good idea to suggest to the reader that they may not agree with your argument.

Demonstrate

1. Continue to the **Show It** and instruct your student to complete the activity.
2. Using the **Show It AK**, work with them to review their response.
3. Now, have your student use their selected text to complete the Application section of the **Show It**.

● ● ●

Inserting Conjunctions

 Activate

1. Ask your student to list the coordinating conjunctions. (Answer: for, and, nor, but, or, yet, so)

 Engage

1. As your student reads the content of the **Read It**, encourage them to write the acronym *FANBOYS* in their notes about conjunctions from Lesson 77.

2. To learn more about conjunctions, have your student open and view the **One Thought or Two? - Watch It**.
    a. Pause the video at 3:00 and 4:00 to allow them to create a compound sentence using the two simple sentences.
    b. Continue the video to see if they are correct.
    c. Afterward, encourage them to call out the answers to the questions from 4:31 to 5:10.

 Demonstrate

1. Move on to the **Show It** and have your student complete the activity.
2. Now, tell them to use the **Show It AK** to check their sentences.

• • •

Spelling Inflected *y* Words

 Engage

1. To review their spelling words, have your student complete the activity in the **Practice It**. If time permits, allow them to play the game more than once. Spelling practice activities for this subtopic will span Lessons 76 through 78.

LESSON 79

Topic	Analyzing Nonfiction

Learning Objectives

The activities in this lesson will help your student meet the following objectives:

- restate the opening idea in an explanatory text
- revise compound sentences containing coordinating conjunctions
- spell words with inflected endings that change *y* to *i*

Materials

- dry erase board and marker
- newspaper article

How to Conclude a Paragraph

Activate

1. Ask your student to think about a story they have read. How did it end? Did everything wrap up? Did the characters live happily ever after?
2. Explain that paragraphs also have conclusions. They serve to wrap up everything that was discussed.

Engage

1. Beginning with the **Read It**, have your student pause after each flip-book and respond to the question aloud before checking the answer.
2. For extra practice, have your student read a newspaper article online or in print, but cover up the conclusion. Encourage them to write a conclusion based on the information in the article. Then, uncover the original conclusion and have your student compare it to the one they wrote.

Demonstrate

1. Continue to the **Show It** and prompt your student to complete the activity.
2. Afterward, remind them to review their concluding sentence using the example in the **Show It AK**.

• • •

Commas before Conjunctions

 Activate

1. Write *FANBOYS* vertically down one side of the dry erase board.
2. Next, have your student write the corresponding conjunctions. (Answer: for, and, nor, but, or, yet, so)

 Engage

1. While reading the content of the **Read It**, encourage your student to combine the sentences in the flip-book before turning the page to see the answer.
2. Now, instruct them to view the **Conjunctions: The Great Wall - Watch It**. Ask them to make note of the username and password provided on the Discovery Education image. Be sure that they click the link for the video and enter the provided username and password to watch.
3. Pause the video at 2:49, 3:29, and 3:58 to allow your student time to choose the correct conjunction before watching for the answer. Encourage them to complete the activity at the end of the video.

 Demonstrate

1. Open the **Assess It** and have your student complete the activity. Ensure they review the expectations of the rubric before and after they complete the activity.
2. When they are finished, scan the document or take a photo of it and upload it to the Dropbox. For additional instructions on how to use the Dropbox, click on the paper clip icon in the upper-left corner of the **Assess It**.

Spelling Inflected *y* Words

 Engage

1. Instruct your student to review and practice the spelling words a few times before they complete the **Assess It**.

 Demonstrate

1. Now move on to the **Assess It**. Have your student write, and correctly spell, the words they hear spoken in the assessment. This assessment covers the spelling words presented in Lessons 76 through 78.
2. When they are finished, scan the document or take a photo of it and upload it to the Dropbox. For additional instructions on how to use the Dropbox, click on the paper clip icon in the upper-left corner of the **Assess It**.
3. The next lesson is a **Mastery Assess It**. Encourage your student to review Lessons 67 through 79 in order to prepare for the assessment.

LESSON 80

Topic | **Analyzing Nonfiction**

Learning Objectives

The activities in this lesson will help your student meet the following objectives:

- not applicable

Materials

- none required

Mastery Assess It 6

1. **Mastery Assess It 6** will cover what your student has learned in Lessons 67 through 79.
2. Click on the **Mastery Assess It 6** icon to begin the online assessment.
3. Have your student read the instructions before they get started. Remind them to take their time and to do their best work.
4. When they are finished and ready for their assessment to be graded, have them click the **Submit** button.

LESSON 81

Topic	Nonfiction Features

Learning Objectives

The activities in this lesson will help your student meet the following objectives:

- compare opposing ideas in different texts
- identify coordinating conjunctions in sentences
- spell words with accented syllables

Materials

- "The Benefits of Vegetarian Diets," "Health Benefits to Eating Meat," and "Rescue at Dunkirk"
- dictionary
- dry erase board and marker
- highlighter
- teacher- or student-selected text
- two small objects

Using T-Charts for Comparison

Activate

1. Place two small objects, such as a golf ball and a baseball, in front of your student. Ask them to compare the objects.
2. Explain that one way to keep track of comparisons is to use a T-chart.

Engage

1. Move on to the **Read It** and have your student work through the content.
2. Discuss which pet is best based on the information in the T-chart.

Demonstrate

1. Next, prompt your student to complete the **Show It** using "The Benefits of Vegetarian Diets" and "Health Benefits to Eating Meat."
2. When they are finished, have them evaluate their response using the example in the **Show It AK**.
3. To extend learning, encourage your student to create a T-chart of pros and cons the next time they need to make a decision.

● ● ●

Identifying Conjunctions

 **Activate**

1. Write the following sentence on the dry erase board: I wanted to see the new play but the tickets were sold out.
2. Ask your student to point out what is wrong with the sentence. (Answer: It is missing a comma between *play* and *but*.) Then, ask them to point out the conjunction. (Answer: but)

 **Engage**

1. Starting with the **Read It**, have your student work through the content. Allow them time to read "Rescue at Dunkirk" and point out the conjunctions.
2. Now, have your student open and view the **Compound Sentences - Watch It** to review conjunctions and how they are used in compound sentences. Pause the video when instructed to allow your student to answer the questions.
3. Next, have them open the **Plutarch's Library-Grammar Speech Game - Play It** to review the parts of speech.

 Demonstrate

1. Continue by instructing your student to complete the activity in the **Show It** and use the **Show It AK** to check their answers.
2. Afterward, have your student complete the Application section of the **Show It** using their selected text.

Spelling Accented Syllables

 **Engage**

1. As your student reads through the **Read It**, direct them to read the list of spelling words.
2. To help them identify the accented syllables of each word, instruct them to write each syllable. For example, for the word *excite*, they would write *ex - cite*. Then, have them say the word aloud and underline the accented syllable. In this example, the second syllable would be underlined.
3. Next, have your student complete the sorting activity to practice their spelling words.
4. Finally, move on to the **Practice It** for your student to complete the activity. Spelling practice activities for this subtopic will span Lessons 81 through 84.

LESSON 82

Topic	Nonfiction Features

Learning Objectives

The activities in this lesson will help your student meet the following objectives:

- set a purpose for reading a text
- complete an outline for an informative essay
- choose correct punctuation for various types of sentences

Materials

- "Outline for 'The Common Crutch: Caffeine'" and "Roberto Clemente, Baseball Hero"
- teacher- or student-selected text
- "Blank Essay Outline" activity page and "Choosing Punctuation" activity page

Purpose

Activate

1. Ask your student why there are billboards. (Answer: to persuade people to buy certain items, shop in a particular store, or believe in something)

Engage

1. As your student reads the **Read It**, encourage them to take notes about setting a purpose and the steps to take before, during, and after reading.

Demonstrate

1. Next, go to the **Show It** and direct your student to complete the activity.
2. Afterward, encourage them to compare their work to the example in the **Show It AK**.
3. Direct your student to use their selected text to complete the Application section of the **Show It**.
4. To reinforce learning, challenge your student to set a purpose for reading and follow the steps before, during, and after reading.

● ● ●

Constructing an Outline

 **Activate**

1. Ask your student if they think that authors write a story in its entirety without doing any planning.
2. Explain that authors use tools such as an outline to plan their writing.

 **Engage**

1. Now, have your student work through the **Read It**. Allow them time to read "Outline for 'The Common Crutch: Caffeine'" before answering the questions in the content.
2. Have your student print and place the Detailed Essay Outline into their journal for future reference.
3. Next, instruct your student to open the **Endangered Animals: An Outline - Watch It**. Ask them to tell you one thing they learned about outlines from the video.

 **Demonstrate**

1. Move on to the **Show It** and have your student complete the "Blank Essay Outline" activity page.
2. Continue to the **Show It AK** and have them use the example provided to review their work.

●●●

Ending Punctuation

 **Engage**

1. As your student reads the content of the **Read It**, encourage them to copy the chart under the Punctuation and Sentence Types section into their journal.
2. Now, have them view the **Watch Its** titled **How Does It End?** and **Types of Sentences** to review the four types of sentences and their punctuation.
3. For extra practice, instruct your student to play the **Plutarch's Library-Sentence Types - Play It**.

 **Demonstrate**

1. Next, prompt your student to complete the "Choosing Punctuation" activity page in the **Show It**.
2. When they are finished, have them use the **Show It AK** to evaluate their answers.
3. To reinforce learning, encourage your student to point out the types of sentences and their punctuation that they see when they are outside of their learning environment.

LESSON 83

Topic	**Nonfiction Features**

Learning Objectives

The activities in this lesson will help your student meet the following objectives:

- assess whether or not the information on a chart clearly summarizes the main ideas of a text
- identify the correct abbreviations for words
- spell words with accented syllables

Materials

- "Compare and Contrast"
- 45 index cards
- "Choosing Abbreviations" activity page

Using Charts to Summarize Text

Activate

1. Ask your student what a Venn diagram, a T-chart, and an outline all have in common. (Answer: They are all used to organize information.)

Engage

1. Starting with the **Read It**, encourage your student to explain why the Space Race chart was effective in summarizing the information. Ask them to explain this before reading the answer below the chart.

Demonstrate

1. Next, instruct your student to complete the **Show It** using "Compare and Contrast."
2. When they are finished, have them evaluate their response using the example in the **Show It AK**.
3. To reinforce learning, encourage your student to use charts when summarizing information, especially in other subjects such as science and social studies.

• • •

Abbreviations

 **Activate**

1. Ask your student to name some abbreviations that they use on a regular basis. They may mention *can't* and *aren't* as well as acronyms such as *BRB* and *LOL*.

 **Engage**

1. Move on to the **Read It**. As your student reads the content, allow them time to create the abbreviation flashcards.
2. Next, prompt them to open and view the **Review for You: Abbreviations - Watch It**. Afterward, ask them which abbreviations they use the most.

 **Demonstrate**

1. Continue to the **Show It** and have your student complete the "Choosing Abbreviations" activity page.
2. Now, have them review their answers using the **Show It AK**.
3. For extra practice, use the index cards to play a review game.
   a. Place all of the cards with the abbreviations face up on the floor in front of your student.
   b. Have them toss a bean bag or similar object onto a card.
   c. Ask them to state the word that the abbreviation stands for.
   d. If they are correct, remove the card from the floor. If they are incorrect, tell them the answer and place the card back on the floor.
   e. Continue until all the cards are off of the floor.

● ● ●

Spelling Accented Syllables

 **Engage**

1. To review their spelling words, have your student complete the activity in the **Practice It**. They may play more than once if time allows. Spelling practice activities for this subtopic will span Lessons 81 through 84.

LESSON 84

Topic	Nonfiction Features

Learning Objectives

The activities in this lesson will help your student meet the following objectives:

- interpret the information in a graph to illustrate how it supports the text
- use the writing process to write an informative essay
- spell words with accented syllables

Materials

- "Saturn" and "Talent Show Growth"

How Graphs Support Content

Activate

1. Instruct your student to use the phrase "graph image" to search the Internet.
2. What do they notice? How many types of graphs do they see? What are the graphs measuring?

Engage

1. Move on to the **Read It** and encourage your student to write the four types of graphs discussed in the content in their journal.

Demonstrate

1. Now, instruct your student to use "Talent Show Growth" to complete the **Show It**.
2. Afterward, have them check their work using the example in the **Show It AK**.
3. To reinforce learning, the next time your student reads something with a graph, ask them to explain how it supports the content. As an added challenge, encourage them to draw their own graph to support nonfiction content they have read.

• • •

Informative Essay

 **Activate**

1. Start by opening **An Informative Essay - Watch It**.
2. After your student watches the video, ask them to summarize the definition of an informative essay in their own words.

 **Engage**

1. Now, prompt your student to read the content of the **Read It**.
2. When they are finished reading, ask them to explain the five steps of the writing process.
3. Next, tell your student to open and view the **Watch It** titled **The Rough Draft**. After they watch the video, ask them which step comes directly before writing a rough draft. (Answer: an outline)
4. Continue by having them open and view the **Mackinac Island: Revised - Watch It**. Pause the video at 0:40 to allow your student time to copy the proofreading checklist in their journal.
5. Finally, have your student view the **A Step Back in Time - Watch It** to review the steps of the writing process and see a final draft.

 **Demonstrate**

1. Open the **Assess It** and have your student complete the activity. Help them to understand the expectations of the rubric before and after writing.
2. When they are finished, scan the document or take a photo of it and upload it to the Dropbox. For additional instructions on how to use the Dropbox, click on the paper clip icon in the upper-left corner of the **Assess It**.

● ● ●

Spelling Accented Syllables

 **Engage**

1. To review their spelling words, prompt your student to complete the activity in the **Practice It**. They may play more than once if time allows. Spelling practice activities for this subtopic span Lessons 81 through 84.

LESSON 85

Topic   Nonfiction Features

Learning Objectives

The activities in this lesson will help your student meet the following objectives:

- write the meaning of *genre* as it relates to the genre of writing being used
- use correct punctuation to write dates

Materials

- teacher- or student-selected texts

Genres of Writing

Activate

1. Ask your student to think of their favorite book. Is it a true story or one that was made up? Is it about something that happened long ago or in the future?
2. Explain that books fall into different categories called *genres*.

Engage

1. While reading the **Read It**, ask your student to think back to the book they discussed in the Activate. To which genre does it belong? Encourage them to justify their answer.
2. Now, have your student open the **Plutarch's Library-Types of Literature - Play It**. If they miss any questions, encourage them to play again.

Demonstrate

1. Next, direct your student to move to the **Show It**. Encourage them to copy the chart below in their journal and used it to complete the activity.

Genre	Description	Type of Story
Fantasy		
Science Fiction		
Realistic Fiction		
Historical Fiction		
Traditional Literature		
Nonfiction and Informational		
Autobiography		

2. When they are finished, remind them to use the **Show It AK** to evaluate their work.
3. Afterward, have your student use their selected text to complete the Application section of the **Show It**.

● ● ●

Punctuation for Written Dates

Engage

1. As your student reads the **Read It**, encourage them to practice writing their birthday using correct punctuation.
2. Next, allow them time to complete the sorting activity.

Demonstrate

1. Move on to the **Show It** and instruct your student to complete the activity.
2. Now, tell them to use the **Show It AK** to check their answers.
3. Finally, remind them to use their selected text to complete the Application section of the **Show It**.
4. To reinforce learning, encourage your student to write dates when they see them.

LESSON 86

Topic | Nonfiction Features

Learning Objectives

The activities in this lesson will help your student meet the following objectives:

- explain how diagrams in an explanatory text help you to understand the content
- construct a sentence with a series of items
- spell words with accented syllables

Materials

- "Electric Current"

How Diagrams Support Text

Activate

1. Ask your student if they have ever put something together using instructions. Did the instructions have pictures? If so, how did the pictures help them?
2. Explain that those pictures are called *diagrams*.

Engage

1. Beginning with the **Read It**, ask your student why diagrams may be helpful. (Answer: They help you visualize what is being explained in the text.)

Demonstrate

1. Now, prompt your student to complete the **Show It** using "Electric Current."
2. When they are finished, tell them to use the **Show It AK** to check their response.
3. To reinforce learning, encourage your student to draw a diagram to help support a nonfiction text that they are reading.

• • •

Commas in a Series

 **Engage**

1. Starting with the **Read It**, have your student work through the content.
2. As they read the flip-book, ask them to point to the commas in each series.
3. Next, have your student open the **Using Commas: Series of Items - Watch It**.
4. Afterward, ask them to tell you one thing they learned from the video.

 **Demonstrate**

1. Move on to the **Show It** and direct your student to complete the activity.
2. Now, go to the **Show It AK** and have them compare their sentences to the examples provided.

• • •

Spelling Accented Syllables

 **Engage**

1. Instruct your student to review and practice the spelling words a few times before they begin the **Assess It**.

 **Demonstrate**

1. Now, move on to the **Assess It**. Have your student write, and correctly spell, the words they hear spoken in the assessment. This assessment covers the spelling words presented in Lessons 81 through 84.
2. When they are finished, scan the document or take a photo of it and upload it to the Dropbox. For additional instructions on how to use the Dropbox, click on the paper clip icon in the upper-left corner of the **Assess It**.

LESSON 87

Topic	Nonfiction Features

Learning Objectives

The activities in this lesson will help your student meet the following objectives:

- create a timeline of important dates with corresponding events
- identify the writing audience of a text
- spell words with silent letters

Materials

- "Landing on the Moon"
- art supplies
- children's book
- colored pencils
- dictionary
- teacher- or student-selected text

Timelines of Dates and Events

Activate

1. Ask your student to list five things they did during the past week. Make sure that they tell you the events in chronological order.

Engage

1. Continue to the **Read It** and prompt your student to work through the content.
2. Encourage them to practice drawing a timeline by plotting the five events from the Activate activity. Instruct them to write details and draw a small picture for each event.

Demonstrate

1. Open the **Assess It** and have your student complete the activity. Be sure they review the expectations of the rubric before, during, and after they complete the activity.
2. When they are finished, scan the document or take a photo of it and upload it to the Dropbox. For additional instructions on how to use the Dropbox, click on the paper clip icon in the upper-left corner of the **Assess It**.

● ● ●

Writing Audience

 **Activate**

1. Show your student a children's book. Ask them for whom it was written. How do they know? They may mention that it was written for young children because it has short sentences, uses small words, and contains illustrations.

 **Engage**

1. As your student reads the **Read It**, ask them how their writing would change if they are writing a letter to an adult instead of sending a text message to a friend.
2. Now, have your student open and view the **Intended Audience - Watch It**. Pause the video at 1:07 so that they can copy the list of ways the audience affects writing.

 **Demonstrate**

1. Next, instruct your student to complete the activity in the **Show It**.
2. Have them use the **Show It AK** to review their work.
3. Afterward, prompt them to complete the activity in the Application section of the **Show It** using their selected text.

• • •

Spelling with Silent Letters

 **Engage**

1. Beginning with the **Read It**, have your student print the chart under the Rules, Patterns, and Examples heading and place it in their journal.
2. Now, instruct your student to read the list of spelling words aloud, making sure they do not pronounce the silent letters.
3. Next, have your student complete the word searches to practice their spelling words.
4. Last, go to the **Practice It** so your student can complete the activity. Spelling practice activities for this subtopic will span Lessons 87 through 89.

LESSON 88

Topic **Nonfiction Features**

Learning Objectives

The activities in this lesson will help your student meet the following objectives:

- explain how the images in an informational text contribute to an understanding of the text
- construct sentences with a series of adjectives
- spell words with silent letters

Materials

- "Fishing"

Images Support Content

Activate

1. Ask your student to imagine a children's book without pictures. Would a young child still be able to understand what is going on in the story?
2. Explain that images are used to help readers visualize and understand what they are reading.

Engage

1. Starting with the **Read It**, discuss how images support the content. Ask how things such as photographs, diagrams, and artwork contribute to what is written.
2. Next, encourage them to think about different types of texts and how images would help enhance the content.

Demonstrate

1. Now, prompt your student to use "Fishing" to complete the **Show It**.
2. When they are finished, have them compare their response to the example in the **Show It AK**.

• • •

Adjectives in a Series

Activate

1. Ask your student to list at least two words that describe themselves.
2. Afterward, ask them to which part of speech the descriptive words belong. (Answer: adjectives)

Engage

1. Now, instruct your student to complete the **Read It**.
2. As they read the flip-book, ask them to point out the adjectives in each sentence as well as the comma that separates the words in a series. Have them check their answers using the chart below the flip-book.

Demonstrate

1. Move on to the **Show It** and have your student complete the activity.
2. Next, remind them to check their answers in the **Show It AK**.
3. As an added challenge, have your student write their own sentence using a series of adjectives. Tell them to describe themselves or their favorite toy.

● ● ●

Spelling with Silent Letters

Engage

1. To review their spelling words, have your student complete the activity in the **Practice It**. If time permits, allow them to play the game more than once. Spelling practice activities for this subtopic will span Lessons 87 through 89.

LESSON 89

Topic	Nonfiction Features

Learning Objectives

The activities in this lesson will help your student meet the following objectives:

- identify the writing purposes of various texts
- use commas to separate city and state names in sentences
- spell words with silent letters

Materials

- none required

Writing Purpose

Activate

1. Ask your student if they would write something humorous to convince an adult that purchasing a new game system is a good idea.
2. They would probably use a more formal and serious tone in their persuasive writing.

Engage

1. While reading the content of the **Read It**, prompt your student to write the four main purposes of writing in their journal.
2. Next, have them open and view the **Author's Purpose - Watch It**. Pause the video from 3:10 to 5:05 to allow them time to determine each author's purpose.

Demonstrate

1. Continue to the **Show It** and instruct your student to complete the activity.
2. When they are finished, have them review their answers using the **Show It AK**.
3. For additional practice identifying the author's purpose, have your student complete the activity in the Application section of the **Show It**.

• • •

City and State Punctuation

Activate

1. Ask your student to write the city and state in which they live in their journal.

Engage

1. Now, go to the **Read It** and direct your student to read through the content. Allow them time to answer any questions in the text.
2. Next, have your student look at what they wrote in their journal for the Activate activity. Did they write the city and state correctly? If not, instruct them to correct it.
3. For a review of comma usage, have them open the **Review for You: Using Commas - Watch It**.

Demonstrate

1. Open the **Assess It** and have your student complete the activity. When they are finished, scan the document or take a photo of it and upload it to the Dropbox. For additional instructions on how to use the Dropbox, click on the paper clip icon in the upper-left corner of the **Assess It**.

Spelling with Silent Letters

Engage

1. To review their spelling words, have your student complete the activity in the **Practice It**. They may play the game more than once if time allows. Spelling practice activities for this subtopic span Lessons 87 through 89.

LESSON 91

| Topic | Nonfiction Features |

Learning Objectives

The activities in this lesson will help your student meet the following objectives:

- list facts about a topic using information presented on a cited website
- record information about a book previously read
- spell words with silent letters

Materials

- planner
- teacher- or student-selected texts
- "Weekly Reading Log" activity page

Using Information on Websites

 ### Activate

1. Ask your student how often and how long they use technology such as a smartphone or computer.
2. Explain that a lot of information exists on the Internet and that it is important to learn how to use it correctly.

 ### Engage

1. Begin with the **Read It** and discuss the content with your student.
2. Instruct them to search the Internet using the phrase "main characteristics of fairy tales" and view the results before reading the answers.
3. Next, have your student open and view the **Internet Research - Watch It**. Ask them to make note of the username and password provided on the Discovery Education image. Be sure that they click the link for the video and enter the provided username and password to watch.
4. While watching the video, pause it from 2:36 until 4:21 to allow them time to answer the questions.

 ### Demonstrate

1. Now, direct your student to complete the activity in the **Show It**. You may need to help them determine reliable sources.
2. Afterward, have them compare their work to the example in the **Show It AK**.
3. As your student continues to use the Internet for research, encourage them to evaluate the websites for credible and useful information.

• • •

Book Review Planner

 **Engage**

1. Starting with the **Read It**, encourage your student to brainstorm books they have read and would like to write a book review about.

 **Demonstrate**

1. Next, prompt your student to complete the **Show It** using a selected text they have previously read.
2. When they are finished, have them evaluate their work using the example in the **Show It AK**.
3. To reinforce learning, encourage your student to use book reviews as a way to record information as they read. The chapter summaries allow them to remember what they have previously read and see how the story builds.

• • •

Spelling with Silent Letters

 **Engage**

1. Instruct your student to review and practice the spelling words a few times before they complete the **Assess It**.

 **Demonstrate**

1. Now move on to the **Assess It**. Have your student write, and correctly spell, the words they hear spoken in the assessment. This assessment covers the spelling words presented in Lessons 87 through 89.
2. When they are finished, scan the document or take a photo of it and upload it to the Dropbox. For additional instructions on how to use the Dropbox, click on the paper clip icon in the upper-left corner of the **Assess It**.
3. The next lesson is a **Mastery Assess It**. Encourage your student to review Lessons 81 through 91 in order to prepare for the assessment.

LESSON 92

Topic	Nonfiction Features

Learning Objectives

The activities in this lesson will help your student meet the following objectives:

- not applicable

Materials

- none required

Mastery Assess It 7

1. **Mastery Assess It 7** will cover what your student has learned in Lessons 81 through 91.
2. Click on the **Mastery Assess It 7** icon to begin the online assessment.
3. Have your student read the instructions before they get started. Remind them to take their time and to do their best work.
4. When they are finished and ready for their assessment to be graded, have them click the **Submit** button.

| **Topic** | **Nonfiction Point of View** |

Learning Objectives

The activities in this lesson will help your student meet the following objectives:

- distinguish between objective and subjective writing
- punctuate appositives in sentences
- spell words with a double consonant *-ed* or *-ing* ending

Materials

- art supplies
- dictionary
- dry erase board and marker
- index cards

Objective and Subjective

Activate

1. Write the following two sentences on the dry erase board: The universe is vast and amazing. We are still discovering new things about the universe.
2. Ask your student which of the two sentences contains an opinion. (Answer: the first)
3. Now, explain that this is a subjective sentence, while the latter is an objective sentence.

Engage

1. Continue to the **Read It**. Tell your student to pay close attention to the differences between objective and subjective writing.
2. Instruct them to copy the chart that summarizes each writing type into their journal.

Demonstrate

1. Next, prompt your student to complete the activity in the **Show It**.
2. Afterward, remind them to evaluate their poster using the example in the **Show It AK**.
3. To extend learning, encourage your student to analyze different writings, such as billboards, menus, and articles, to determine whether they are objective or subjective.

● ● ●

Punctuating Appositives

 **Engage**

1. As your student reads the **Read It**, instruct them to write the definition of appositive in their journal. (Answer: renames another noun in a sentence)
2. For extra practice, challenge your student to write another sentence that includes an appositive about the girl, Elizabeth. An example sentence may be: Elizabeth, the girl in the pink shirt, sat in the front of the theater.

 **Demonstrate**

1. Move on to the **Show It** and have your student complete the activity.
2. Finally, have them refer to the **Show It AK** to check their answers.

• • •

Spelling Double Consonants

 **Engage**

1. While reading the **Read It**, have your student copy the chart under the heading Rules, Patterns, and Examples into their journal.
2. Now, have your student read the list of spelling words and write them on a sheet of paper or index cards (one word per card).
3. Next, prompt your student to complete the word searches to practice the spelling words.
4. Last, move on to the **Practice It** so your student can complete the activity. Spelling practice activities for this subtopic will span Lessons 93 through 95.

LESSON 94

Topic	**Nonfiction Point of View**

Learning Objectives

The activities in this lesson will help your student meet the following objectives:

- express an opinion based on the topic of a text
- place commas in sentences that contain introductory words and phrases
- spell words with a double consonant *-ed* or *-ing* ending

Materials

- "A Letter to Mom"

Personal Bias

Activate

1. Ask your student to explain the difference between subjective and objective writing. If they need help, tell them to reference Lesson 93. (Answer: Subjective writing is based on feelings and opinions, while objective writing is based on facts.)

Engage

1. Now, go to the **Read It** and instruct your student to work through the content.
2. Discuss the example response with your student. Is it something they agree with? Why or why not?

Demonstrate

1. Open the **Assess It** and have your student complete the activity. Be sure that they review the expectations of the rubric before and after writing.
2. When they are finished, scan the document or take a photo of it and upload it to the Dropbox. For additional instructions on how to use the Dropbox, click on the paper clip icon in the upper-left corner of the **Assess It**.

• • •

Introductory Words and Phrases

 **Activate**

1. Ask your student to define the word *introduction*. Explain that sentences can have introductions, too.

 **Engage**

1. As your student reads the **Read It**, encourage them to write their own sentence that contains an introductory word or phrase. Ensure that they place the comma correctly in the sentence.
2. Next, have them open the **Using Commas: Introductory - Watch It**.
3. Afterward, ask them to define the term *dependent clause*. (Answer: a part of a sentence that cannot stand on its own)

 **Demonstrate**

1. Now, have your student complete the activity in the **Show It**.
2. When they are finished, remind them to check their paragraph using the **Show It AK**.
3. To reinforce learning, encourage your student to point out introductory words and phrases when they see them.

• • •

Spelling Double Consonants

 **Engage**

1. To review their spelling words, prompt your student to complete the activity in the **Practice It**. If time permits, allow them to play the game more than once. Spelling practice activities for this subtopic will span Lessons 93 through 95.

LESSON 95

Topic **Nonfiction Point of View**

Learning Objectives

The activities in this lesson will help your student meet the following objectives:

- compare texts by different authors based on the same subject matter
- write a book review
- spell words with a double consonant *-ed* or *-ing* ending

Materials

- "The Value of Chores" and "The Awfulness of Chores"
- previously read teacher- or student-selected text
- "Book Review Template" activity page

Point of View Shapes Content

Activate

1. Ask your student to tell you their favorite movie and explain why.
2. Now, take the opposite stance and explain why that same movie is your least favorite.
3. Tell your student that even though you were both discussing the same movie, your point of view shaped what was said.

Engage

1. While reading the content of the **Read It**, discuss which point of view your student agrees with.
2. Continue by having your student complete the **Practice It**. They may reference the passages in the activity as needed.

Demonstrate

1. Next, direct your student to complete the **Show It** using "The Value of Chores" and "The Awfulness of Chores."
2. When your student is finished, have them use the **Show It AK** to evaluate their response.

● ● ●

Book Review

 **Engage**

1. As your student reads the **Read It**, allow them time to answer the question at the end of the content.
2. Now, instruct them to open and view the **Watch It** titled **The Very Best Book Report**.
3. Next, ask them what steps they should take after writing the first draft. (Answer: Proofread, revise, edit, and write the final draft.)

 **Demonstrate**

1. Open the **Assess It** and have your student complete the activity. Ensure that they understand the expectations of the rubric before and after writing.
2. When they are finished, scan the document or take a photo of it and upload it to the Dropbox. For additional instructions on how to use the Dropbox, click on the paper clip icon in the upper-left corner of the **Assess It**.

● ● ●

Spelling Double Consonants

 **Engage**

1. To review their spelling words, have your student complete the activity in the **Practice It**. If time permits, allow them to play the game more than once. Spelling practice activities for this subtopic span Lessons 93 through 95.

LESSON 96

Topic | **Nonfiction Point of View**

Learning Objectives

The activities in this lesson will help your student meet the following objectives:

- list characteristics of persuasive writing
- construct a personal letter using correct punctuation

Materials

- "Opening a Savings Account" and "The Team Sport of Lacrosse"

Components of Persuasive Genre

Activate

1. Ask your student if they have ever tried to persuade someone to do something. How did they do it? What did they say or do?

Engage

1. As your student reads the content of the **Read It**, instruct them to write the three components of persuasive writing in their journal. (Answer: a clear point of view, reasons and facts to support the point of view, and a strong conclusion)
2. Allow them time to read "Opening a Savings Account." Encourage them to answer the questions aloud before checking their answers.
3. Next, have them open the **Plutarch's Library-Healthful Habits - Play It**. If time permits, allow them to play until they achieve a perfect score.

Demonstrate

1. Continue to the **Show It** and prompt your student to use "The Team Sport of Lacrosse" to complete the activity.
2. Now, have them use the **Show It AK** to check their work.

● ● ●

Punctuating a Personal Letter

Engage

1. Beginning with the **Read It**, talk to your student about sending letters. When was the last time they sent one? To whom did they write? What about an email? Ask them if an email should still contain proper punctuation. What about a text message?

Demonstrate

1. Open the **Assess It** and have your student complete the activity. Be sure that they review the expectations of the rubric before and after writing.
2. When they are finished, scan the document or take a photo of it and upload it to the Dropbox. For additional instructions on how to use the Dropbox, click on the paper clip icon in the upper-left corner of the **Assess It**.

LESSON 97

Topic	Nonfiction Point of View

Learning Objectives

The activities in this lesson will help your student meet the following objectives:

- compare a firsthand account and a secondhand account of an event
- describe how an author validates a point of view
- spell words with a double consonant *-ed* or *-ing* ending

Materials

- "The Golden Spike: A Firsthand Account," "Completion of the Transcontinental Railroad: A Secondhand Account," and "Recycling"

Comparing Perspectives

Activate

1. Ask your student to tell you about something they have experienced, such as a birthday party or their favorite vacation.
2. Explain that this is called a *firsthand account* because they were present.
3. Now, ask your student to imagine that you told another person about the experience.
4. Explain that this is called a *secondhand account* because you were not present.

Engage

1. Start by having your student copy the following table in their journal.

	Source Type	Definition	Examples
Firsthand Account			
Secondhand Account			

2. As your student reads the content of the **Read It**, instruct them to use the table to name the source type, definition, and examples of a firsthand and secondhand account.
3. Encourage your student to verbalize the difference between the two examples before reading the answer.

Demonstrate

1. Open the **Assess It** and have your student complete the activity. Be sure that they understand the expectations of the rubric before and after writing.
2. When they are finished, scan the document or take a photo of it and upload it to the Dropbox. For additional instructions on how to use the Dropbox, click on the paper clip icon in the upper-left corner of the **Assess It**.

• • •

Validating Point of View

 **Engage**

1. Begin with the **Read It** and allow your student time to complete the example before checking the answers.
2. To practice, ask your student their opinion about a topic, such as elementary students having a smartphone. Encourage them to support their opinion, or perspective, with at least two valid reasons.

 **Demonstrate**

1. Move on to the **Show It** and have your student use "Recycling" to complete the activity.
2. Now, tell them to compare their work to the example in the **Show It AK**.
3. As your student continues to develop opinions, challenge them to support their perspectives with reasons and facts.

● ● ●

Spelling Double Consonants

 **Engage**

1. Instruct your student to review and practice the spelling words a few times before they complete the **Assess It**.

 **Demonstrate**

1. Now move on to the **Assess It**. Have your student write, and correctly spell, the words they hear spoken in the assessment. This assessment covers the spelling words presented in Lessons 93 through 95.
2. When they are finished, scan the document or take a photo of it and upload it to the Dropbox. For additional instructions on how to use the Dropbox, click on the paper clip icon in the upper-left corner of the **Assess It**.

LESSON 98

Topic | **Nonfiction Point of View**

Learning Objectives

The activities in this lesson will help your student meet the following objectives:

- identify the author's point of view in a persuasive text
- construct a business letter using correct punctuation
- spell words in which the silent *e* is dropped before adding *-ed*, *-es*, or *-ing*

Materials

- dictionary
- highlighter
- index cards
- newspaper articles
- "Persuasive Point of View" activity page

Explain Author's Point of View

Activate

1. Ask your student to state their opinion about trampolines and whether they are a safe form of exercise for children.
2. Explain that this is called a point of view.

Engage

1. Starting with the **Read It**, instruct your student to verbalize the author's point of view in the example and the question before reading the answers.
2. Now, tell them to go back to their opinion from the Activate activity. What strong language could they include to make their opinion more persuasive and understandable?

Demonstrate

1. Next, direct your student to complete the "Persuasive Point of View" activity page in the **Show It**.
2. When they are finished, have them evaluate their response using the example in the **Show It AK**.
3. To reinforce learning, encourage your student to read newspaper articles in the Opinion section. Ask them to explain the author's perspective and to point out the language that helped them draw their conclusions.

● ● ●

Punctuating a Business Letter

 **Engage**

1. While completing the **Read It**, encourage your student to take notes about the parts of a business letter, including the address, date, greeting, body, closing, and signature.
2. Ask your student to point out the difference between the greeting of a personal letter and a business letter. (Answer: In a personal letter, the greeting is followed by a comma, while in a business letter, the greeting is followed by a colon.)

 **Demonstrate**

1. Now, go to the **Show It** and prompt your student to complete the activity.
2. Afterward, instruct them to check their letter using the example in the **Show It AK**.

● ● ●

Spelling Dropped Silent *e*

 **Engage**

1. As your student reads the **Read It**, have them copy the chart under the heading Rules, Patterns, and Examples"into their journal.
2. Now, prompt your student to read the list of spelling words and write them on a sheet of paper or index cards (one card per word).
3. Next, have your student complete the word searches to practice the spelling words.
4. Last, move on to the **Practice It** and instruct your student to complete the activity. Spelling practice activities for this subtopic will span Lessons 98 through 100.

LESSON 99

Topic | **Nonfiction Point of View**

Learning Objectives

The activities in this lesson will help your student meet the following objectives:

- describe the topic of an informational text using only facts or details
- correctly punctuate times of day
- spell words in which the silent *e* is dropped before adding *-ed*, *-es*, or *-ing*

Materials

- "Hunting Season Announcement"
- digital and analog clock
- teacher- or student-selected text

Using Facts or Details

Activate

1. Ask your student to state a fact and an opinion about ice cream. They might say that there are many flavors of ice cream and that mint chocolate chip is the best.

Engage

1. Move on to the **Read It** and direct your student to answer any questions in the content.
2. Next, have them open and view the **Fact or Opinion? - Watch It**. Pause the video at 2:46, 2:55, and 3:10 and ask them whether each statement is a fact or an opinion.
3. Afterward, ask your student to explain the meaning of *superlative* and how it is used in opinions. (Answer: a word that exaggerates meaning, such as *greatest* or *worst*, and helps identify opinions)
4. For extra practice discerning facts from opinions, encourage your student to use the **Plutarch's Library-Fact or Opinion - Play It**. If time permits, allow them to play until they achieve a perfect score.
5. Now, have them complete the activity in the **Practice It**.

Demonstrate

1. Continue to the **Show It** and instruct your student to use "Hunting Season Announcement" to complete the activity.
2. When they are finished, have them evaluate their response using the example in the **Show It AK**.
3. Finally, prompt them to complete the Application section of the **Show It**.

• • •

Punctuating Times of Day

 **Activate**

1. Ask your student to point out a digital and an analog clock. If they are unfamiliar with the term *analog clock*, explain that it is the clock with hands.

 **Engage**

1. After your student reads the content of the **Read It**, ask them how to punctuate the time in number form. (Answer: with a colon)

 **Demonstrate**

1. Next, go to the **Show It** and prompt your student to complete the activity.
2. Instruct them to review their answers using the **Show It AK**.
3. To reinforce learning, when you see an analog clock, encourage your student to tell you the time and where to place the colon when writing it in number form.

● ● ●

Spelling Dropped Silent *e*

 **Engage**

1. To review their spelling words, instruct your student to complete the activity in the **Practice It**. They may play the game more than once if time allows. Spelling practice activities for this subtopic will span Lessons 98 through 100.

LESSON 100

Topic   **Nonfiction Point of View**

Learning Objectives

The activities in this lesson will help your student meet the following objectives:

- list details that support an author's point of view
- revise sentences containing lists of items to include colons
- spell words in which the silent *e* is dropped before adding *-ed*, *-es*, or *-ing*

Materials

- none required

Supporting Facts

Activate

1. Instruct your student to ask you why you think students should have classes all year long. Answer by saying, "Because."
2. If they ask why, respond with, "Because I said so."
3. Now, ask your student if that is a valid reason. When they say no, explain that they will learn about supporting opinions with facts.

Engage

1. Beginning with the **Read It**, prompt your student to verbalize the answers to the excerpt before checking if they are correct.
2. Go back to the question in the Activate. This time, respond that students should have year-long classes because they would retain information better and not forget what they learned. Discuss why this is a better answer than "Because."

Demonstrate

1. Open the **Assess It** and have your student complete the activity. When they are finished, scan the document or take a photo of it and upload it to the Dropbox. For additional instructions on how to use the Dropbox, click on the paper clip icon in the upper-left corner of the **Assess It**.

● ● ●

Punctuate a List

 **Engage**

1. As your student reads the **Read It**, encourage them to answer the questions in the content.
2. For extra practice, ask them to write a list of things they would take to the beach. Ensure that they include a colon. For example: I would take the following items to the beach: a towel, sunscreen, a water bottle, and a surfboard.

 **Demonstrate**

1. Next, instruct your student to complete the activity in the **Show It**.
2. When they are finished, have them use the **Show It AK** to check their answers.

• • •

Spelling Dropped Silent *e*

 **Engage**

1. To review their spelling words, have your student complete the activity in the **Practice It**.
2. As an added challenge, encourage them to unscramble the spelling word before listening to it being read. If time permits, allow them to play more than once.
3. Spelling practice activities for this subtopic span Lessons 98 through 100.

LESSON 101

Topic Nonfiction Point of View

Learning Objectives

The activities in this lesson will help your student meet the following objectives:

- compare and contrast the positive and negative aspects of a chosen topic
- express an opinion about a topic

Materials

- none required

Compare Positive and Negative

Activate

1. Ask your student to tell you one positive aspect of eating dessert before dinner and one negative aspect.
2. They may say that one pro is that they get to eat their favorite part of the meal first and one con is that they will not have room to eat a nutritious meal.

Engage

1. Move on to the **Read It** and discuss the content with your student.
2. Next, discuss why it is important to understand and explore both sides of an argument. If possible, bring a current event into the conversation and help your student explore both sides so they can form a well-thought-out opinion.

Demonstrate

1. Now, direct your student to complete the activity in the **Show It**. As an added challenge, encourage them to choose a topic that is prevalent in the news.
2. When they are finished, have them evaluate their chart using the example in the **Show It AK**.
3. To extend learning, as your student becomes more involved in the world around them, encourage them to explore both sides of every issue before forming an opinion.

• • •

Expressing an Opinion

 ## Activate

1. Based on their answer in the previous Activate, ask your student to tell you their opinion about having dessert before dinner.

 ## Engage

1. While reading the **Read It**, encourage your student to form an opposing opinion about the villain argument before reading the three possible responses.
2. Next, have them open and view the **Fact and Opinion - Watch It**.
3. Afterward, ask them to explain the difference between facts and opinions.

 ## Demonstrate

1. Continue by prompting your student to complete the **Show It**.
2. Finally, remind them to check their sentences using the examples in the **Show It AK**.

LESSON 102

Topic   **Nonfiction Point of View**

Learning Objectives

The activities in this lesson will help your student meet the following objectives:

- evaluate whether or not the reasons an author uses in a text to support a point of view are sufficient
- use quotation marks to identify the titles of short works in sentences
- spell words in which the silent *e* is dropped before adding *-ed*, *-es*, or *-ing*

Materials

- "School Should Start Later"

Reasons Which Support Opinion

Activate

1. Tell your student that you believe people should sleep during the day and play and work at night.
2. Ask them to generate a reason to support your opinion. For example, they may say that if you sleep all day, it will be easier to stay up all night.

Engage

1. As your student reads the content of the **Read It**, ask them if the reasons supporting the opinion that body checking should not be allowed are sufficient.

Demonstrate

1. Open the **Assess It** and have your student complete the activity. Be sure that they review the expectations of the rubric before and after writing.
2. When they are finished, scan the document or take a photo of it and upload it to the Dropbox. For additional instructions on how to use the Dropbox, click on the paper clip icon in the upper-left corner of the **Assess It**.

• • •

Quotation for Short Works

Activate

1. Ask your student to look at the materials section for today's lesson. What do they notice about the story title? (Answer: It is surrounded by quotation marks.)

Engage

1. Begin with the **Read It** and discuss the content with your student.
2. Encourage them to copy the chart under the Tips section into their journal.

Demonstrate

1. Move on to the **Show It** and instruct your student to complete the activity.
2. Now, go to the **Show It AK** and have them review their answers.

• • •

Spelling Dropped Silent *e*

Engage

1. Instruct your student to review and practice the spelling words a few times before they complete the **Assess It**.

Demonstrate

1. Now move on to the **Assess It**. Have your student write, and correctly spell, the words they hear spoken in the assessment. This assessment covers the spelling words presented in Lessons 98 through 100.
2. When they are finished, scan the document or take a photo of it and upload it to the Dropbox. For additional instructions on how to use the Dropbox, click on the paper clip icon in the upper-left corner of the **Assess It**.

LESSON 103

Topic	Nonfiction Point of View

Learning Objectives

The activities in this lesson will help your student meet the following objectives:

- identify the proof an author uses to claim that a theory is correct
- distinguish between possessive nouns and plural nouns
- spell words with the long *i* or long *e* ending sound using the letter *y*

Materials

- "Earth: The Blue Marble"
- dictionary
- index cards

Proving a Theory Is Correct

 ## Activate

1. Ask your student to explain why there are no longer dinosaurs on Earth. Their answer may be based on facts or just something that they think.
2. Explain that they will learn about how authors support their theories.

 ## Engage

1. Starting with the **Read It**, have your student work through the content.
2. Discuss dinosaur extinction.
   a. Did the author present information about a theory already known to them?
   b. What support did the author include?

 ## Demonstrate

1. Continue to the **Show It** and have your student use "Earth: The Blue Marble" to complete the activity. You may need to explain that BCE stands for Before Common Era and is similar to the dating system BC, or Before Christ.
2. When they are finished, have them evaluate their response using the example in the **Show It AK**.
3. To reinforce learning, encourage your student to research scientific theories.

• • •

Possessive or Plural Nouns

 **Engage**

1. Begin by having your student draw the following chart in their journal.

	Definition	How to Form	Example
Possessive Noun			
Plural Noun			

2. As your student works through the **Read It**, encourage them to fill in the chart with information from the content.
3. Now, instruct your student to view the **Possessive or Plural Nouns - Watch It**. Pause the video at 2:00 and 2:32 to allow them time to choose the appropriate noun.

 **Demonstrate**

1. Next, direct your student to complete the **Show It** activity.
2. Afterward, prompt them to check their answers using the **Show It AK**.

• • •

Spelling Words Ending in *y*

 **Engage**

1. As your student reads the **Read It**, instruct them to play the sound clips and repeat the sounds aloud.
2. Then, have your student read the list of spelling words and write them on a sheet of paper or index cards (one card per word).
3. Next, have your student complete the sorting activity to determine which spelling words have a long *i* sound and which have a long *e* sound.
4. Now, direct them to open the **Y as a Vowel - Watch It**. Ask them to make note of the username and password provided on the Discovery Education image. Be sure that they click the link for the video and enter the provided username and password to watch.
5. Last, move on to the **Practice It** for your student to complete the activity. Spelling practice activities for this subtopic will span Lessons 103 through 105.

LESSON 104

Topic **Nonfiction Point of View**

Learning Objectives

The activities in this lesson will help your student meet the following objectives:

- identify words and phrases used in texts about different subject areas
- convert pairs of words into contractions
- spell words with the long *i* or long *e* ending sound using the letter *y*

Materials

- dry erase board and marker
- highlighter
- "Content Vocabulary" activity page

Comparing Vocabulary Usage

Activate

1. Write the word *science* in the center of the dry erase board.
2. Now, give your student one minute to write as many words relating to science as possible.
3. After the minute is up, review the words and erase the board. This time, write *mathematics* in the center.
4. Again, give your student one minute to write as many words relating to math as possible.
5. After the minute is up, review the words. Which category was easier to complete?
6. Explain that each subject has its own vocabulary.

Engage

1. Starting with the **Read It**, have your student work through the content.
2. After they read the example, allow them time to pick out any content-related words before reading the answers.

Demonstrate

1. Move on and have your student complete the **Show It** by printing and using the "Content Vocabulary" activity page. Encourage them to label the highlighted words with the corresponding subject.
2. When they are finished, have them review their work using the **Show It AK**.

• • •

Contractions

 **Activate**

1. On the dry erase board, write the word *can't*. Ask your student what that word means. (Answer: to be unable to do something)
2. Ask them which word means the same thing. (Answer: cannot)
3. Explain that *can't* is a contraction of *cannot*.

 **Engage**

1. While reading the **Read It**, tell your student to pay close attention to the chart containing acceptable contractions.
2. Now, have your student open and view the **Crazy Contractions - Watch It** for more information about forming contractions.
3. Next, have them watch the **Review: Using Contractions - Watch It**. Pause the video at 2:55 and 3:34 to allow them time to form the contractions.
4. For extra practice, prompt your student to open the **Carnival Racers-Contractions - Play It**. They will need to choose a course and a racer before playing. Allow them to play more than once if time allows.

 **Demonstrate**

1. Continue by prompting your student to complete the **Show It**.
2. Finally, have them review their answers using the **Show It AK**.
3. To reinforce learning, make a game of spotting contractions when they are outside of the learning environment. Challenge your student to call out any contractions they see and say the two words that form the contraction, and vice versa.

● ● ●

Spelling Words Ending with *y*

 **Engage**

1. To review their spelling words, instruct your student to complete the activity in the **Practice It**. They may play the game more than once if time allows. Spelling practice activities for this subtopic will span Lessons 103 through 105.

LESSON 105

Topic	Nonfiction Point of View

Learning Objectives

The activities in this lesson will help your student meet the following objectives:

- describe how words create a specific tone
- create an outline for a persuasive paragraph
- spell words with the long *i* or long *e* ending sound using the letter *y*

Materials

- none required

How Words Create Tone

Activate

1. Prompt your student to read the following sentence in a happy voice: May I please borrow a pencil?
2. Now, have them read the sentence in a shy voice and then a grumpy voice.
3. Explain that the tone of voice is similar to the tone of writing. Your tone of voice indicates how you feel about something, while an author's tone tells the reader how they feel about a topic.

Engage

1. Beginning with the **Read It**, tell your student to focus on how certain words let the reader know the author's feelings.
2. Discuss the similarities and differences between tone and mood. Remind your student that tone affects mood and that both are generally similar. For example, if an author uses a friendly tone, the reader's mood will be happy.
3. Next, instruct your student to open and view the **Analyzing Tone - Watch It**.
4. Afterward, ask them to tell you one interesting thing they learned from the video.

Demonstrate

1. Open the **Assess It** and have your student complete the activity. Ensure they review the expectations of the rubric before and after they complete the activity.
2. When they are finished, scan the document or take a photo of it and upload it to the Dropbox. For additional instructions on how to use the Dropbox, click on the paper clip icon in the upper-left corner of the **Assess It**.

● ● ●

Persuasive Paragraph Outline

 **Engage**

1. As your student reads the **Read It**, encourage them to copy or print and place the persuasive paragraph outline planner into their journal for future reference.
2. Now, help your student brainstorm possible topics for a persuasive paragraph.

 **Demonstrate**

1. Move on to the **Show It** and have your student complete the activity using one of the topics they brainstormed from the Engage section.
2. When they are finished, have them evaluate their response using the example in the **Show It AK**.

• • •

Spelling Words Ending with *y*

 **Engage**

1. To review their spelling words, have your student complete the activity in the **Practice It**. If time permits, allow them to play the game more than once. Spelling practice activities for this subtopic span Lessons 103 through 105.

LESSON 106

Topic	Nonfiction Point of View

Learning Objectives

The activities in this lesson will help your student meet the following objectives:

- write the plural forms of letters and numbers
- write a persuasive paragraph about a topic of interest

Materials

- dry erase board and marker

Plural Letters and Numbers

Activate

1. Ask your student to illustrate the word plural on the dry erase board. They may draw multiple people, animals, or objects.
2. Next, ask them to write the word that corresponds to their drawing. For example, if they drew a picture of three dogs, they would write dogs underneath the picture.

Engage

1. Starting with the **Read It**, instruct your student to explain how to write the different plural letters and numbers, including a single number, a single letter, and a number greater than one digit. (Answer: Add an apostrophe and the letter *s*.)

Demonstrate

1. Now, go to the **Show It** and prompt your student to complete the activity.
2. Remind them to use the **Show It AK** to check their answers.

● ● ●

Write a Persuasive Paragraph

Engage

1. While reading the **Read It**, challenge your student to brainstorm a single topic.
2. Next, have them open and view the **Persuasive Writing - Watch It**.
3. Afterward, ask them what the goal of persuasive writing is. (Answer: to take a closer look at your own views)

Demonstrate

1. Open the **Assess It** and have your student complete the activity. Be sure that they review the expectations of the rubric before and after writing.
2. When they are finished, scan the document or take a photo of it and upload it to the Dropbox. For additional instructions on how to use the Dropbox, click on the paper clip icon in the upper-left corner of the **Assess It**.

LESSON 107

| Topic | Nonfiction Point of View |

Learning Objectives

The activities in this lesson will help your student meet the following objectives:

- explain how words influence the meaning of content
- explain the difference between reason and fact
- spell words with the long *i* or long *e* ending sound using the letter *y*

Materials

- "Children Should Have Limited TV Time," "Opinion: Television Viewing Should be Limited for Children," and "Waiting on Saturday"

How Words Develop Meaning

Activate

1. Read the following sentence and ask your student to tell you what they visualize: Betsy flung the clothes out of her closet as she frantically searched for her missing phone.
2. Now, read this sentence and ask them what they see: Bob looked through the clothes in his closet, methodically searching for his missing phone.
3. Finally, ask them which words helped them create the picture in their mind.

Engage

1. As your student reads the **Read It**, allow them to answer any questions in the content.
2. For extra practice, prompt your student to write a sentence describing a small child making a mess in a restaurant. Encourage them to use words that will create a clear picture.

Demonstrate

1. Next, direct your student to use "Waiting on Saturday" to complete the **Show It**.
2. Afterward, instruct them to compare their work to the example in the **Show It AK**.

● ● ●

Reason versus Fact

 ## Activate

1. Ask your student to state how they felt about the last movie they saw. Ensure that they give a reason to support their opinion.
2. Next, ask them to state one fact about the movie.

 ## Engage

1. As your student reads the content of the **Read It**, have them write down definitions for the words *fact* and *reason*. (Answer: A fact is something that is commonly known to be true, while a reason is an explanation that is often based on emotion.)
2. Now, allow them time to read "Children Should Have Limited TV Time" and "Opinion: Television Viewing Should be Limited for Children" before answering the question.
3. For extra practice discerning the difference between facts and opinions, have your student complete the **Practice It** activity.

 ## Demonstrate

1. Continue to the **Show It** and instruct your student to complete the activity.
2. When they are finished, tell them to compare their work to the example in the **Show It AK**.
3. To reinforce learning, have your student write a statement about spiders that includes an opinion, a reason, and a fact. For example, they may write the following: People should not be afraid of spiders because they are awesome and only a small number of species are considered dangerous.

Spelling Words Ending with *y*

 ## Engage

1. Instruct your student to review and practice the spelling words a few times before they complete the **Assess It**.

 ## Demonstrate

1. Now move on to the **Assess It**. Have your student write, and correctly spell, the words they hear spoken in the assessment. This assessment covers the spelling words presented in Lessons 103 through 105.
2. When they are finished, scan the document or take a photo of it and upload it to the Dropbox. For additional instructions on how to use the Dropbox, click on the paper clip icon in the upper-left corner of the **Assess It**.

LESSON 108

Topic	Nonfiction Point of View

Learning Objectives

The activities in this lesson will help your student meet the following objectives:

- read a passage aloud at an appropriate rate
- create a list of words that use hyphens to form compound words
- spell words with the consonant digraphs *sh* and *ch*

Materials

- "Excerpt from 'The Queen of the Golden Heart'" and "Summer Vacation"
- children's book
- colored pencils
- dictionary
- index cards

Prose Presentation Skills

Activate

1. Tell your student to stand up and pretend that there is an audience in front of them.
2. Ask them to introduce themselves to the audience.
3. Now, ask them how they would feel if they had to do that in front of a real audience.

Engage

1. Beginning with the **Read It**, allow your student time to read "Excerpt from 'The Queen of the Golden Heart'" to themselves and then again out loud. Discuss any changes they could make to increase fluency and rate before reading it a final time.

Demonstrate

1. Next, prompt your student to read "Summer Vacation" to complete the **Show It**.
2. Afterward, have them use the **Show It AK** to confirm that they have met the criteria for the activity.
3. To extend learning, have your student read a children's book aloud to an audience. The audience may be friends, family, or even toys. Ensure that they read fluently and at an appropriate pace.

● ● ●

Compound Words

 **Engage**

1. Starting with the **Read It**, instruct your student to write the definitions of the three types of compound words in their journal.
2. Allow them time to rewrite the example sentence using the correct punctuation for the compound words.
3. For extra practice identifying the different types of compound words, have your student complete the activity in the **Practice It**.

 **Demonstrate**

1. Move on to the **Show It** and direct your student to complete the activity.
2. When they are finished, tell them to compare their words to the examples in the **Show It AK**.
3. As an added challenge, prompt your student to draw pictures of each part of the compound words they found.

• • •

Spelling Digraphs *sh* and *ch*

 **Engage**

1. As your student reads the **Read It**, have them play the sound clips and repeat the sounds aloud.
2. Now, instruct your student to read the list of spelling words and write them on a sheet of paper or index cards (one card per word). Prompt them to underline the digraph in each word.
3. Next, have your student complete the sorting activity to determine which spelling words have a *sh* digraph and which have a *ch* digraph.
4. Finally, move on to the **Practice It** so your student can complete the activity. Spelling practice activities for this subtopic will span Lessons 108 through 110.

LESSON 109

Topic **Nonfiction Point of View**

Learning Objectives

The activities in this lesson will help your student meet the following objectives:

- read aloud a text with changes in pitch, rhythm, volume, and tone
- convert numbers to words
- spell words with the consonant digraphs *sh* and *ch*

Materials

- "Night and the Grandson"
- dictionary
- teacher- or student-selected text

Prose Oral Expression

Activate

1. Ask your student if they have ever seen a play. What did they notice about the actors and their voices? Did they speak with a lot of expression and changes in volume and tone, or did they speak in a monotone voice? Which would be more interesting to the audience?
2. If your student has not seen a play, ask them what they have noticed about actors' voices in movies or TV shows.

Engage

1. Continue to the **Read It** and encourage your student to do the following as they work through the slide show:
   - **Pitch**: When reading the example sentence, practice the three pitches mentioned.
   - **Rhythm**: Tap out the rhythm as they speak.
   - **Volume**: Whisper and yell to show volume.
   - **Tone**: Read the last sentence multiple times, each time using a different tone.

Demonstrate

1. Open the **Assess It** and have your student complete the activity. Ensure that they review the expectations of the rubric before and after they complete the activity.
2. When they are finished, scan the document or take a photo of it and upload it to the Dropbox. For additional instructions on how to use the Dropbox, click on the paper clip icon in the upper-left corner of the **Assess It**.

● ● ●

Hyphenated Numbers

Engage

1. While reading the **Read It**, ask your student why numbers that are compound words need to be written with hyphens. (Answer: It makes the numbers easier to read.)
2. Afterward, ask them where to place the hyphen when writing numbers above ninety-nine. (Answer: between the numbers in the tens and ones places)

Demonstrate

1. Now, prompt your student to complete the **Show It**.
2. Next, go to the **Show It AK** and have them check their answers.
3. Finally, remind them to use their selected text to complete the Application section of the **Show It**.

● ● ●

Spelling Digraphs *sh* and *ch*

Engage

1. To review their spelling words, direct your student to complete the activity in the **Practice It**. They may play the game more than once if time allows. Spelling practice activities for this subtopic will span Lessons 108 through 110.

LESSON 110

Topic	Nonfiction Point of View

Learning Objectives

The activities in this lesson will help your student meet the following objectives:

- recognize that facts support opinions in a persuasive text
- convert fractions to words
- spell words with the consonant digraphs *sh* and *ch*

Materials

- recipe
- "Facts and Reasons" activity page

Facts Support Reasons

Activate

1. Ask your student to imagine that a scientist and a clown are having a debate about conserving water. Who do they think will win? Why?
2. Explain that though it seems likely that the scientist would win, it is still an opinion.
3. What if your student knew that the clown actually went to school to study water conservation while the scientist studied astronomy? Explain that these facts help to support their opinion.

Engage

1. Begin with the **Read It** and discuss how to use facts to support reasons.
2. Ask your student what would happen in the debate from the Activate if the scientist began every statement with "I think." Encourage them to explain their thoughts.

Demonstrate

1. Now, instruct your student to complete the "Facts and Reasons" activity page in the **Show It**.
2. When they are finished, have them review their answers using the example in the **Show It AK**.
3. To reinforce learning, have a debate with your student about a topic of their choice. As you debate, encourage them to use facts to support their reasons.

● ● ●

Hyphenated Fractions

 **Engage**

1. While reading the **Read It**, ask your student where to place the hyphen in a fraction. (Answer: between the numerator and denominator)
2. Allow them time to complete the question in the example before checking the answer.

 Demonstrate

1. Continue to the **Show It** and prompt your student to complete the activity.
2. Now, go to the **Show It AK** and have them review their answers.
3. For extra practice, the next time you are cooking from a recipe, have your student convert the fractions to words.

● ● ●

Spelling Digraphs *sh* and *ch*

 **Engage**

1. To review their spelling words, have your student complete the activity in the **Practice It**. They may play the game more than once if time allows. Spelling practice activities for this subtopic span Lessons 108 through 110.

LESSON 111

Topic	Nonfiction Point of View

Learning Objectives

The activities in this lesson will help your student meet the following objectives:

- respond to a statement by providing reasons to support this point of view
- recognize how an author develops an argument with supporting reasons in a persuasive text
- spell words with the consonant digraphs *sh* and *ch*

Materials

- "Buy American"
- colored pencils

Respond with Reasons

Activate

1. First, have your student draw a picture to show an unhappy person at the beach.
2. Next, ask them to explain the reason why the person in their picture feels that way.

Engage

1. As your student reads the **Read It**, encourage them to write the reasons for the example point of view before reading the possibilities.

Demonstrate

1. Now, prompt your student to complete the activity in the **Show It**.
2. Afterward, remind them to use the example in the **Show It AK** to evaluate their work.

• • •

Reasons Support Point of View

Engage

1. Starting with the **Read It**, encourage your student to reflect on how some of their major opinions have been formed.
2. Discuss some of their opinions and how they came to be.

Demonstrate

1. Move on to the **Show It** and have your student use "Buy American" to complete the activity.
2. Next, remind them to check their reasons using the **Show It AK**.
3. To extend learning, prompt your student to choose one of their major opinions from the Engage section. Challenge them to write a persuasive paragraph about the opinion and include at least two reasons why the reader should agree with them.

• • •

Spelling Digraphs *sh* and *ch*

Engage

1. Instruct your student to review and practice the spelling words a few times before they complete the **Assess It**.

Demonstrate

1. Now move on to the **Assess It**. Have your student write, and correctly spell, the words they hear spoken in the assessment. This assessment covers the spelling words presented in Lessons 108 through 110.
2. When they are finished, scan the document or take a photo of it and upload it to the Dropbox. For additional instructions on how to use the Dropbox, click on the paper clip icon in the upper-left corner of the **Assess It**.
3. The next lesson is a **Mastery Assess It**. Encourage your student to review Lessons 93 through 111 in order to prepare for the assessment.

LESSON 112

Topic	Nonfiction Point of View

Learning Objectives

The activities in this lesson will help your student meet the following objectives:

- not applicable

Materials

- none required

Mastery Assess It 8

1. **Mastery Assess It 8** will cover what your student has learned in Lessons 93 through 111.
2. Click on the **Mastery Assess It 8** icon to begin the online assessment.
3. Have your student read the instructions before they get started. Remind them to take their time and to do their best work.
4. When they are finished and ready for their assessment to be graded, have them click the **Submit** button.

LESSON 113

Topic | **Collaborating with Others**

Learning Objectives

The activities in this lesson will help your student meet the following objectives:

- identify guidelines for preparing for a discussion
- write compound sentences with the coordinating conjunction *and*
- spell words with the digraphs *th*, *ph*, and *wh*

Materials

- art supplies

Preparing for a Discussion

Activate

1. Ask your student what happens when a group of people are all talking over each other at the same time. They may mention that no one can clearly hear what is being said.

Engage

1. Beginning with the **Read It**, prompt your student to list the guidelines for preparing for a discussion in their journal.

Demonstrate

1. Next, direct your student to complete the **Show It** activity.
2. Now, instruct them to check their poster using the example in the **Show It AK**.
3. To extend learning, remind them to reference their poster while participating in a discussion.

Compound Sentences with *And*

Engage

1. As your student reads the **Read It**, ask them to explain the relationship between conjunctions and compound sentences. (Answer: Compound sentences depend on a conjunction to join two thoughts.)
2. Next, prompt them to note the tips for writing compound sentences with *and* in their journal.

Demonstrate

1. Continue by instructing your student to complete the compound sentences in the **Show It**.
2. Move on to the **Show It AK** and have your student check their sentences.

Spelling Digraphs *th, ph, wh*

Activate

1. Begin by having your student view the **Watch Its** titled **Digraph: ph** and **Digraphs: th & wh**. Ask them to make note of the username and password provided on the Discovery Education image. Be sure that they click the link for the video and enter the provided username and password to watch.
2. Prompt them to repeat the sounds of the digraphs as they are presented in the video.

Engage

1. After your student listens to the audio clips in the **Read It**, ask them if they can think of other words that have the digraphs *ph*, *th*, and *wh* in them.
2. Next, instruct them to write the list of spelling words in their journal and circle the spelling digraphs.
3. Finally, direct them to complete the activity in the **Practice It**. Spelling practice activities for this subtopic will span Lessons 113 through 115.

LESSON 114

Topic   **Collaborating with Others**

Learning Objectives

The activities in this lesson will help your student meet the following objectives:

- identify ways to participate in a discussion
- state a reason to support a point of view and corroborate it with a fact
- spell words with the digraphs *th*, *ph*, and *wh*

Materials

- "Tomato, Tomato"
- highlighter

Participating in a Discussion

Activate

1. Take turns telling a story with your student.
   a. Explain that you will take turns adding a sentence to tell a story.
   b. Start with, "Once upon a time," and complete the sentence.
   c. Direct your student to tell the next part in one sentence.
   d. Continue taking turns until the story seems to come to an end, and prompt your student to say the last sentence.
2. Now, discuss how you both had to be good listeners to know what to add to the story. Also, emphasize that you both took turns speaking.

Engage

1. While your student reads the **Read It**, prompt them to share times they have used the guidelines for participating in a group conversation.
2. Afterward, have your student copy the "Guidelines for Group Discussions" in their journal for future reference.

Demonstrate

1. Next, direct your student to complete the activity in the **Show It**.
2. Tell them to compare their responses to the example in the **Show It AK**.
3. To extend learning, remind them of the group discussion guidelines while having a conversation at the dinner table.

● ● ●

Corroborate Reason with Fact

Engage

1. As your student reads the **Read It**, allow them to print "Tomato, Tomato" to mark the supporting reasons and facts with a highlighter.
2. After reading, ask them to explain why it is important to support a point of view with reasons and corroborate those reasons with facts. (Answer: It creates a stronger argument.)

Demonstrate

1. Continue to the **Show It** and instruct your student to complete the activity.
2. Now, have them reference the **Show It AK** to evaluate their response and compare it to the example provided.

● ● ●

Spelling Digraphs *th*, *ph*, *wh*

Engage

1. Begin by having your student review the list of spelling words in their journal from Lesson 113. Prompt them to circle the words that are the most difficult and spell them out loud at least three times.
2. Finally, instruct them to play the game in the **Practice It**. Spelling practice activities for this subtopic will span Lessons 113 through 115.

LESSON 115

Topic | **Collaborating with Others**

Learning Objectives

The activities in this lesson will help your student meet the following objectives:

- prepare for a small group discussion
- write compound sentences with the coordinating conjunction *but*
- spell words with the digraphs *th*, *ph*, and *wh*

Materials

- "Margaret and Gert"
- playing cards
- sticky notes
- teacher- or student-selected text

Small Group Discussion Prep

Activate

1. Begin by playing a couple of rounds of Go Fish with your student.
2. Discuss how it is important to listen and remember what cards the other player(s) ask for. By listening and remembering well, they can ask for those cards later in the game.

Engage

1. Move on to the **Read It** and have your student reference the literature circle jobs list.
2. Ask which literature circle job they would like the most and why.

Demonstrate

1. Now, instruct your student to go to the **Show It** and complete the activity. Allow them to print the text to place their sticky notes directly on the paper.
2. Continue to the **Show It AK** and have your student review their work.
3. Afterward, direct your student to complete the Application section of the **Show It** by using the sticky note method with their selected text.

● ● ●

Compound Sentences with *But*

Engage

1. As your student reads the **Read It**, ask them how the conjunction *but* helps join the clauses in each sentence of the flip-book. (Answer: The conjunction *but* is used to show a contrast between two things.)

Demonstrate

1. Next, prompt your student to complete the sentence activity in the **Show It**.
2. Use the **Show It AK** to have them check their answers.
3. To extend learning, encourage your student to point out when and how *but* is used in various texts they read.

●●●

Spelling Digraphs *th, ph, wh*

Engage

1. Finally, instruct your student to complete the spelling exercise in the **Practice It**. Spelling practice activities for this subtopic span Lessons 113 through 115.

LESSON 116

Topic	Collaborating with Others

Learning Objectives

The activities in this lesson will help your student meet the following objectives:

- summarize your contribution to a small group discussion
- write a persuasive paragraph that contains reasons and supporting facts

Materials

- "The Porcupine and the Firefly" and "Yogurt"
- highlighters

Small Group Discussion

Activate

1. Begin by asking your student, "If you were to have a discussion about your favorite movie or TV show, what would you share about it?"
2. Next, ask them how they might start this discussion with another person. They may respond that they would begin by asking, "Do you know of the show _____?"
3. Discuss how it would be polite to ask the other person about their favorite movie or TV show.

Engage

1. As your student reads the **Read It**, discuss any challenges they have faced while working in a group. Prompt them to share solutions to those problems.
2. Afterward, ask your student how people benefit from engaging in small group discussions. They may mention that they can share ideas and learn from each other in a small group.

Demonstrate

1. Open the **Assess It** and have your student complete the activity. When they are finished, scan the document or take a photo of it and upload it to the Dropbox. For additional instructions on how to use the Dropbox, click on the paper clip icon in the upper-left corner of the **Assess It**.

● ● ●

Reasons and Supporting Facts

Engage

1. While reading the **Read It**, tell your student to pay special attention to the paragraph outline chart. Discuss how it could be helpful in organizing their work.
2. After reading the example persuasive paragraph, "Yogurt," prompt your student to identify the reasons and supporting facts about the benefits of serving yogurt in schools.
3. Encourage them to print the reading and highlight the reasons in one color and the supporting facts in another color.

Demonstrate

1. Next, instruct your student to complete the persuasive paragraph in the **Show It**. If they cannot think of a topic that interests them, tell them to write about a topic provided in the activity.
2. Last, encourage them to compare their response to the example in the **Show It AK**.

LESSON 117

Topic	Collaborating with Others

Learning Objectives

The activities in this lesson will help your student meet the following objectives:

- recognize words and phrases that help to link opinions and reasons
- write complex sentences using subordinating conjunctions
- spell words with the digraphs *th*, *ph*, and *wh*

Materials

- none required

Linking Opinions and Reasons

 **Activate**

1. Begin by asking your student the following questions and challenging them to give a reason for each:
   - What is your favorite color? Why?
   - What is your favorite animal? Why?
   - What is your favorite food? Why?
2. Next, discuss how these are their personal opinions and that they can give reasons for their opinions.

 **Engage**

1. Now, go to the **Read It** and instruct your student to note the chart of linking words and phrases in their journal.

 **Demonstrate**

1. Continue by having your student complete the **Show It**. It may help to print the activity so they can circle the linking words and phrases in the passage.
2. Afterward, have them check their answers in the **Show It AK**.

• • •

232

Punctuating Complex Sentences

Activate

1. Prompt your student to open and view the **Complex Sentences - Watch It**.
2. Now, ask them to explain the meaning of a complex sentence. (Answer: A complex sentence has an independent and a dependent clause.)

Engage

1. Begin with the **Read It** and discuss the difference between independent and dependent clauses.
2. Next, instruct your student to note the list of subordinating conjunctions in their journal.

Demonstrate

1. Move on to the **Show It** and prompt your student to complete the activity.
2. Finally, remind them to compare their answers to the examples in the **Show It AK**.

Spelling Digraphs *th, ph, wh*

Engage

1. Encourage your student to review the list of spelling words from Lesson 113 before they complete the **Assess It**.

Demonstrate

1. Now move on to the **Assess It**. Have your student write, and correctly spell, the words they hear spoken in the assessment. This assessment covers the spelling words presented in Lessons 113 through 115.
2. When they are finished, scan the document or take a photo of it and upload it to the Dropbox. For additional instructions on how to use the Dropbox, click on the paper clip icon in the upper-left corner of the **Assess It**.

LESSON 118

Topic	**Collaborating with Others**

Learning Objectives

The activities in this lesson will help your student meet the following objectives:

- reflect on a discussion
- list rules for collaborative discussions
- spell words with consonant blends

Materials

- art supplies
- dictionary
- index cards
- markers
- poster board

Reflecting on a Discussion

Activate

1. Begin by typing the words "fourth grade group discussion video" in the search bar of an Internet browser.
2. Next, select a video of a group discussion and show it to your student.
3. Prompt your student to share what they saw and heard in the group discussion.

Engage

1. Continue to the **Read It** and instruct your student to note the reflection categories in their journal. Encourage them to include one question for each category type.

Demonstrate

1. Continue to the **Show It** and have your student complete the activity. If peers are not available to have the group discussion, have the discussion with them so they can reflect on it.
2. Now, discuss their responses and help them determine if the reflection questions were fully answered.

Follow Agreed-Upon Rules

Engage

1. As your student reads the **Read It**, ask them which rules they like most when working with others. Why?

Demonstrate

1. Instruct your student to complete the **Show It** activity. If they are unable to work with a group, have them create the rules and share them with another peer or adult at a later time.
2. Next, encourage them to evaluate their poster using the **Show It AK**.

● ● ●

Spelling with Consonant Blends

Engage

1. As your student works through the **Read It**, instruct them to repeat the sounds of the consonant blends from the audio clips in the content.
2. Now, direct them to write the spelling words on a sheet of paper or index cards (one card per word).
3. Last, remind them to complete the activity in the **Practice It**. Spelling practice activities for this subtopic will span Lessons 118 through 120.

LESSON 119

Topic Collaborating with Others

Learning Objectives

The activities in this lesson will help your student meet the following objectives:

- choose transitional words and phrases to support an opinion on a graphic organizer
- use an online dictionary to write the meanings of unknown words
- spell words with consonant blends

Materials

- markers
- online dictionary
- spelling flashcards
- stapler
- strips of paper
- teacher- or student-selected text
- "Persuasive Connecting Words" activity page

Choosing Connecting Words

 ## Activate

1. Start by having your student write the phrase *I believe* on a strip of paper.
2. Next, instruct them to write an opinion statement on another strip of paper. For example, *I believe… that human products should not be tested on animals.*
3. Now, have them loop the first strip and staple it to make a chain link.
4. Finally, have them thread the second strip through the first chain link. Loop it around to staple it and make a second chain link.

 ## Engage

1. As your student reads the **Read It**, instruct them to make a list of connecting words in their journal.

 ## Demonstrate

1. Continue to the **Show It** and have your student complete the activity.
2. When they have finished, work with them to compare their answers and paragraph with the examples provided in the **Show It AK**.

• • •

Consulting Online References

 **Engage**

1. After your student reads the **Read It**, help them find an online dictionary. Encourage them to choose a word to look up in order to become familiar with the website.

 Demonstrate

1. Now, instruct your student to complete the activity in the **Show It**.
2. Afterward, help them check their responses with the examples in the **Show It AK**.
3. Finally, prompt them to use their selected text to complete the Application section of the **Show It**.

● ● ●

Spelling with Consonant Blends

 **Engage**

1. Direct your student to pull out and mix up the spelling flashcards they made in Lesson 118. Then, have them sort the cards by consonant blend.
2. Prompt them to spell each word aloud before they complete the exercise in the **Practice It**. Spelling practice activities for this subtopic will span Lessons 118 through 120.

LESSON 120

| Topic | Collaborating with Others |

Learning Objectives

The activities in this lesson will help your student meet the following objectives:

- choose a discussion role and prepare accordingly for a discussion
- use an online dictionary to determine the proper pronunciations of words
- spell words with consonant blends

Materials

- "The Importance of Protecting Endangered Species"
- spelling flashcards
- teacher- or student-selected text

Discussion Roles

Activate

1. Begin by having your student open and view the **Group Discussion - Watch It**. Ask them to make note of the username and password provided on the Discovery Education image. Be sure that they click the link for the video and enter the provided username and password to watch.
2. Afterward, prompt them to share an aspect of the group discussion that they liked. For example, they may have liked the experiences all of the students were sharing.

Engage

1. As your student reads the **Read It**, instruct them to take note of common discussion roles in their journal. Encourage them to include any information they learn about each role.
2. Next, ask them which role they would like most and why.

Demonstrate

1. Now, direct your student to complete the **Show It**.
2. When they are finished, have them reference the **Show It AK** to compare their response to the example provided.

• • •

Determining Pronunciation

Engage

1. While your student reads the **Read It**, have them repeat the pronunciation of the audio clips.
2. Next, help them use an Internet source to find the pronunciation of a particular word.

Demonstrate

1. Move on to the **Show It** and have your student complete the activity.
2. Help them check their answers with the **Show It AK**.
3. Now, direct your student to use their selected text to complete the Application section of the **Show It**.

●●●

Spelling Consonant Blends

Engage

1. Instruct your student to review their spelling words by working with the flashcards they made in Lesson 118.
2. Finally, prompt them to open the **Practice It** and play the game. Spelling practice activities for this subtopic span Lessons 118 through 120.

LESSON 121

Topic	Collaborating with Others

Learning Objectives

The activities in this lesson will help your student meet the following objectives:

- recognize connecting words and phrases used in persuasive writing
- use a glossary or dictionary to describe the differences between weather events

Materials

- dictionary, glossary, or reference books
- teacher- or student-selected text
- "Weekly Reading Log" activity page

Connecting Words and Phrases

 ## Activate

1. Start by having your student use the word *additionally* in a sentence. For example: There were many fruits and vegetables at the market. Additionally, many vendors were selling fresh eggs.
2. Then, discuss the use of the word *additionally*. It is similar to using the word *also* in order to give more information.

Engage

1. As your student reads the **Read It**, have them make a table in their journal to organize the categories of connecting words. An example has been provided below.
2. As they read, prompt them to complete the table by listing the example words.

Add Information	Show Contrast	Introduce Examples	Show Consequences	Conclude Writing

 ## Demonstrate

1. Now, direct your student to complete the activities in the **Show It**.
2. Then, help them check their answers with the **Show It AK**.

• • •

Consulting a Dictionary

 Activate

1. Begin by having your student open and view the **Using a Dictionary - Watch It** to learn about the aspects of a dictionary.
2. Be sure they pause the video at 3:36 to identify the words based on the pronunciation symbols.

 **Engage**

1. While your student reads the **Read It**, prompt them to explain the purpose of a dictionary and a glossary. (Answer: A dictionary allows the user to look up information about things. A glossary is often found in a nonfiction text. It allows the user to find information about the topic of the text.)

 Demonstrate

1. Open the **Assess It** and have your student complete the activity. Be sure that they review the expectations of the rubric before and after writing.
2. When they are finished, scan the document or take a photo of it and upload it to the Dropbox. For additional instructions on how to use the Dropbox, click on the paper clip icon in the upper-left corner of the **Assess It**.

LESSON 122

Topic	Collaborating with Others

Learning Objectives

The activities in this lesson will help your student meet the following objectives:

- write a persuasive paragraph using connecting words or phrases
- spell words with consonant blends

Materials

- spelling flashcards
- "Blank Paragraph Outline" activity page

Using Connecting Words

Activate

1. Direct your student to review the connecting words and phrases table they created in their journal in Lesson 121.
2. Then, ask them if they can think of any other examples.

Engage

1. While your student reads the **Read It**, discuss the importance of using connecting words and phrases to make smooth transitions from reason to reason in a persuasive paragraph.
2. Consider having your student print out the "Blank Paragraph Outline" activity page to use later in the **Assess It**.
3. Then, discuss how an outline helps the writer to formulate their thoughts before they write.

Demonstrate

1. Open the **Assess It** and have your student complete the activity. Be sure that they review the expectations of the rubric before and after writing. Encourage them to use the "Blank Paragraph Outline" activity page they printed out in the Engage section to organize their paragraph.
2. When they are finished, scan the document or take a photo of it and upload it to the Dropbox. For additional instructions on how to use the Dropbox, click on the paper clip icon in the upper-left corner of the **Assess It**.

• • •

Spelling with Consonant Blends

Engage

1. Encourage your student to review their spelling flashcards from Lesson 118 before they complete the **Assess It**.

Demonstrate

1. Now, move on to the **Assess It**. Have your student write, and correctly spell, the words they hear spoken in the assessment. This assessment covers the spelling words presented in Lessons 118 through 120.

2. When they are finished, scan the document or take a photo of it and upload it to the Dropbox. For additional instructions on how to use the Dropbox, click on the paper clip icon in the upper-left corner of the **Assess It**.

LESSON 123

Topic | **Collaborating with Others**

Learning Objectives

The activities in this lesson will help your student meet the following objectives:

- build on the ideas of others in a discussion
- explain how the opening and closing sentences in a persuasive text are similar
- spell contractions

Materials

- "Bicycle: The Gift that Keeps on Giving"

Building on Discussion Ideas

Activate

1. Begin by prompting your student to find a way to combine the following two ideas in a scenario: You and your friend want to play two different games. You want to play tag, and he wants to play forts and knights.
2. One possible solution is to play forts and knights tag. Have a discussion with your student about how this solution builds on both ideas.

Engage

1. As your student reads the **Read It**, have them write the list of sentence stems in their journal. Then, have them circle the stem that they would be most likely to use in a conversation about pedestrian safety.
   a. For example, if they were listening to rules about how to be safe while walking near a busy street, what could they add to the conversation?
   b. Your student may respond by saying, "**I would add the idea that** it is important to keep your head up to be aware of moving objects. Looking at your phone while walking can be dangerous."

Demonstrate

1. Now, direct your student to complete the activity in the **Show It**.
2. Then, help them reference the **Show It AK** and compare their response to the sample provided.
3. To extend learning, challenge your student to use the sentence stems during dinner conversations.

• • •

Opening and Closing Sentences

 **Engage**

1. While your student reads the **Read It**, discuss the reasons why the opening and closing sentences in paragraphs or essays should have similar messages.

 **Demonstrate**

1. Now, instruct your student to move on to the **Show It** activity. Allow them to print the text to annotate their thoughts on the edges of the paper.
2. Then, work with them to compare their response to the sample in the **Show It AK**.

• • •

Spelling Contractions

 Activate

1. Start by having your student use the word *you've* in a sentence. For example: If *you've* been stung by a bee, you should carefully remove the stinger with the edge of a card.

 **Engage**

1. After your student reads the **Read It**, have them choose five of the contractions from the spelling list and verbally expand the words. For example: shouldn't = should + not.
2. Then, instruct them to write the list of spelling words in their journal.
3. Next, prompt them to open the **Carnival Racers-Contractions - Play It** to play the game.
4. Finally, guide your student to complete the exercise in the **Practice It**. Spelling practice activities for this subtopic will span Lessons 123 through 125.

LESSON 124

Topic | **Collaborating with Others**

Learning Objectives

The activities in this lesson will help your student meet the following objectives:

- respond to questions about a text during a discussion
- restate the main idea of the opening statement in a persuasive text
- use a thesaurus to determine the meanings of unfamiliar words
- spell contractions

Materials

- "The World at Your Fingertips"
- highlighter
- thesaurus

Classroom Conversation

Activate

1. Begin by having your student pretend they are a reporter interviewing a guest. Have them think of three questions they can ask about any topic.
2. Then, have them act out the interview by asking you the questions, just like a reporter might do.

Engage

1. Next, have your student move to the **Read It** and read the content.
2. While reading, have them list the questions from the Using Questions to Check for Understanding section in their journal.

Demonstrate

1. Now, have your student move on to the **Show It** activity. Allow them to print "The World at Your Fingertips" to work with the story directly. Encourage them to read the entire text and then go back through it to mark the answers to the **Show It** questions with a highlighter. If peers are not available, have the discussion with your student about the text.
2. Finally, check that they can answer the overarching question with sufficient reasoning, "Do you think people would have a difficult time if the Internet was no longer available?"

• • •

Restating Opening Statement

 ## Activate

1. Have your student open the **Main Idea - Watch It** to view the video on how to identify the main idea in a story or paragraph.
2. Pause the video at 3:16 and allow your student time to determine the main idea of the passage. Continue the video to check their response.

 ## Engage

1. As your student reads the **Read It**, have them determine the message from the example opening statement about pesticides before they try to create a closing statement.
2. After reading, ask them to share the purpose of an opening and a closing statement. Encourage them to refer to the **Read It** to locate the answer. (Answer: An opening statement introduces a point of view or opinion. A closing statement ends the writing and brings the attention back to the point of view.)

 ## Demonstrate

1. Now, instruct your student to complete the writing activities in the **Show It**.
2. Then, work with them to compare their response to the **Show It AK**.

Consulting a Thesaurus

 ## Activate

1. Direct your student to open the **Using a Thesaurus - Watch It** to learn about aspects of a thesaurus.
2. Then, have them verbally explain the meaning of the term *synonym* in their own words. A synonym is a word with a similar meaning to another word.

 ## Engage

1. As your student reads the **Read It**, discuss the difference between the terms *synonym* and *antonym*. Synonyms have the same meaning as another word, whereas antonyms have the opposite meaning.

 ## Demonstrate

1. Now, guide your student to find synonyms and antonyms for the list of words in the **Show It**.
2. Then, help them review their answers with the **Show It AK**.
3. Direct your student to use their selected text to complete the Application section of the **Show It**.

Spelling Contractions

 **Engage**

1. Guide your student to complete the spelling activity in the **Practice It**. Encourage them to repeat the activity multiple times, if necessary. Spelling practice activities for this subtopic will span Lessons 123 through 125.

LESSON 125

Topic	Collaborating with Others

Learning Objectives

The activities in this lesson will help your student meet the following objectives:

- ask clarifying questions during a partner discussion
- present an introduction of yourself
- spell contractions

Materials

- index cards
- slideshow presentation program
- video recording software

Clarify with a Partner

Activate

1. Start by asking your student, "What do you do when you don't understand something?" They should respond by saying that they ask questions.
2. Discuss how it can be helpful to ask questions when they do not understand something.

Engage

1. While your student reads the **Read It**, have them list the sentence starters from the flip-book in their journal. Explain that these sentence starters will help them to ask clarifying questions.
2. Then, discuss your student's thoughts about the Guidelines for Clarifying. Do they think these guidelines are useful? Why or why not?

Demonstrate

1. Open the **Assess It** and have your student complete the activity. You may have to be their partner if a peer is not available. Help them to understand the expectations of the rubric before they begin writing. When they are finished, help them to review their work to make sure they have met the rubric expectations.
2. When they are finished, scan the document or take a photo of it and upload it to the Dropbox. For additional instructions on how to use the Dropbox, click on the paper clip icon in the upper-left corner of the **Assess It**.

Presentation Choice

 **Engage**

1. As your student reads the **Read It**, discuss a time they were in a new group setting and had to introduce themselves. Ask them to describe what they shared about themselves such as their name, where they live, etc.
2. Then, ask your student to list the presenting techniques in their journal. Ask them to read the list and circle any techniques they need to work on personally.

 **Demonstrate**

1. Now, instruct your student to complete the activity in the **Show It**.
2. Then, help them evaluate their presentation based on the criteria noted in the **Show It AK**.

• • •

Spelling Contractions

 **Engage**

1. Guide your student to complete the spelling activity in the **Practice It**. Encourage them to repeat the activity multiple times, if necessary. Spelling practice activities for this subtopic will span Lessons 123 through 125.

LESSON 126

Topic | **Collaborating with Others**

Learning Objectives

The activities in this lesson will help your student meet the following objectives:

- rephrase comments or questions stated during a discussion
- explain the purpose of a concluding sentence

Materials

- none required

Rephrase with a Partner

Activate

1. Begin by telling your student a short story about your childhood.
2. Then, ask them if they have any questions about the story.
3. Next, have them retell the story in their own words.

Engage

1. As your student reads through the content of the **Read It**, have them read the sentence starters aloud. Ask them why these sentence starters are useful. (Answer: They are a way to rephrase what the speaker said.)

Demonstrate

1. Now, direct them to complete the activity in the **Show It**. Act as your student's partner if a peer is not available.
2. Then, check that your student has used two of the sentence starters to clarify their partner's thoughts or ideas.

Concluding Statement Purpose

 **Activate**

1. Start by having your student open the **Concluding Statement - Watch It** to view the video.
2. Then, have them explain the purpose of a concluding statement. A concluding statement helps to bring an end to a written piece.

 **Engage**

1. While your student reads the **Read It**, have them compare the examples of opening and closing statement pairs. Ask them to identify what is similar between the statements? (Answer: They both focus on the main idea.)

 **Demonstrate**

1. Now, instruct your student to complete the **Show It** activity.
2. Finally, work with them to evaluate their response with the **Show It AK**.

LESSON 127

Topic	Collaborating with Others

Learning Objectives

The activities in this lesson will help your student meet the following objectives:

- use formal presentation or informal discourse in a persuasive attempt to change a school rule
- write a paragraph with a concluding sentence that restates the main idea of your topic
- spell contractions

Materials

- presentation software
- store advertisements
- video recording software

Persuading Others

Activate

1. Have your student look through some store advertisements and determine the products the companies are trying to persuade the reader to buy.
2. Then, ask your student, "How is the store trying to convince the reader to buy the products?" Most often, the store shows the discounted price on the advertisement to get the reader's attention.

Engage

1. While your student reads the **Read It**, discuss the differences between formal and informal presentations.
2. Then, prompt them to describe how they would try to convince their friends to spend the day picking up trash on the beach.
   a. For example, they could begin by sharing the ways in which trash on the beach affects animals. Animals end up eating the trash, which can cause them to get very ill or even die.
   b. Finally, they could ask their friends, "Do you want to save some animals by picking up trash on the beach?"
3. Next, discuss your student's approach to convincing their friends to clean up the beach. Was it formal or informal? They likely used an informal approach. An informal approach addresses small groups and allows the speaker to engage in a conversation about the topic.
4. Last, have them open the **Plutarch's Library-Media Messages - Play It** to play the game.

Demonstrate

1. Now, instruct your student to complete the presentation activity in the **Show It**.
2. Then, help them to evaluate their presentation with the **Show It AK**.

• • •

Write a Concluding Sentence

 **Engage**

1. Have your student read the content of the **Read It**.
2. After they read the example paragraph at the end of the text, ask them to determine what the author is persuading the reader to think. The author is persuading the reader to think that writing is a great tool for self-expression.

 **Demonstrate**

1. Now, direct your student to complete the writing activity in the **Show It**.
2. Then, work with them to compare their paragraph to the example in the **Show It AK**.

• • •

Spelling Contractions

 **Engage**

1. Encourage your student to review the list of spelling words in their journal from Lesson 123 before they complete the **Assess It**.

 **Demonstrate**

1. Now, move on to the **Assess It**. Have your student write, and correctly spell, the words they hear spoken in the assessment. This assessment covers the spelling words presented in Lessons 123 through 125.
2. When they are finished, scan the document or take a photo of it and upload it to the Dropbox. For additional instructions on how to use the Dropbox, click on the paper clip icon in the upper-left corner of the **Assess It**.

LESSON 128

Topic **Collaborating with Others**

Learning Objectives

The activities in this lesson will help your student meet the following objectives:

- express original ideas, thoughts, or opinions during a partner discussion
- present a book report

Materials

- colored pencils
- index cards
- teacher- or student-selected text

Original Ideas with a Partner

Activate

1. Start by asking your student what comes to mind when they hear the word *cooperate*. Ask them to draw a picture of what they think about and add words for what they hear.
2. Explain that when they work with a partner, both partners must cooperate with each other to share their ideas, thoughts, and opinions.

Engage

1. Have your student work through the content of the **Read It**.
2. Then, ask them to think about how they could work cooperatively with others in an online learning environment. What might that look like? Have they ever tried it?

Demonstrate

1. Now, help your student complete the activity in the **Show It**. If a peer is not available, have the discussion with them.
2. Finally, check that they wrote down an original idea that they contributed to the conversation.

● ● ●

Presenting a Book Report

 **Engage**

1. While your student reads the **Read It**, prompt them to take notes on the key elements of a book report. Consider having your student copy the chart below into their notebook. They can complete it with the information from the **Read It** and use it as a reference.

Book Report Key Elements	
Introduction	
Summary	
Opinion	
Conclusion	

2. Then, ask them to discuss how they would present a book report using these key elements.

 **Demonstrate**

1. Now, instruct your student to complete the book report activity in the **Show It**. If an audience is not available, they can give their presentation to you.
2. Finally, work with them to evaluate their report. Reference the **Show It AK** to check that your student's work meets the activity's requirements.
3. The next lesson is a **Mastery Assess It**. Encourage your student to review Lessons 113 through 128 in order to prepare for the assessment.

LESSON 129

Topic **Collaborating with Others**

Learning Objectives

The activities in this lesson will help your student meet the following objectives:

- not applicable

Materials

- none required

Mastery Assess It 9

1. **Mastery Assess It 9** will cover what your student has learned in Lessons 113 through 128.
2. Click on the **Mastery Assess It 9** icon to begin the online assessment.
3. Have your student read the instructions before they get started. Remind them to take their time and to do their best work.
4. When they are finished and ready for their assessment to be graded, have them click the **Submit** button.

LESSON 130

Topic **Presenting Ideas**

Learning Objectives

The activities in this lesson will help your student meet the following objectives:

- paraphrase one portion of a text read aloud
- create a persuasive writing piece that supports a point of view
- spell words with the /ou/ sound spelled *ou*, *ow*, or *ough*

Materials

- "Save the Sumatran Orangutan"
- dictionary
- index cards
- teacher- or student-selected text

Orally Paraphrase Read Aloud

Activate

1. Start by having your student retell their favorite story.
2. Then, explain that they just paraphrased, which means to summarize a text in your own words.

Engage

1. While your student reads the **Read It**, prompt them to explain the difference between paraphrasing and plagiarism. Paraphrasing is summarizing written work, while plagiarism is copying it word for word.

Demonstrate

1. Now, direct your student to move on to the **Show It** activity. Encourage them to take notes while listening to the audio clip. Prompt them to refer to the tips for taking notes in the **Read It** if needed.
2. Then, help them check their response with the **Show It AK**.
3. Use your student's selected text and help them to complete the Application section of the **Show It**.

• • •

Persuasive Writing

Engage

1. Have your student work through the content of the **Read It**, and review the purpose of a persuasive piece of writing.
2. Consider printing out the "Save the Sumatran Orangutan" text. Instruct your student to identify the reasons and supporting details of the argument by circling the reasons and underlining the supporting details.
3. Then, discuss the structure of the persuasive essay. Guide them to notice that the first three body paragraphs use transition words to organize the three reasons of the argument.

Demonstrate

1. Next, open the **Assess It** and have your student complete the activity. Help them to understand the expectations of the rubric before they begin writing. When they are finished, help them to review their work to make sure they have met the rubric expectations.
2. When they are finished, scan the document or take a photo of it and upload it to the Dropbox. For additional instructions on how to use the Dropbox, click on the paper clip icon in the upper-left corner of the **Assess It**.

● ● ●

Spelling with Vowel Patterns

Activate

1. Begin by saying the words *about* and *cow* to your student.
2. Then ask them, "What sound do these words have in common?" They both have the /ou/ sound.
3. Next, discuss how the /ou/ sound is spelled differently in each word. The sound /ou/ is spelled with the letters *ou* in the word *about* and *ow* in the word *cow*.

Engage

1. Prompt your student to repeat the /ou/ sounds from the audio clips in the **Read It**. Then, have them spell the example words aloud.
2. Next, instruct them to write the spelling words on index cards to make flashcards. Tell them to underline the *ou* spelling pattern in each word.
3. Last, guide them to open the **Practice It** to complete the exercise. Spelling practice activities for this subtopic will span Lessons 130 through 132.

LESSON 131

Topic **Presenting Ideas**

Learning Objectives

The activities in this lesson will help your student meet the following objectives:

- restate evidence provided by a speaker to support particular points
- differentiate between situations that call for formal English and those where informal English is appropriate
- spell words with the /ou/ sound spelled *ou*, *ow*, or *ough*

Materials

- spelling flashcards

Evidence

Activate

1. Start by having your student look outside to determine the weather conditions.
2. Then, prompt them by asking, "What evidence can you give that validates the current weather?" For example, if it is sunny, they may state that the presence of the sun not being covered by clouds is evidence.

Engage

1. As your student reads the **Read It**, prompt them to explain the difference between reasons and evidence. Evidence includes the information and facts that support the reasons.

Demonstrate

1. Instruct your student to move on to the **Show It**. Direct them to open the **Being Safe with Electricity - Watch It** and view the video to complete the activity. Ask them to make note of the username and password provided on the Discovery Education image. Be sure that they click the link for the video and enter the provided username and password to watch.
2. Then, work with them to check their response with the **Show It AK**.

● ● ●

Formal and Informal Context

 **Engage**

1. While your student reads the **Read It**, ask them, "How would you recognize formal versus informal language?" They may respond by saying that someone who is speaking informally will sound more relaxed, while a formal speech sounds serious.

 **Demonstrate**

1. Now, direct your student to create the announcement in the **Show It** and present it to you or others.
2. Then, help them review the criteria and example in the **Show It AK** to evaluate their work.

● ● ●

Spelling with Vowel Patterns

 **Engage**

1. Start by having your student mix up the spelling flashcards they created in Lesson 130. Then, instruct your student to sort them by their spelling patterns.
2. Last, have your student complete the activity in the **Practice It**. Encourage them to repeat the activity multiple times, if necessary. Spelling practice activities for this subtopic will span Lessons 130 through 132.

LESSON 132

Topic **Presenting Ideas**

Learning Objectives

The activities in this lesson will help your student meet the following objectives:

- revise a story by placing main events in a logical sequence
- determine the meanings of unfamiliar words
- spell words with the /ou/ sound spelled *ou*, *ow*, or *ough*

Materials

- glue
- scissors
- teacher- or student-selected text

Logical Sequence

Activate

1. Begin by asking your student to describe the events of their day if the day was backward. They may give the following details:
   - eat dinner
   - sports practice
   - school work
   - lunch
   - school work
   - breakfast
2. Then, discuss how viewing these events backward makes them hard to follow because they are not in the correct order.

Engage

1. Now, have your student work through the content of the **Read It**.
2. Ask them to verbally explain the events that need to be reordered in the example. Then, allow them to continue to finish the activities.
3. Then, direct your student to complete the activity in the **Practice It**.
4. Next, guide them to play the game in the **Plutarch's Library-Story Sequence - Play It**.

Demonstrate

1. Now, have your student reorder the passage in the **Show It**.
   a. Consider having them print the passage.
   b. Then, instruct them to cut the paragraph apart by separating the sentences.
   c. Next, direct them to sequence the sentences from beginning to end and glue them on a piece of paper.
2. Use the **Show It AK** to help them check their work.
3. Finally, direct your student to complete the activity in the Application section in the **Show It**.

• • •

Context Clues Synonyms

 **Engage**

1. As your student reads the **Read It**, prompt them to use context clues to identify the unknown word in the examples before they read the answers.
2. Then, have them open the **Carnival Racers-Synonyms - Play It** to play the game.

 **Demonstrate**

1. Now, direct your student to use context clues to define unknown words in the **Show It**. Consider printing the sentences for your student.
2. Then, have them reference the **Show It AK** to check their responses.

• • •

Spell with Vowel Patterns

 **Engage**

1. Instruct your student to review their spelling flashcards. Have them separate the words that are harder for them to spell. Encourage them to spell the difficult words aloud a few times.
2. Finally, have them complete the activity in the **Practice It**. Spelling practice activities for this subtopic will span Lessons 130 through 132.

LESSON 133

Topic | **Presenting Ideas**

Learning Objectives

The activities in this lesson will help your student meet the following objectives:

- revise the vocabulary in the paragraph
- tell a story in an organized manner using appropriate facts and relevant, descriptive details
- spell words with the /ou/ sound spelled *ou*, *ow*, or *ough*

Materials

- dictionary
- highlighter
- spelling flashcards
- "Revising Vocabulary" activity page

Revise Sample Paragraphs

 ## Activate

1. Begin by asking your student, "What other words have the same meaning as the word *play*?" Possible answers may include *amusement*, *pleasure*, or *recreation*.
2. Then, discuss why variety in word choice is important when revising written pieces.

 ## Engage

1. While your student reads the **Read It**, discuss the original and revised paragraph in the example. Emphasize how the revised version elaborates on the details so that the reader has a broader understanding of the topic.
2. Then, ask your student to explain why it is important to make revisions to their writing. They may mention that revising vocabulary or including additional details helps to make the writing strong and easier to follow.

 ## Demonstrate

1. Now, instruct your student to move on to the activities in the **Show It** and complete the "Revising Vocabulary" activity page.
2. Then, help them compare their responses to the examples in the **Show It AK**.

• • •

Story

 **Engage**

1. After your student reads the example story in the **Read It**, have them describe the images they saw in their mind while they read.
2. Then, prompt them to explain how the writer told the story in sequential order. Ask them to identify what happened in the beginning, middle, and end of the story?

 Demonstrate

1. Now, direct your student to complete the **Show It** activity. Be sure they review the rubric before they tell their story.
2. Then, work with them to check that they met the requirements of the rubric. Allow them to reference the **Show It AK** to view a sample story.

● ● ●

Spelling Vowels Patterns

 Engage

1. Encourage your student to review the spelling flashcards before they complete the **Assess It**.

 Demonstrate

1. Now, move on to the **Assess It**. Have your student write, and correctly spell, the words they hear spoken in the assessment. This assessment covers the spelling words presented in Lessons 130 through 132.
2. When they are finished, scan the document or take a photo of it and upload it to the Dropbox. For additional instructions on how to use the Dropbox, click on the paper clip icon in the upper-left corner of the **Assess It**.

LESSON 134

Topic | **Presenting Ideas**

Learning Objectives

The activities in this lesson will help your student meet the following objectives:

- identify the reasons a speaker provides to support particular points
- speak clearly and at an understandable pace when presenting information
- spell words with *eigh*

Materials

- dictionary

Reasons

Activate

1. Begin by prompting your student to give three reasons that kids need to have free time. They may respond by saying that kids need free time to play with friends, do creative projects, and choose their own activities.

Engage

1. After your student reads the **Read It**, prompt them to answer the following question: How are reasons part of presenting an argument? (Answer: Reasons explain why an argument is valid.)

Demonstrate

1. Now direct your student to move on to the **Show It** activity. Instruct them to open the **Being Safe with Electricity - Watch It** and take note of the reasons presented by the speaker. Ask them to make note of the username and password provided on the Discovery Education image. Be sure that they click the link for the video and enter the provided username and password to watch.
2. Then, work with your student to check their answers with the **Show It AK**.

●●●

Speak Clearly

 **Engage**

1. Have your student move on and work through the content of the **Read It**.
2. While they read, instruct them to list the tips for speaking in their journal.
3. After your student listens to the audio clip, prompt them to share what they like about the pace, tone, and expression of the speaker.

 Demonstrate

1. Now, instruct your student to complete the activity in the **Show It**. Encourage them to take about ten minutes to jot down notes or ideas that they will be presenting in their speech. Consider printing the checklist before they give their speech.
2. Then, review the checklist with your student and share what they did well and what they can improve upon.

Spelling with *eigh* Pattern

 Activate

1. Start by having your student write as many words as they can that use the *eigh* spelling pattern. Examples include *height*, *weight*, *eight*, *neighbor*, etc.

 Engage

1. Have your student repeat the sounds they hear in the audio clips in the **Read It**.
2. Then, after they have completed the sorting activity, ask them, "Does the spelling pattern *eigh* say long /ā/ or long /ī/ more often?" It says long /ā/ more often.
3. Finally, instruct them to play the game in the **Practice It**. Spelling practice activities for this subtopic will span Lessons 134 through 136.

LESSON 135

Topic	Presenting Ideas

Learning Objectives

The activities in this lesson will help your student meet the following objectives:

- revise an informative writing piece by adding details
- use definitions to find the meanings of unknown words in context
- spell words with *eigh*

Materials

- "The Polar Bear"
- research materials

Revise Informative Writing

 Activate

1. Begin by having your student quickly glance out a window and describe what they see.
2. Then, have them peer out the window for at least a minute and describe what they see.
3. Ask them to think about the details they shared. Discuss whether or not they saw more details when they took the time to go back and look more deeply at the setting.

 Engage

1. As your student reads the **Read It**, review the purpose of informative writing and the steps of the writing process.
2. Then, have them compare the example draft of the writing about polar bears to the revised text. Ask them to share what they notice and what they wonder about the revisions.

 Demonstrate

1. Now, direct your student to complete the activity in the **Show It**.
2. Then, work with them to compare their revised paragraph to the example in the **Show It AK**.

• • •

Context Clues Definitions

 **Engage**

1. Have your student open the **Review: What's the Meaning? - Watch It** to learn about how to define an unknown word.
2. Then, ask them to explain two ways to define a word. (Answer: Use a dictionary or use context clues.)
3. Next, direct your student to read the content of the **Read It**.
4. Then, allow them to play the game in the **Plutarch's Library-Context Clues - Play It**.

 **Demonstrate**

1. Now, instruct your student to identify the context clues in the **Show It** activity. Consider having them print the sentences before they begin.
2. Then, help them reference the **Show It AK** to check their answers.

● ● ●

Spelling with *eigh* Pattern

 **Engage**

1. Begin by having your student write the list of spelling words from Lesson 134 in their journal.
2. Then, guide them to complete the exercise in the **Practice It**. Spelling practice activities for this subtopic will span Lessons 134 through 136.

LESSON 136

Topic	Presenting Ideas

Learning Objectives

The activities in this lesson will help your student meet the following objectives:

- recount an experience you had in an organized manner using appropriate facts and relevant, descriptive details
- use examples to find the meanings of unknown words in context
- spell words with *eigh*

Materials

- "Using Example Context Clues" activity page

Experience

Activate

1. Start by asking your student, "What is one of your earliest memories?" Tell them to share as much of the story as they can remember and include as many details as possible.
2. Then, prompt them to think about why they remember this event in their life. Help them focus on the emotional connection and discuss how their feelings have a big impact on what they remember.

Engage

1. As your student reads the **Read It**, emphasize the importance of sharing their feelings about a personal experience. Discuss the ways in which including emotion in a story helps to bring the story to life.
2. Consider having them copy or print the graphic organizer in the **Read It** as a reference.

Demonstrate

1. Now, direct your student to complete the **Show It** activity. Be sure they review the rubric before they begin. Allow them to brainstorm their experience by writing notes or using a graphic organizer. Explain that they do not need to write full sentences while brainstorming. Instead, they can simply note a few words about the events they are going to share.
2. Finally, print the rubric and use it to help your student evaluate their recount of an experience. Discuss the strengths of their story and how they might improve it.

• • •

Context Clues Examples

 **Engage**

1. Guide your student to open the **Use Context to Get Your Clues - Watch It** and view the video.
2. Then, pause the video at 1:12, and ask your student to share what they think the made up words could mean based on the context.
   - *Zushed* may mean that the speaker is exhausted because he worked out hard in the morning.
   - *Poff* could mean healthy because the doctor wants him to get exercise to be healthy.
3. Continue the video so that your student can compare their responses to those presented by the speaker.
4. While your student reads the **Read It**, encourage them to determine the meaning of the unknown words in the sample sentences before they read the answers.

 **Demonstrate**

1. Open the **Assess It** and have your student complete the activity using the "Using Example Context Clues" activity page.
2. When they are finished, scan the document or take a photo of it and upload it to the Dropbox. For additional instructions on how to use the Dropbox, click on the paper clip icon in the upper-left corner of the **Assess It**.

• • •

Spelling with *eigh* Pattern

 **Engage**

1. Have your student review the list of spelling words in their journal. If they have not yet copied the words into their journal, return to Lesson 134 and direct them to do so.
2. Then, instruct them to complete the activity in the **Practice It**. Encourage them to repeat the activity, if necessary. Spelling practice activities for this subtopic will span Lessons 134 through 136.

LESSON 137

Topic **Presenting Ideas**

Learning Objectives

The activities in this lesson will help your student meet the following objectives:

- create a checklist to facilitate the editing process
- use antonyms to define unknown words in context
- spell words with *eigh*

Materials

- markers
- poster board
- "Antonyms as Context Clues" activity page

Editing Checklist

Activate

1. Begin by having your student open the **Editing - Watch It** to view the process of editing written work.
2. Then, ask them, "What strategies can you use to edit your writing?" For example, *back to front* is a strategy where the writer reads their writing backwards. Also, the spell checker on a computer can identify misspelled words.

Engage

1. While your student reads the content of the **Read It**, direct them to take note of the editing symbols in their journal.
2. Next, have them work through the questions in the **Beaker's Big Buzz-Punctuation - Play It**.

Demonstrate

1. Now, instruct your student to create a checklist as directed in the **Show It**. Encourage them to make a poster of their checklist to reference while editing any written work.
2. Then, help them to compare their checklist to the sample in the **Show It AK**.
3. To extend learning, encourage your student to use editing symbols as they check their writing for errors.

● ● ●

Context Clues Antonyms

Engage

1. As your student reads the text of the **Read It**, have them determine the meaning of the unknown word in the example before they read the answer. Direct them to identify the antonym in the sentence first.
2. Your student may use the **Carnival Racers-Antonyms - Play It** and the **Practice It** as needed.

Demonstrate

1. Now, guide your student to complete the "Antonyms as Context Clues" activity page in the **Show It**.
2. Then, use the **Show It AK** and work with your student to check their answers.

• • •

Spelling with *eigh* Pattern

Engage

1. Encourage your student to review any challenging words from the spelling list before they complete the **Assess It**.

Demonstrate

1. Now, move on to the **Assess It**. Have your student write, and correctly spell, the words they hear spoken in the assessment. This assessment covers the spelling words presented in Lessons 134 through 136.
2. When they are finished, scan the document or take a photo of it and upload it to the Dropbox. For additional instructions on how to use the Dropbox, click on the paper clip icon in the upper-left corner of the **Assess It**.

LESSON 138

Topic	Presenting Ideas

Learning Objectives

The activities in this lesson will help your student meet the following objectives:

- rewrite one piece of writing to meet the criteria for the highest level of a rubric
- list interesting facts about a topic you researched
- spell words with the middle sound /er/ spelled *er*, *ir*, or *ur*

Materials

- chocolate chip cookie
- dictionary
- index cards
- markers

Writing Rubric

Activate

1. Begin by placing a chocolate chip cookie in front of your student to observe. Then ask them, "What expectations do you have of a chocolate chip cookie?" They may say that it should have a lot of chocolate chips, and it should be sweet and crunchy.
2. Prompt them to assess the cookie based on their criteria. For example, they can answer the following questions to determine its quality. Allow them to taste the cookie to see if it meets their criteria.
   - Does the cookie have a lot of chocolate chips?
   - Is it sweet?
   - Is it crunchy?

Engage

1. Have your student begin with the **Read It**.
2. As they read, instruct them to list the three main parts to any rubric.
3. Once they finish the reading, prompt them to verbally explain what the rubric in the example is assessing.

Demonstrate

1. Open the **Assess It** and have your student complete the activity. Be sure they review the expectations of the rubric before, during, and after they complete the activity.
2. When they are finished, scan the document or take a photo of it and upload it to the Dropbox. For additional instructions on how to use the Dropbox, click on the paper clip icon in the upper-left corner of the **Assess It**.

● ● ●

Internet Research

Engage

1. While your student reads the **Read It**, allow them to search for information about beagles on the Internet. Help them to use a kid-friendly search engine such as Kiddle.

Demonstrate

1. Now, instruct your student to complete the **Show It** activity. If time allows, encourage them to include images that correlate with their listed facts.
2. Then, work with them to evaluate their responses using the examples in the **Show It AK**.
3. Help your student to complete the activity in the Application section of the **Show It**. They may consider researching a question pertaining to another subject area such as science or social studies.

● ● ●

Spelling with *er*, *ir*, *ur*

Activate

1. Start by asking your student to write the following words in their journal: *paper*, *thirsty*, and *turning*. Help them to make any necessary corrections.
2. Then ask them, "What sound do these words have in common? They all have the /er/ sound.

Engage

1. After your student reads through the content of the **Read It**, instruct them to write the spelling words on index cards to make flashcards.
2. Then, have them underline the /er/ spelling pattern in each word.
3. Next, direct them to complete the exercise in the **Practice It**. Spelling practice activities for this subtopic will span Lessons 138 through 140.

LESSON 139

Topic | Presenting Ideas

Learning Objectives

The activities in this lesson will help your student meet the following objectives:

- present your thoughts on a topic using appropriate facts and relevant, descriptive details
- correct errors in grammar and sentence structure in a paragraph
- spell words with the middle sound /er/ spelled *er*, *ir*, or *ur*

Materials

- art supplies
- spelling flashcards
- tri-fold poster board

Presentation Organization

Activate

1. Ask your student what they think of when they hear the word *organize*. They may think of having to clean their room or sort their socks.
2. Let them know that they will learn about the importance of organizing their writing.

Engage

1. Begin with the **Read It** and have a discussion with your student about the purpose of an outline. Ask them if they have ever used an outline in the past.
2. After they read, ask them to share any interesting details or facts they learned from the presentation outline.

Demonstrate

1. Now instruct your student to move on to the **Show It** activity. Be sure they review the expectations of the rubric before and after they complete the presentation poster.
2. Then, use the rubric and work with them to evaluate their poster.

• • •

Sentence Structure

 **Engage**

1. As your student reads the **Read It**, have them pay special attention to the description of compound-complex sentences.
2. Then, encourage them to write their own compound-complex sentence.
3. Next, direct them to open the **Enlighten Maze-Editing - Play It** to practice their editing skills.

 **Demonstrate**

1. Now, guide your student to complete the activities in the **Show It**. Allow them to print the paragraph to revise it directly on the paper.
2. Then, use the **Show It AK** and allow your student to compare their work to the example answer.
3. Next, direct your student to complete the exercise in the Application section of the **Show It**. If they do not have a sample available, prompt them to write a paragraph about a personal experience.

● ● ●

Spelling with *er*, *ir*, *ur*

 **Engage**

1. Prompt your student to review the flashcards they made in Lesson 138.
2. Then, guide them to complete the exercise in the **Practice It**. Spelling practice activities for this subtopic will span Lessons 138 through 140.

LESSON 140

Topic   **Presenting Ideas**

Learning Objectives

The activities in this lesson will help your student meet the following objectives:

- create an engaging presentation that expresses information on a topic
- write sentences using social studies vocabulary terms
- spell words with the middle sound /er/ spelled *er*, *ir*, or *ur*

Materials

- "Playground Safety" slide show presentation
- presentation software
- spelling flashcards

Creating Multimedia

Activate

1. As a review, begin by having your student open the **Review: Oral Presentations - Watch It** to view the video.
2. Then, discuss the aspects that make a good presentation. Help your student name the following elements:
   - Speak loudly and clearly.
   - Organize information so it is in order.
   - Use note cards, but don't read them.
   - Use visual aids such as posters or a digital presentation.

Engage

1. Then, have your student move on to the **Read It**.
2. As they read, have them note the types of multimedia in their journal.
3. After reading, ask them to list at least three pieces of information from the presentation.

Demonstrate

1. Open the **Assess It** and have your student complete the activity. Help them to understand the expectations of the rubric before they begin writing. When they are finished, help them to review their work to make sure they have met the rubric expectations.
2. When they are finished, scan the document or take a photo of it and upload it to the Dropbox. For additional instructions on how to use the Dropbox, click on the paper clip icon in the upper-left corner of the **Assess It**.

● ● ●

Government Sentences

 **Engage**

1. While your student reads the **Read It**, have them use the vocabulary words verbally in sentences. If they are struggling with a word, help them to think of a sentence.

 **Demonstrate**

1. Now, instruct your student to complete the **Show It** activity.
2. As an added challenge, have your student use their sentences to create a short story. Encourage them to revise the sentences, if necessary.
3. Then, allow them to compare their sentences with the examples in the **Show It AK**.

● ● ●

Spelling with *er, ir, ur*

 **Engage**

1. Guide your student to mix up their spelling flashcards from Lesson 138 and sort them by their /er/ spelling pattern.
2. Finally, have them complete the activity in the **Practice It**. Spelling practice activities for this subtopic will span Lessons 138 through 140.

LESSON 141

Topic | **Presenting Ideas**

Learning Objectives

The activities in this lesson will help your student meet the following objectives:

- identify differences between formal and informal English
- compare and contrast animal adaptations using terms related to the topic

Materials

- none required

Formal and Informal English

Activate

1. Start by having your student open the **Formal and Informal Style - Watch It** to learn about different writing styles.
2. Then, prompt them to explain the differences between formal and informal writing styles. Formal is more serious, while informal is more casual.

Engage

1. Direct your student to create a T-chart in their journal. Tell them to label the left side, *Formal English* and the right side *Informal English*.

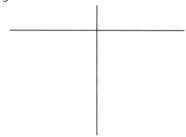

2. As they read the **Read It**, ask them to define the headings and list examples for each side of the T-chart.
3. After your student reads, have them act out formal and informal speaking For example, they can act as though they are giving a presentation and then pretend that they are talking to a friend.

Demonstrate

1. Now, instruct your student to move on to the **Show It** activity.
2. Then, work with them to compare their paragraph to the sample in the **Show It AK**.
3. To extend learning, encourage your student to listen to others talking each day (in person, on television, over the phone, etc.). Ask them to identify when people are speaking formally or informally.

• • •

Compare and Contrast Animals

Engage

1. Direct your student to read through the content of the **Read It**.
2. Then, have them verbally create three sentences to compare a walrus and a polar bear using the information in the Venn diagram.

Demonstrate

1. Now, guide your student to complete the Venn diagram activity in the **Show It**.
2. Finally, help them check to make sure their Venn diagram compares the similarities and differences between two animals. They should have at least two adaptations in each section of the Venn diagram.

LESSON 142

Topic | Presenting Ideas

Learning Objectives

The activities in this lesson will help your student meet the following objectives:

- illustrate one aspect of a topic
- describe the journey of electricity through an electric current
- spell words with the middle sound /er/ spelled *er*, *ir*, or *ur*

Materials

- art supplies
- dry erase board and marker
- spelling flashcards
- timer

Visual Illustrations

Activate

1. Using a dry erase board, play a few rounds of Pictionary with your student. Set a timer for 60 seconds, and take turns drawing while the other person guesses the picture.
2. Then, discuss how an illustration can provide a lot of information about a topic.

Engage

1. As your student reads the **Read It**, prompt them to explain how the images about basketball help the reader better understand the topic. They may respond by saying that one of the images shows what a basketball court looks like without the writer having to describe it.

Demonstrate

1. Now, guide your student to complete the illustration activity in the **Show It**. If time allows, encourage them to illustrate multiple pictures for their topic.
2. Then, have them reference the **Show It AK** examples to see other ways to represent the suggested topics.

• • •

Electric Current Journal Entry

Engage

1. While your student reads the **Read It**, have them draw the diagram of the simple circuit in their journal.
2. Then, instruct them to verbally explain how the circuit works.

Demonstrate

1. Now, have your student move on to the **Show It** activity.
2. Then, help them to compare their journal entry to the sample in the **Show It AK**.

Spelling with *er*, *ir*, *ur*

Engage

1. Encourage your student to review their spelling flashcards before they complete the **Assess It**.

Demonstrate

1. Now, move on to the **Assess It**. Have your student write, and correctly spell, the words they hear spoken in the assessment. This assessment covers the spelling words presented in Lessons 138 through 140.
2. When they are finished, scan the document or take a photo of it and upload it to the Dropbox. For additional instructions on how to use the Dropbox, click on the paper clip icon in the upper-left corner of the **Assess It**.

LESSON 143

Topic	Presenting Ideas

Learning Objectives

The activities in this lesson will help your student meet the following objectives:

- self-correct errors while reading
- locate statistics that give insight into one aspect of a topic

Materials

- "Liftoff"
- children's magazine or online news article
- colored pencils
- poster board

Rereading

Activate

1. Prompt your student to skim a children's magazine article or an online news article. Ask them what they think it will be about.
2. Then, tell them to read a paragraph from the article out loud. Ask them if anything is unclear in the section they read. If so, ask them, "How can you figure out what it means?" They may say they could use context clues or reread the article.
3. Next, guide them to reread the paragraph to make sense of the information.

Engage

1. While your student reads the **Read It**, instruct them to list the reading tips in their journal.
2. Then, emphasize that rereading doesn't mean they have to reread every single word, but it may be helpful to scan the paragraph or section again to get some clarity.

Demonstrate

1. Now, direct your student to complete the activity in the **Show It**. Encourage them to read the text out loud and reread sections they do not understand. While they read, try to notice if your student is unclear about a section and goes back to reread it.
2. Then, check that your student reread sections of the text to better understand them. If they did not, ask them if there are parts of the text that did not make sense. Help them reread those sentences.

• • •

Statistics

Engage

1. Have your student read the **Read It**.
2. Ask them if they have noticed any statistics recently. They may have watched the news or read a cereal box, for example. Ask them to share any examples.
3. Then, discuss the ways in which the statistics in the example about cyber bullying help them better understand how often cyber bullying occurs.

Demonstrate

1. Now, instruct your student to move on to the **Show It** activity. Guide them to use a kid-friendly search engine, such as *Kiddle*, to look for statistics.
2. Finally, help them compare their results to the examples in the **Show It AK**.
3. To extend learning, encourage your student to use their statistical information to create a visual display.

Topic	Presenting Ideas

Learning Objectives

The activities in this lesson will help your student meet the following objectives:

- present ideas on a topic
- summarize a text

Materials

- "Fingerprints"
- index cards
- markers
- poster board

Presenting a Report

Activate

1. Start by having your student open the **Using Voice and Body Language - Watch It** to view the video.
2. Pause the video at 1:16, and prompt your student to explain why pace is important in a presentation. (Answer: Pace is how fast or slowly the presenter speaks, which affects the audience's ability to process the information.)

Engage

1. Instruct your student to read the content of the **Read It**.
2. Then ask them, "What part of giving an oral presentation is most difficult for you?" Help your student to find strategies to make the difficult parts easier for them.

Demonstrate

1. Now, guide your student to prepare and deliver an oral presentation for the **Show It**. Encourage them to use index cards to prepare their presentation.
2. Then, use the **Show It AK** to determine if your student's presentation met the expectations. Discuss any ways they can make improvements.

• • •

Summarizing

Engage

1. As your student reads the **Read It**, instruct them to make a poster of the summarizing questions from the text. Have them hang it in a location that is easy to reference.

Demonstrate

1. Open the **Assess It** and have your student complete the activity. Help them to understand the expectations of the rubric before they begin writing. When they are finished, help them to review their work to make sure they have met the rubric expectations.

2. When they are finished, scan the document or take a photo of it and upload it to the Dropbox. For additional instructions on how to use the Dropbox, click on the paper clip icon in the upper-left corner of the **Assess It**.

3. To extend learning, encourage your student to reference their summarizing questions poster after reading texts.

4. The next lesson is a **Mastery Assess It**. Encourage your student to review Lessons 130 through 144 in order to prepare for the assessment.

LESSON 145

Topic | **Presenting Ideas**

Learning Objectives

The activities in this lesson will help your student meet the following objectives:

- not applicable

Materials

- none required

Mastery Assess It 10

1. **Mastery Assess It 10** will cover what your student has learned in Lessons 130 through 144.
2. Click on the **Mastery Assess It 10** icon to begin the online assessment.
3. Have your student read the instructions before they get started. Remind them to take their time and to do their best work.
4. When they are finished and ready for their assessment to be graded, have them click the **Submit** button.

LESSON 146

Topic	Poetry

Learning Objectives

The activities in this lesson will help your student meet the following objectives:

- explain one major theory or idea within a topic
- identify the meanings of words that contain roots and prefixes
- spell words with the ending sound /er/ spelled *ar*, *er*, or *or*

Materials

- dictionary
- dry erase board and marker
- index cards
- "Matching Definitions: Prefixes" activity page

Topic Theory

Activate

1. Tell your student that they were going on a trip to the zoo; however, the trip got canceled. Ask them to guess why the trip was canceled. They may say that the weather was bad or the transportation broke down.
2. Explain that they just developed a theory, which they will learn more about.

Engage

1. Begin with the **Read It**, and have your student read through the content.
2. Encourage them to develop a theory about why Annabelle decided not to go to the party before reading the possibilities.

Demonstrate

1. Now, have your student complete the activity in the **Show It**.
2. Work with them to check their theory using the example in the **Show It AK**.
3. To reinforce learning, encourage your student to develop theories about the characters in books that they are reading. Why do the characters do the things they do?

Studying Roots and Prefixes

Activate

1. Write the words *do* and *redo* on the dry erase board. Ask your student what each word means. (Answer: *Do* means to complete or accomplish something. *Redo* means to do something again.)
2. Ask your student to circle the part of the word that changes the meaning of *redo*. (Answer: *re-*)
3. Explain that *re-* is a prefix.

Engage

1. Starting with the **Read It**, have your student work through the content. Consider having them print the two charts. Then, ask them to fasten the charts into their journal for future reference. Alternatively, they can copy the charts into their journal by hand.
2. It may help your student to verbally explain the difference between *root words* and *base words*. A *base word* is an actual word that can stand alone, while a *root word* is part of a word that comes from another language and cannot stand alone. For example, *spect* is a root word meaning "see" that cannot stand alone. However, *inspect*, which is part of *inspection*, is a base word since it can stand alone.
3. Next, have your student open the **Watch It** titled **That Changes Things**.
4. After they view the video, encourage your student to write a word that uses the base word *direct* and another word using the prefix *pre-*. Examples include *indirect*, *direction*, *misdirection*, *director*, *prequel*, *precook*, *preheat* and *preview*.

Demonstrate

1. Move on to the **Show It** and have your student complete the "Matching Definitions: Prefixes" activity page.
2. When your student is finished, have them use the **Show It AK** to evaluate their responses.
3. To extend learning, encourage your student to call out root words and prefixes as they see them on billboards, advertisements, and other signs.

• • •

Spelling with *er, or, ar*

Engage

1. Begin with the **Read It**. As your student reads the content, make sure they understand that this list of words uses *er, or,* and *ar* to turn verbs into nouns.
2. Then, have your student read the list of spelling words. You may want them to write each word on a sheet of paper or index cards. Prompt them to point out the verb in many of the nouns.
3. Next, have your student complete the sorting activity to practice their spelling words.
4. Last, move on to the **Practice It** for your student to complete the activity. Spelling practice activities for this subtopic will span Lessons 146 through 148.

LESSON 147

Topic | Poetry

Learning Objectives

The activities in this lesson will help your student meet the following objectives:

- use context clues to determine the meanings of unfamiliar words and phrases
- identify the meanings of words that contain roots and suffixes
- spell words with the ending sound /er/ spelled *ar*, *er*, or *or*

Materials

- "John Adams and the Boston Massacre"
- "Matching Definitions: Suffixes" activity page

Using Context Clues

Activate

1. Tell your student they are going to be a detective. They will need to look at clues to determine the meanings of words.
2. Read them the following sentence: The conspicuous man wore a neon green shirt and polka dot shorts.
3. Ask them to determine the meaning of *conspicuous* based on the context clues. (Answer: easily seen)

Engage

1. As your student reads the content of the **Read It**, encourage them to remain a detective as they search for clues to define the words in the example.
2. Next, have them open the **Vocabulary Using Context Clues - Watch It**. Pause the video at 3:39, 4:08, and 4:45 to allow your student time to determine the meaning of the words using context clues.
3. Afterward, have your student write down LPR3 in their journal and explain the mnemonic device.
   - L - Look -- Look before, at, and after the word whose meaning you do not know.
   - P - Predict -- Predict the meaning of the unknown word.
   - R - Reason -- Think carefully about the word's meaning.
   - R - Resolve -- Recognize you may need to use a dictionary or ask for help.
   - R - Redo -- You can redo the steps as necessary.

Demonstrate

1. Using the text "John Adams and the Boston Massacre," have your student complete the activity in the **Show It**.
2. When they are finished, have them evaluate their work using the **Show It AK**.
3. To extend learning, as your student reads independently, encourage them to use context clues to determine the meaning of unknown words before looking them up in a dictionary or asking an adult for help.

Studying Roots and Suffixes

 ## Engage

1. Start by reading the content of the **Read It** with your student. Consider having them print the two charts. Then, ask them to fasten the charts into their journal for future reference. Alternatively, they can copy the charts by hand.
2. Then, have your student open and view the **Use Keys to Unlock the Meaning - Watch It**.
3. Afterward, encourage your student to write a word that uses the root *aud* and another word using the suffix *-ful*. Examples include *audiobook*, *inaudible*, *audience*, *mouthful*, *painful*, and *careful*.
4. Now, have your student complete the **Practice It** activity for extra practice determining the meanings of words.

 ## Demonstrate

1. Move on to the **Show It** and have your student complete the "Matching Definitions: Suffixes" activity page.
2. Use the **Show It AK** and work with your student to check their answers.
3. To extend learning, encourage your student to call out root words and suffixes as they see them when they are out and about. To help your student determine a word's meaning, encourage them to break down unfamiliar words into their roots and affixes when reading independently.

Spelling with *er, or, ar*

 ## Engage

1. Have your student open the **Practice It** and complete the activity. If time allows, your student may complete the activity more than once. Spelling practice activities for this subtopic will span Lessons 146 through 148.

LESSON 148

Topic	Poetry

Learning Objectives

The activities in this lesson will help your student meet the following objectives:

- locate reasons that support an aspect of a topic
- identify the origin of a common idiom
- spell words with the ending sound /er/ spelled *ar*, *er*, or *or*

Materials

- colored pencils

Topic Positives

Activate

1. Read the following paragraph to your student.
   The castle, though once beautiful, is now in disrepair. The paint is peeling, the windows are cracked, and a funny smell permeates much of the downstairs. It's on sale, so you better move quick!"
2. Ask your student if they would want to live in the castle described. Why or why not?
3. Now, read this paragraph.
   The castle needs a little love and attention to achieve its former glory. Behind the paint are the original brick walls. The windows let in sunlight and fresh air. It smells of history and a future full of opportunities. It's on sale, so you better move quick!"
4. Would your student want to live in the castle after hearing this description? Why or why not?
5. Explain that, when persuading someone, it is helpful to focus on the positives of your topic.

Engage

1. Begin with the **Read It**. Have your student read through the content.
2. Next, have them think about the castle from the Activate. What else could be said that would help persuade someone to buy it? Perhaps they could focus on the history, the living space, the potential, or the large yard.

Demonstrate

1. Open the **Assess It** and have your student complete the activity. Be sure they review the expectations of the rubric before, during, and after they complete the activity.
2. When they are finished, scan the document or take a photo of it and upload it to the Dropbox. For additional instructions on how to use the Dropbox, click on the paper clip icon in the upper-left corner of the **Assess It**.

• • •

Idiom Origins

Activate

1. Say to your student, "Look! It's raining cats and dogs!"
2. Ask them what they picture in their mind. Do they see cats and dogs falling from the sky? Is that really what you meant?
3. Then, ask them what the saying actually means. (Answer: It's pouring rain.)
4. Explain that the saying is called an idiom.

Engage

1. Starting with the **Read It**, have your student work through the content.
2. Next, have your student open the **Idioms, Similes, and Metaphors - Watch It**.
3. Afterward, engage your student in a discussion about idioms that they have used. Consider using the Internet to look up a list of common idioms and pointing out some of your favorites.

Demonstrate

1. Now, have your student complete the activity in the **Show It**.
2. When they are finished, have them evaluate their response using the example in the **Show It AK**.
3. To reinforce learning, instruct your student to choose one of the idioms from the **Watch It** or from their previous discussion and illustrate both its literal and figurative meaning. For example, they might draw a picture of cats and dogs falling from the sky and another of pouring rain.

• • •

Spelling with *er, or, ar*

Engage

1. Have your student open the **Practice It** and complete the activity. If time allows, encourage them to play the game more than once. Spelling practice activities for this subtopic will span Lessons 146 through 148.

LESSON 149

Topic | Poetry

Learning Objectives

The activities in this lesson will help your student meet the following objectives:

- locate reasons that negate an aspect of a topic
- spell words with the ending sound /er/ spelled *ar*, *er*, or *or*

Materials

- advertisements

Topic Negatives

Activate

1. Tell your student that you are thinking about becoming a knight and going to fight a dragon.
2. Ask them to help you make your decision by naming one positive aspect of your plan and one negative aspect. For example, they might say that a positive aspect is that you would be able to go on a grand adventure, but a negative aspect is that you could be eaten by a dragon.
3. Based on their argument, inform your student of your decision.

Engage

1. Together with your student, read the content of the **Read It** aloud.
2. Engage them in a discussion about why it is important to address both the positive and negative aspects of a topic. (Answer: Addressing both positive and negative aspects of a topic allows for a more well-rounded position.)

Demonstrate

1. Now, have your student complete the activity in the **Show It**. Allow them to reference the **Idiom Origins - Read It** in Lesson 148 for a refresher on how to cite their sources.
2. When they are finished, help them evaluate their response using the example in the **Show It AK**.
3. To extend learning, have your student look at advertisements in newspapers and magazines, as well as those on TV. Do they notice more negative or positive ads? Which are more effective? Why? Are there an equal number of positive and negative ads or did they find that one type was more common than the other?

• • •

Spelling with *er*, *or*, and *ar*

 **Engage**

1. Instruct your student to review and practice the spelling words a few times before they complete the **Assess It**.

 **Demonstrate**

1. Now, move on to the **Assess It**. Have your student write, and correctly spell, the words they hear spoken in the assessment. This assessment covers the spelling words presented in Lessons 146 through 148.

2. When they are finished, scan the document or take a photo of it and upload it to the Dropbox. For additional instructions on how to use the Dropbox, click on the paper clip icon in the upper-left corner of the **Assess It**.

LESSON 150

Topic	Poetry

Learning Objectives

The activities in this lesson will help your student meet the following objectives:

- annotate a poem before summarizing
- write important facts from a text
- spell words with the trigraph *tch*

Materials

- "A Fish in a Bowl" and "California Gold Rush"
- dictionary
- index cards
- teacher- or student-selected text

Poetry Summary

Activate

1. Engage your student in a discussion about poetry. Use the following sentence stems to encourage conversation.
   - When I think of poetry, I think of…
   - The best thing about poetry is…
   - Song lyrics are/aren't the same as poetry because…
   - The worst thing about poetry is..
   - Something I would like to know about poetry is…
   - Poetry is easy/difficult for me to understand because…
2. Explain that they will learn more about poetry and how to better understand what has been written.

Engage

1. Starting with the **Read It**, have your student work through the content.
2. Have them pause to formulate a summary for the example poem before they reference the answer key within the text.
3. Next, have your student open the **Poetry Summary - Watch It**. Pause the video at 0:45, and prompt them to copy down the steps for annotating poems.
4. Then, have your student open the **Plutarch's Library-Free Verse - Play It**. If time allows, encourage them to play again until they achieve a perfect score.
5. For extra practice with annotation and summarizing, have your student complete the **Practice It** activity.

Demonstrate

1. Using the poem "A Fish in a Bowl," have your student complete the activity in the **Show It**.
2. When they are finished, work together to review their annotated poem and summary using the example in the **Show It AK**.
3. As your student continues to read poetry, encourage them to annotate the text. This is especially helpful if they feel they struggle with understanding poetry. Consider having them try it using appropriate song lyrics or another poem.

• • •

Facts

 **Engage**

1. Begin with the **Read It**. Have your student read the content.
2. After reading, encourage them to go a reliable website to find at least three facts about their favorite wild animal.

 **Demonstrate**

1. Move on to the **Show It**, and have your student complete the activity using the text, "California Gold Rush."
2. Next, direct your student to the **Show It AK**, and have them compare their facts to the examples provided.
3. Then, have your student complete the Application section of the **Show It** using their selected text.

● ● ●

Spelling Trigraph *tch*

 **Engage**

1. Begin with the **Read It**. As your student reads the content, encourage them to listen to the recording of the trigraph and repeat the sound aloud.
2. Then, have your student read the list of spelling words. You may want them to write each word on a sheet of paper or index cards and underline the trigraph *tch*.
3. Next, have your student complete the word searches to practice the spelling words.
4. Last, move on to the **Practice It** for your student to complete the activity. Spelling practice activities for this subtopic will span Lessons 150 through 152.

LESSON 151

Topic	Poetry

Learning Objectives

The activities in this lesson will help your student meet the following objectives:

- summarize a poem using details from the text
- compare the literal meaning of a common idiom or adage to the figurative meaning
- spell words with the trigraph *tch*

Materials

- colored pencils
- teacher- or student-selected text
- "Weekly Reading Log" activity page

Poem Summary Questions

Activate

1. Ask your student to tell you the five *W*s and one *H*. (Answer: Who?, What?, Where?, When?, Why?, How?)
2. Explain that these questions, along with annotating, can be used to help summarize a poem. Your student learned about annotating poems in Lesson 150.

Engage

1. As your student reads the content of the **Read It**, encourage them to verbalize the answers to *who*, *why*, *what*, *when*, and *how* based on the poem in the text. Then, encourage them to check their answers below the poem.
2. Next, have your student open the **Play Its** titled **Plutarch's Library-Acrostic**, **Plutarch's Library-Diamante**, and **Plutarch's Library-Haiku**. If time allows, feel free to permit your student to play each game until they achieve a perfect score.

Demonstrate

1. Now, have your student complete the activity in the **Show It**.
2. When they are finished, have them evaluate their summary using the example in the **Show It AK**.
3. To reinforce learning, encourage your student to use these questions to help them annotate and summarize poems.

● ● ●

Literal vs. Figurative

 ## Activate

1. Say to your student, "I am literally so hot I could melt."
2. Ask them if you are actually melting. As you are not, explain that *literally* is misused in this sentence. What you meant is that you are figuratively melting.

 ## Engage

1. Begin with the **Read It**. Have your student read all of the content.
2. Next, engage them in a discussion about why writers use idioms and adages. Explain that they help to paint pictures in the mind of the reader and create humorous mental images.
3. Then, have your student open and view the **Literal versus Figurative - Watch It**. Pause the video at 3:25 to allow your student time to answer the question posed.

 ## Demonstrate

1. Move on to the **Show It**, and have your student complete the activity. As an added challenge, encourage them to draw a picture of both the literal and figurative meanings of the idiom.
2. Then, go to the **Show It AK** and work with them to review their paragraph.
3. To reinforce learning, challenge your student to use an idiom or adage in casual conversation. They can also keep a running list of idioms and adages they hear so that they may use the sayings in the future.

• • •

Spelling Trigraph *tch*

 ## Engage

1. For extra practice with their spelling words, have your student complete the **Practice It** activity. If time allows, encourage them to play the game more than once. Spelling practice activities for this subtopic will span Lessons 150 through 152.

LESSON 152

Topic	Poetry

Learning Objectives

The activities in this lesson will help your student meet the following objectives:

- determine the theme of a poem from details in the text
- create a skit to portray a common proverb
- spell words with the trigraph *tch*

Materials

- "Different Colors: A Poem"
- props for a skit

Theme of a Poem

Activate

1. Ask your student to think about a favorite poem, nursery rhyme, or song. What message is the author trying to get across?
2. Explain that this message is the theme, which they will learn more about in this lesson.

Engage

1. Starting with the **Read It**, have your student work through the content.
2. Pause to allow your student time to say the theme of the example poem out loud before checking the answer.
3. Next, have your student open and view the **William Shakespeare: Sonnet 30 - Watch It**.
4. Afterward, engage them in a discussion about the poem. Did they like it? Why or why not? Did discovering the theme change their mind?

Demonstrate

1. Using the text "Different Colors: A Poem," have your student complete the **Show It** activity.
2. Then, work with them to check their theme and details using the examples in the **Show It AK**.

• • •

Proverb Skit

 **Engage**

1. Begin with the **Read It**. Have your student read the content.
2. As they read the skit, consider reading it with them. Encourage your student to use different voices for the different parts.

 Demonstrate

1. Move on to the **Show It**, and have your student complete the activity. You may need to help your student brainstorm ways to incorporate a proverb into a skit. Encourage them to be creative and to have fun!
2. Be sure that they review the expectations of the rubric before, during, and after they complete the activity.
3. Have them use the rubric and the **Show It AK** to confirm that they have met the criteria for the activity.

● ● ●

Spelling Trigraph *tch*

 **Engage**

1. For extra practice of their spelling words, have your student complete the **Practice It** activity. If time allows, encourage them to play the game more than once. Spelling practice activities for this subtopic will span Lessons 150 through 152.

LESSON 153

Topic	Poetry

Learning Objectives

The activities in this lesson will help your student meet the following objectives:

- categorize research about a topic
- explain the meanings of common idioms, adages, and proverbs
- spell words with the trigraph *tch*

Materials

- "Saturn"
- art supplies
- dry erase board and marker
- small candies

Graphic Organizer

Activate

1. Pour out small candies, such as Skittles® or M&Ms®, in front of your student.
2. Ask them to organize the candy. They may choose to organize by color or some other way.
3. Explain that, much like the candies, thoughts can be organized into something called a graphic organizer.

Engage

1. Begin with the **Read It**. As your student reads the content, encourage them to draw an example of the three types of graphic organizers in their journal for future reference.
2. Next, have your student open the **Prewriting: Graphic Organizers - Watch It**. Ask them to make note of the username and password provided on the Discovery Education image. Be sure that they click the link for the video and enter the provided username and password to watch.
3. As they watch, instruct them to think about the best way to organize the information about knights.

Demonstrate

1. Now, have your student complete the activity in the **Show It**. It may help your student to skim the text before deciding which graphic organizer to use when taking notes.
2. When your student is finished, have them use the **Show It AK** to evaluate their responses.

• • •

Idioms, Adages, and Proverbs

 **Activate**

1. Play a game with idioms. Get your student to guess the idiom by either drawing it on the dry erase board or acting it out. After your student guesses, have them take a turn.
2. The list below provides some possible idioms to use for the game.
   - Bite your tongue.
   - Barking up the wrong tree
   - Costs an arm and a leg
   - A race against time
   - Give someone the cold shoulder

 **Engage**

1. Starting with the **Read It**, have your student read through the content.
2. Then, have your student open the **Idioms, Adages, and Proverbs - Watch It**. While watching the video, encourage them to pay close attention to the strategies for decoding the types of figurative language while reading.

 **Demonstrate**

1. Move on to the **Show It** and prompt your student to complete the activity. They may use the listed idioms, adages, and proverbs or they may research their own.
2. Work with them to check their meanings and illustrations using the examples in the **Show It AK**.
3. To reinforce learning, encourage your student to use context clues while reading to decode the meaning of idioms, adages, and proverbs in a text.

Spelling Trigraph *tch*

 **Engage**

1. Instruct your student to review and practice the spelling words a few times before they complete the **Assess It**.

 **Demonstrate**

1. Now move on to the **Assess It**. Have your student write, and correctly spell, the words they hear spoken in the assessment. This assessment covers the spelling words presented in Lessons 150 through 152.
2. When they are finished, scan the document or take a photo of it and upload it to the Dropbox. For additional instructions on how to use the Dropbox, click on the paper clip icon in the upper-left corner of the **Assess It**.

LESSON 154

Topic	Poetry

Learning Objectives

The activities in this lesson will help your student meet the following objectives:

- organize the information in a set of notes in a logical sequence
- spell words with the trigraph *dge*

Materials

- "John Adams and the Boston Massacre"
- dictionary
- index cards
- "Essay Planner" activity page

Essay Planner

Activate

1. Ask your student if they have ever made a plan. Examples might include planning a surprise party, planning a play in during a sporting event, or planning what to see on vacation.
2. Engage your student in a discussion about how that plan made things better. For example, if they did not have a plan for what to see on vacation, they might have missed something they wanted to visit.

Engage

1. Begin with the **Read It**. Have your student read the content.
2. Ask your student why the topic sentence in Essay Planner A is better than the topic sentence in Essay Planner B. (Answer: Essay Planner B's topic sentence is too specific, and the rest of the details do not help to support it. Essay Planner A's topic sentence is better because it is broad and covers all of the details.)

Demonstrate

1. Using the text, "John Adams and the Boston Massacre," have your student complete the "Essay Planner" activity page in the **Show It**.
2. When they are finished, help them evaluate their response using the example in the **Show It AK**.

● ● ●

Spelling Trigraph *dge*

 **Engage**

1. Begin with the **Read It**. As your student reads the content, encourage them to listen to the recordings of the trigraph. Prompt them to repeat the sounds aloud after listening to each audio clip.
2. Then, have your student read the list of spelling words. You may want them to write each word on a sheet of paper or index cards and underline the trigraph *dge*.
3. Then, direct them to complete the vowel sorting activity.
4. Last, move on to the **Practice It** for your student to complete the activity. Spelling practice activities for this subtopic will span Lessons 154 through 156.

LESSON 155

Topic	Poetry

Learning Objectives

The activities in this lesson will help your student meet the following objectives:

- interpret a poem
- list sources that provide information about a research topic
- spell words with the trigraph *dge*

Materials

- "Farewell, Summer"
- dictionary

Poetry Interpretation

Activate

1. Ask your student what they think an interpreter does.
2. Explain that an interpreter translates for speakers of different languages. They may have seen interpreters on TV who were translating spoken words into American Sign Language (ASL), which is used by the Deaf community.
3. Then, ask them what it means to interpret. (Answer: explain the meaning of something) To continue with the example, the interpreters explain the meaning of the spoken words to the Deaf community using ASL.

Engage

1. Starting with the **Read It**, have your student work through the content.
2. Allow them time to read the example poem and interpret it using the steps in the reading before moving on to check the accuracy of their interpretation.
3. Next, have your student open and view the **Poetry Interpretation - Watch It**. Encourage them to pay close attention to the process of interpreting a poem.
4. Your student may use the **Play Its** titled **Plutarch's Library-The Long Ride** and **Plutarch's Library-Cinquain** as needed.

Demonstrate

1. Open the **Assess It** and have your student complete the activity using the text "Farewell, Summer."
2. When they are finished, scan the document or take a photo of it and upload it to the Dropbox. For additional instructions on how to use the Dropbox, click on the paper clip icon in the upper-left corner of the **Assess It**.

● ● ●

Sources

 **Engage**

1. As your student reads the content of the **Read It**, encourage them to write down the types of reliable sources they would be able to use when researching.
2. Then, have them open and view the **Research Sources - Watch It**.
3. Afterward, ask your student why it is important to get information from a variety of sources. (Answer: to get a broader picture of the topic)

 **Demonstrate**

1. Move on to the **Show It** and have your student complete the activity.
2. When they are finished, have them evaluate their list using the example in the **Show It AK**.
3. As your student continues to research and learn about a variety of topics, work with them to choose sources that are reliable, especially those on the Internet. Encourage your student to read carefully, looking for bias or misleading information.

● ● ●

Spelling Trigraph *dge*

 **Engage**

1. For extra practice with their spelling words, have your student complete the **Practice It** activity. If time allows, encourage them to play the game more than once. Spelling practice activities for this subtopic will span Lessons 154 through 156.

LESSON 156

Topic | Poetry

Learning Objectives

The activities in this lesson will help your student meet the following objectives:

- read a poem at an appropriate rate
- research a topic on the Internet
- spell words with the trigraph *dge*

Materials

- "Our Nature" and "Night Flying: A Roundabout"
- dictionary

Poetry Presentation Skills

Activate

1. Find a poem that is read aloud online. A good search phrase to use is "spoken word poetry for kids."
2. Encourage your student to listen to the poem. Then, ask them the following questions.
   - What do they notice about the poem?
   - Is it easier to understand when it is read aloud?
   - Do they think the poem would be better if they could just read it silently?

Engage

1. Now, have your student read the content of the **Read It**.
2. As they read the poem "Our Nature" aloud, give them feedback about their strengths and areas in which they can improve. Encourage them to read the poem several times until they are satisfied with their performance.

Demonstrate

1. Now, have your student complete the activity in the **Show It** using "Night Flying: A Roundabout."
2. Prompt them to use the **Show It AK** to confirm that they have met the criteria for the activity.

• • •

Research Topic

Engage

1. As your student reads the content of the **Read It**, encourage them to pay close attention to the guidelines for determining a website's reliability.
2. Engage your student in a discussion about the sites they visit frequently. How do they know that they are reliable?

Demonstrate

1. Move on to the **Show It** and have your student complete the activity. You may need to work with them to determine if the websites they have chosen are reliable. It may be helpful to show your student an unreliable site so that they are able to compare the two.
2. When they are finished, have them evaluate their response using the example in the **Show It AK**.

• • •

Spelling Trigraph *dge*

Engage

1. For extra practice with their spelling words, have your student complete the **Practice It** activity. They may play multiple rounds of the game for extra practice, each time trying to complete the activity faster than the previous time. Spelling practice activities for this subtopic will span Lessons 154 through 156.

LESSON 157

Topic | Poetry

Learning Objectives

The activities in this lesson will help your student meet the following objectives:

- read aloud a poem with changes in pitch, rhythm, volume, and tone
- describe items using simile comparisons
- spell words with the trigraph *dge*

Materials

- "The Lumberjack"
- colored pencils
- dictionary
- dry erase board and marker

Poetry Oral Expression

Activate

1. Prompt your student to look up another poem online that is read aloud. Have them use the search phrase, "spoken word poetry for kids."
2. After watching, ask them the following questions.
   - What do they notice about the speaker?
   - Does their expression change or remain the same throughout the poem?
   - Do they think the poem would be better if they could just read it silently?

Engage

1. Next, have your student read the content of the **Read It**.
2. Encourage them to look up another spoken word poem, and, this time, have them focus on the pitch, rhythm, volume, and tone of the speaker. Now, use the search phrase, "clean spoken word poetry." This search yields results with more experienced poets, which may help your student to pick out their various expressions.

Demonstrate

1. Open the **Assess It** and have your student complete the activity. Be sure they review the expectations of the rubric before, during, and after they complete the activity.
2. When they are finished, scan the checklist or take a photo of it and upload it to the Dropbox. You may also want to include notes about your student's performance. For additional instructions on how to use the Dropbox, click on the paper clip icon in the upper-left corner of the **Assess It**.

● ● ●

Simile Comparisons

Activate

1. Read the following simile to your student, and ask them to draw what they picture in their mind on the dry erase board.
   - This is as boring as watching paint dry.

Engage

1. Begin with the **Read It**. Have your student read the content.
2. Encourage them to brainstorm similes for the images in the flip-book before reading the examples given below.

Demonstrate

1. Move on to the **Show It**, and have your student complete the activity. As an added challenge, have them illustrate one or two of their similes.
2. When your student is finished, have them use the **Show It AK** to evaluate their work.
3. To reinforce learning, when your student sees a simile in a text they are reading, have them point it out and explain its meaning.

• • •

Spelling Trigraph *dge*

Engage

1. Instruct your student to review and practice the spelling words a few times before they complete the **Assess It**.

Demonstrate

1. Now, move on to the **Assess It**. Have your student write, and correctly spell, the words they hear spoken in the assessment. This assessment covers the spelling words presented in Lessons 154 through 156.
2. When they are finished, scan the document or take a photo of it and upload it to the Dropbox. For additional instructions on how to use the Dropbox, click on the paper clip icon in the upper-left corner of the **Assess It**.
3. The next lesson is a **Mastery Assess It**. Encourage your student to review Lessons 146 through 157 in order to prepare for the assessment.

LESSON 158

Topic	Poetry

Learning Objectives

The activities in this lesson will help your student meet the following objectives:

- not applicable

Materials

- none required

Mastery Assess It 11

1. **Mastery Assess It 11** will cover what your student has learned in Lessons 146 through 157.
2. Click on the **Mastery Assess It 11** icon to begin the online assessment.
3. Have your student read the instructions before they get started. Remind them to take their time and to do their best work.
4. When they are finished and ready for their assessment to be graded, have them click the **Submit** button.

LESSON 159

Topic	Drama

Learning Objectives

The activities in this lesson will help your student meet the following objectives:

- summarize a drama
- use word processing skills to type a paragraph
- spell words with the soft *c* sound

Materials

- *The Great Aluminum Knight* and *The Secret Club*
- colored pencils
- dictionary
- word processing program

Sum It Up

Activate

1. Ask your student to draw three pictures in their journal that show the beginning, middle, and end of their favorite story.
2. Then, ask them to explain the pictures and summarize the story.

Engage

1. While your student reads the dramas in the **Read It**, consider dividing up the roles so that you both take turns reading from the script.
2. Then, have them summarize the drama before they read the sample summary.

Demonstrate

1. Now, direct your student to complete the **Show It** activity.
2. Then, work with them to compare their summary to the example in the **Show It AK**.
3. To reinforce learning, instruct your student to complete the activities in the **Extend It**. Prompt them to check their response using the answer key at the bottom of the page.

● ● ●

Word Processing

 **Engage**

1. As your student reads the content of the **Read It**, help them to open a new document in a word processing program as they follow the steps in the text.

 **Demonstrate**

1. Have your student move on to the **Show It** activity. Help them brainstorm a topic to write about.
2. Then, use the **Show It AK** to check that your student's paragraph meets the expectations for the activity. If they need help getting started, allow them to view the sample paragraph.

● ● ●

Spelling with Soft *c*

 **Activate**

1. Have your student write the words *city* and *cat* in their journal. Then, instruct them to circle the letter *c* in each word.
2. Next, ask them, "What sound does the letter *c* make in these words?" (Answer: The *c* makes an /s/ sound in the word *city*, and it makes a /k/ sound in the word *cat*.)

 **Engage**

1. As your student reads the **Read It**, have them write the rules for hard and soft *c* in their journal.
2. Then, instruct them to write the spelling words in their journal. Direct them to use a dictionary to look up the definitions of any unknown words. Have them include the definitions in their journal as well.
3. Finally, guide them to open the **Practice It** and complete the exercise. Spelling practice activities for this subtopic will span Lessons 159 through 161.

LESSON 160

Topic	Drama

Learning Objectives

The activities in this lesson will help your student meet the following objectives:

- incorporate similes in a character sketch
- use spell-check to check a document for spelling errors
- spell words with the soft *c* sound

Materials

- colored pencils
- magazine article
- word processing software

Similes Character Sketch

Activate

1. Begin by instructing your student to open the **Just a Figure of Speech - Watch It** to view the video.
2. Then, have them explain the meaning of the term *figurative language*. Figurative language is used to describe something by using words that are not literal.

Engage

1. Guide your student to read the text of the **Read It**.
2. Ask them to explain why similes are used in writing. (Answer: Similes compare things and can provide the reader with a better mental picture.)
3. Then, prompt your student to verbally create their own simile that describes a character from their favorite movie or TV show.

Demonstrate

1. Now, direct your student to complete the activity in the **Show It**. Encourage them to include an illustration with their character sketch.
2. Finally, allow your student to compare their character sketch to the sample in the **Show It AK**.

● ● ●

Spell-Check

 Activate

1. Begin by having your student read a paragraph from a magazine article, starting at the bottom and working their way to the top.
2. Then ask them, "What did you notice when you read the sentences backward?" They may have noticed that they read more slowly. Discuss how this practice will help them catch spelling errors because their eyes will slow down to look at each word more carefully.

 Engage

1. As your student reads through the **Read It**, help them find the spell-check function in a word processing program while they follow the steps in the text.
2. If the steps are different than those presented in the text, help them to write a set of steps in their journal that they can follow independently.

 Demonstrate

1. Now, have your student move on to the **Show It** activities.
   a. Help them copy and paste the paragraph by highlighting it with the mouse.
   b. Then, right-click the mouse button and select "Copy."
   c. Next, open a blank word processing document and right-click again and select "Paste." The paragraph should appear on the word processing document.
2. Then, use the **Show It AK** to help your student check their answers.

Spelling with Soft *c*

 Engage

1. Begin by reviewing the soft *c* rule with your student. The letter *c* is soft when followed by the letters *i*, *e*, or *y*.
2. Last, guide them to complete the exercise in the **Practice It**. Spelling practice activities for this subtopic will span Lessons 159 through 161.

LESSON 161

Topic	Drama

Learning Objectives

The activities in this lesson will help your student meet the following objectives:

- describe people using metaphors
- determine the theme of a drama from details in the text
- spell words with the soft *c* sound

Materials

- *Different Colors: A Play*
- colored pencils

Metaphor Descriptions

Activate

1. Guide your student to open the **Similes and Metaphors - Watch It** to view the video.
2. Then, discuss the difference between similes and metaphors. Similes use the words *like* or *as* to compare two things. Metaphors call an object something else and do not use the words *like* or *as*.

Engage

1. After your student reads the contents of the **Read It**, prompt them to use a metaphor to describe themselves. Instruct them to write the sentence in their journal and draw a picture to go with it.

Demonstrate

1. Now, instruct your student to complete the activity in the **Show It**. Have them create a chart in their journal, similar to the one below. Tell them to include ten rows so that they can list 10 people for the metaphor-writing activity.

Person	Metaphor

2. Then, help them compare their metaphors to the samples provided in the **Show It AK**. Prompt them to explain why they chose each metaphor for the person they are describing.

• • •

318

Theme of a Drama

 ## Activate

1. Ask your student to think about their favorite movie, story, or fable. Ask them if they can identify the theme, the central idea or message the author is trying to get across. If you student is unsure, continue to the **Read It** and then come back to this question.

 ## Engage

1. Instruct your student to read the **Read It**. Divide the roles for the example drama and read it with your student.
2. Then, discuss the author's message. Ask them, "What does the author want you to learn from the script?"

 ## Demonstrate

1. Now, guide your student to determine the theme of the drama in the **Show It**. Offer to read some of the lines in the script so that it becomes more interactive. Encourage them to print the script, reread it, and mark supporting details that connect with the theme.
2. Then, work with your student to check their response with the **Show It AK**.
3. To extend learning, reread the drama with your student while acting out the character's movements.

Spelling Soft *c*

 ## Engage

1. Have your student complete the activity in the **Practice It**. Spelling practice activities for this subtopic will span Lessons 159 through 161.

LESSON 162

Topic	Drama

Learning Objectives

The activities in this lesson will help your student meet the following objectives:

- read and comprehend a drama
- publish a final copy of an essay
- spell words with the soft *c* sound

Materials

- *The Vision of Gwen* and *Making Dad Stay*
- previously written essay draft
- stuffed animals
- word processing software

Drama Comprehension

Activate

1. Start by having your student act out a story with stuffed animals like a puppet show. Allow them to make up a story or retell one that they know.
2. Then, discuss what they had to make the stuffed animals do in order to tell the story well. They may respond by saying that the animals needed to say parts of the story so that the audience knew what was happening in the play.

Engage

1. Have your student read the content of the **Read It**. Then, allow them to choose a role in the play to read while you read for the other character. If they are unclear about the plot of the drama, have them reread it.
2. Then, guide them to play the game in the **Plutarch's Library-Romeo and Juliet - Play It**.

Demonstrate

1. Now, instruct your student to complete the **Show It** activity.
2. Then, help them check their answers with the **Show It AK**.

• • •

Final Copy

 ## Activate

1. Start by having your student open and view the **Publishing - Watch It** to learn about writing a final draft.
2. Then, discuss when a piece of writing is ready for publishing. A piece of writing is ready for publishing when it has been revised and edited.

 ## Engage

1. As your student reads the **Read It**, show them how to open a new document in a word processing program on a computer.
2. If the steps are different than those presented in the text, help them to write a set of steps in their journal that they can reference.

 ## Demonstrate

1. Open the **Assess It** and have your student complete the activity. Be sure that they review the expectations of the rubric before and after writing.
2. When they are finished, scan the document or take a photo of it and upload it to the Dropbox. For additional instructions on how to use the Dropbox, click on the paper clip icon in the upper-left corner of the **Assess It**.

Spelling with Soft *c*

 ## Engage

1. Encourage your student to review the list of spelling words from Lesson 159 before they complete the **Assess It**.

 ## Demonstrate

1. Now, move on to the **Assess It**. Have your student write, and correctly spell, the words they hear spoken in the assessment. This assessment covers the spelling words presented in Lessons 159 through 161.
2. When they are finished, scan the document or take a photo of it and upload it to the Dropbox. For additional instructions on how to use the Dropbox, click on the paper clip icon in the upper-left corner of the **Assess It**.

LESSON 163

| Topic | Drama |

Learning Objectives

The activities in this lesson will help your student meet the following objectives:

- create a character map for a main character in a drama
- compare the literal meaning of a metaphor to its figurative meaning
- spell words with the soft *g* sound

Materials

- *Making Dad Stay*
- dictionary
- index cards
- markers
- "Character Map" activity page

Drama Character

Activate

1. Start by having your student open the **Character Traits - Watch It** to view the video.
2. Then, ask them to name the three main types of character traits. (Answer: Physical, emotional, and behavioral traits are three ways to describe a character's qualities.)

Engage

1. Instruct your student to read through the content of the **Read It**.
2. Have them take notes in their journal on the ways in which they can learn more about a character.
3. Direct your student to focus on the "Character Map" activity page and discuss its content. They will use this activity page in the **Show It**.

Demonstrate

1. Now, guide your student to complete the **Show It** using the "Character Map" activity page as they read *Making Dad Stay*.
2. Then, use the **Show It AK** and help your student to compare their response to the sample.

● ● ●

Metaphor Meanings

 ## Activate

1. Have your student open the **Metaphor Meanings - Watch It** to review the use of metaphors.
2. Then, ask them to explain the difference between literal and figurative language. Literal language says exactly what something is while figurative language calls it something else based on similar qualities.

 ## Engage

1. As your student reads the **Read It**, have them pay special attention to the literal and figurative comparison paragraph for the following metaphor: The slide on the playground was an oven.
2. Explain to your student that this paragraph shows the type of response they will need to give in the **Show It**.

 ## Demonstrate

1. Now, have your student move on to the activity in the **Show It**.
2. Then, help them reference the sample paragraph in the **Show It AK** to compare their response.

Spelling with Soft *g*

 ## Activate

1. Begin by reading the following sentence to your student:
   The generous gentle giant gestured gingerly to the gypsy.
2. Then ask them, "What sound did you hear the most?" (Answer: /j/ sound)
3. Next, discuss that the /j/ sound in these words is spelled with the letter *g*.

 ## Engage

1. As your student reads through the **Read It**, prompt them to make a connection between the soft *c* and soft *g* rule. Both letters make a soft sound when the letters *e*, *i*, or *y* follow them.
2. Instruct your student to write the list of spelling words on index cards. Then, tell them to underline the soft *g* and the letter that makes it soft. For example, the letters *gi* in the word *gigantic* should be underlined.
3. Then, direct them to play the spelling game in the **Practice It**. Spelling practice activities for this subtopic will span Lessons 163 through 165.

LESSON 164

Topic	Drama

Learning Objectives

The activities in this lesson will help your student meet the following objectives:

- describe and illustrate the setting of a text
- write a poem that contains a metaphor
- spell words with the soft *g* sound

Materials

- "A Battle among the Stars"
- art supplies
- spelling flashcards
- teacher- or student-selected text

Setting

Activate

1. Start by having your student open the **Setting - Watch It** to view the video.
2. Then ask them, "What are the three main parts of a setting?" (Answer: Time, place, and environment are the three main parts of a setting.)

Engage

1. After your student reads the content of the **Read It**, prompt them to describe the setting of their last birthday. Tell them to describe the time, place, and environment.

Demonstrate

1. Now, instruct your student to complete the **Show It** activity.
2. Then, have them reference the **Show It AK** to review an example answer.
3. Finally, direct your student to complete the activity in the Application section of the **Show It**.

Metaphor Poem

Engage

1. While your student reads the **Read It**, have them share what they visualize when reading the poems.

Demonstrate

1. Now, open the **Assess It** and have your student complete the activity. Help them to understand the expectations of the rubric before they begin writing. When they are finished, help them to review their work to make sure they have met the rubric expectations.
2. Then, scan the document or take a photo of it and upload it to the Dropbox. For additional instructions on how to use the Dropbox, click on the paper clip icon in the upper-left corner of the **Assess It**.

Spelling with Soft *g*

Engage

1. Guide your student to shuffle their spelling flashcards from Lesson 163. Then, prompt them to sort the words by their soft *g* spelling patterns: *gi*, *ge*, or *gy*.
2. Last, have them complete the activity in the **Practice It**. Spelling practice activities for this subtopic will span Lessons 163 through 165.

LESSON 165

Topic	Drama

Learning Objectives

The activities in this lesson will help your student meet the following objectives:

- create an in-depth profile of a character from a text
- replace words in a poem with synonyms
- spell words with the soft *g* sound

Materials

- "Friendly Competition"
- "Blank Character Profile" activity page

Character Profile

Activate

1. Ask your student to describe themselves. What do they look like physically? What is their personality like? What are their interests?
2. Explain to them that these traits are the things an author considers when developing a character in a story.

Engage

1. Begin with the **Read It**. Have your student read all of the content, pausing to discuss the five categories of a character profile. As your student reads, encourage them to write these categories in their journal.
2. Then, ask your student to think of their favorite character from a story they have read and describe them using the character profile.

Demonstrate

1. Open the **Assess It** and have your student complete the activity. Help them to understand the expectations of the rubric before they begin writing. When they are finished, help them to review their work to make sure they have met the rubric expectations.
2. Then, scan the document or take a photo of it and upload it to the Dropbox. For additional instructions on how to use the Dropbox, click on the paper clip icon in the upper-left corner of the **Assess It**.

● ● ●

Synonyms in Poems

 ## Activate

1. Ask your student to explain the meaning of the word synonym. (Answer: a word that has the same or similar meaning as another word.)
2. Then, ask them to share a word that is more descriptive than the word *good*.

 ## Engage

1. As your student reads the content of the **Read It**, engage them in a discussion about how the words in the second version of "Roller Coaster Ride" create imagery that is more vivid than in the first version.
2. Then, have your student match synonyms by completing the drag and drop activity.

 ## Demonstrate

1. Open the **Assess It** and have your student complete the activity. Be sure that they review the expectations of the rubric before and after writing.
2. When they are finished, scan the document or take a photo of it and upload it to the Dropbox. For additional instructions on how to use the Dropbox, click on the paper clip icon in the upper-left corner of the **Assess It**.
3. To extend learning, occasionally challenge your student to think of an alternative word in the stories or poems they read. Can they think of a more descriptive word than the existing one?

Spelling with Soft *g*

 ## Engage

1. To give your student extra practice with their spelling words, instruct them to complete the activity in the **Practice It**. If time permits, encourage them to play the game more than once. Spelling practice activities for this subtopic will span Lessons 163 through 165.

Topic	Drama

Learning Objectives

The activities in this lesson will help your student meet the following objectives:

- make a connection between the text of a drama and how it is read aloud
- compare and contrast the character traits of main characters in a text

Materials

- "Friendly Competition," *The Great Aluminum Knight*, and *The Hat*
- teacher- or student-selected text
- "Character Traits" activity page

Drama Connections

Activate

1. Ask your student if they have ever seen a play. If they have, ask them to share details about their experience. If they have not, ask them to share details about a television program that they enjoy watching. What is the setting like? How do the characters interact?
2. Explain to them that characters, or actors, in a play or television show have to memorize a script that includes their spoken lines and stage directions.
3. Tell your student that a drama, or play, is a text that is meant to be acted out.

Engage

1. Then, have your student read through the content of the **Read It**. When they are finished, have them return to the script example for David and act it out.
2. Ask them to point out the different details in the script, such as the character's name, his lines, and the stage directions noted in italics and brackets.
3. Next, direct your student to open and view the **Act It Out: The Play - Watch It**. Ask them to explain why the setting is important in a play. How do costumes and props enhance a play or performance?

Demonstrate

1. Next, have your student complete the activity in the **Show It**.
2. Using the **Show It AK**, work with your student and help them to compare their answers to the samples provided.
3. To extend the learning, encourage your student to act out the play *The Great Aluminum Knight* with several friends. Have them think about what the setting should look like. What props are needed? Have them rehearse the play, following the stage directions and reading the script. Then, have them perform for an audience.

• • •

Compare and Contrast

 Engage

1. Begin with the **Read It**, and have your student read the content. Consider having them print out a copy of the "Examples of Character Traits" table and asking them to fasten it into their journal. This list can also be found in the **Show It**.

2. As your student compares the character traits of two characters in the play *The Hat*, suggest that they use a Venn diagram to organize their thoughts.

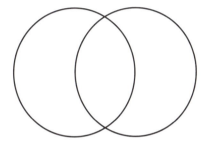

3. Next, have your student engage in the **Plutarch's Library-Characterization - Play It** and decide which words best describe each character.

Demonstrate

1. Now, have your student move on to the **Show It** to complete the activity.

2. Work with your student to evaluate their responses with the **Show It AK**. Invite them to add more details to their table.

3. Finally, direct your student to complete the activity in the Application section of the **Show It**.

LESSON 167

Topic | **Drama**

Learning Objectives

The activities in this lesson will help your student meet the following objectives:

- compare a written skit to a visual presentation of that skit
- replace words in a poem with antonyms
- spell words with the soft *g* sound

Materials

- *The Secret Club*

Skit Connections

Activate

1. Ask your student to share their thoughts about whether or not illustrations can enhance a story.
2. Tell them that illustrations help the reader visualize what a setting may look like.

Engage

1. After your student has read the content of the **Read It**, have them describe the similarities and differences between a play and a skit.
2. Then, discuss why authors include illustrations with their scripts.

Demonstrate

1. Next, have your student move on to the **Show It** to complete the Venn diagram in their journal, comparing the script and illustration in the skit *The Secret Club*.
2. Finally, instruct your student to compare their response to the sample in the **Show It AK**.

• • •

Antonyms in a Poem

 Activate

1. Ask your student to explain the meaning of the word *antonym*. (Answer: a word that means the opposite of another word)
2. Then, ask them to share an antonym for the word *terrific*.

 Engage

1. As your student reads the content of the **Read It**, engage them in a discussion about how the words in the second version of the "The Big Game" create imagery that is more vivid than in the first version.
2. Then, have your student match antonyms by completing the drag-and-drop activity.
3. Prompt your student to open the **Antonyms & Synonyms Search - Watch It** to view the video.
4. During the video, pause as necessary to allow your student to play Jungle Trivia. They will need to identify antonyms for a given word and replace words in a sentence with a synonym.

 Demonstrate

1. Open the **Assess It** and have your student complete the activity. Be sure that they review the expectations of the rubric before and after writing.
2. When they are finished, scan the document or take a photo of it and upload it to the Dropbox. For additional instructions on how to use the Dropbox, click on the paper clip icon in the upper-left corner of the **Assess It**.

Spelling with Soft *g*

 Engage

1. Encourage your student to review the list of spelling words from Lesson 163 before they complete the **Assess It**.

 Demonstrate

1. Now move on to the **Assess It**. Have your student write, and correctly spell, the words they hear spoken in the assessment. This assessment covers the spelling words presented in Lessons 163 through 165.
2. When they are finished, scan the document or take a photo of it and upload it to the Dropbox. For additional instructions on how to use the Dropbox, click on the paper clip icon in the upper-left corner of the **Assess It**.

Topic | Drama

Learning Objectives

The activities in this lesson will help your student meet the following objectives:

- illustrate the similarities and differences between a scene from a drama and the visual or oral presentation of that drama
- write a poem that incorporates precise actions
- spell words in which the digraph *gh* is not silent

Materials

- *The Great Leap*
- "Two Scenes from *The Thief of Camelot*"
- art supplies
- dictionary
- highlighter
- index cards
- shoe box
- "Drama Diorama Comparison" activity page

Drama Comparisons

 ## Activate

1. Ask your student to explain the meaning of the words *similarities* and *differences*. (Answer: *Similarities* means things that are same, and *differences* means things that are different.)
2. Then, ask them to describe similarities they share with a family member. Then, thinking of the same family member, ask them to describe differences. Perhaps, they both enjoy swimming. However, your student may say that spaghetti is their favorite food, but their family member may like tacos.

 ## Engage

1. After your student has read the content of the **Read It**, have them describe the similarities and differences between the play and the illustrations.
2. Take time to review the parts of a script with them including the cast, setting, stage directions, etc.
3. Now, have your student brainstorm ideas of when dioramas would be useful.

 ## Demonstrate

1. Open the **Assess It** and have your student complete the activity. Be sure that they review the expectations of the rubric before and after writing.
2. When they are finished, scan the document or take a photo of it and upload it to the Dropbox. For additional instructions on how to use the Dropbox, click on the paper clip icon in the upper-left corner of the **Assess It**.
3. To extend learning, have your student share their completed diorama with you or a family member. Ask them to explain how it is a 3-D representation of the similarities and differences between the script and illustrations seen in the two scenes from *The Thief of Camelot*.

● ● ●

Precise Action Poem

 Activate

1. Ask your student to explain what it means to do something precisely. (Answer: Doing something precisely means to do something with complete accuracy.)
2. Tell them they will read poems with precise actions, meaning that the verbs in the poems are specific.

 Engage

1. As your student reads the content of the **Read It**, encourage them to share alternative precise action words for the bold words in the examples.
2. Next, explain to them that a thesaurus is a dictionary of synonyms and antonyms. Encourage your student to search the Internet for an online thesaurus. This resource can be used to select precise action words.

 Demonstrate

1. Now, have your student complete the **Show It** activity. Encourage them to read their poem aloud. Then, have them point out the precise action words.
2. Consider allowing your student to read the example poem in the **Show It AK** before they begin the assignment. Doing so may help them to understand the expectations of the activity.
3. To extend learning, consider visiting the library with your student and having them check out a book of poetry. Then, have them identify the precise action words in a few poems of their choice.

Spelling Digraph *gh*

 Engage

1. Begin by instructing your student to read the content of the **Read It**. Consider having them copy the chart provided in the Rules, Patterns, and Examples section into their journal.
2. Next, have your student listen to audio clips of the different sounds made by the digraph *gh*. Encourage them to practice saying the words aloud.
3. Direct your student to read the list of spelling words. You may want them to write each word and its definition in their journal or on an index card.
4. Have your student complete the drag and drop activity to practice using the spelling words.
5. As an opportunity for your student to review their spelling words, have them complete the **Practice It** activity. Encourage them to play multiple rounds of the game so that they can practice spelling all the words. Spelling practice activities for this subtopic will span Lessons 168 to 170.

Topic	Drama

Learning Objectives

The activities in this lesson will help your student meet the following objectives:

- write a drama from provided illustrations
- analyze an author's purpose for creating conflict between two characters in a text
- spell words in which the digraph *gh* is not silent

Materials

- "Liftoff" and "Fingerprints"
- teacher- or student-selected texts

Script Writing

 ### Activate

1. Ask your student to explain the difference between a play and story. (Answer: A play and a story can be similar, but a play is meant to be acted out.)

 ### Engage

1. As your student reads the **Read It**, have them review the parts of a script.
2. Then, have a discussion with them about how a script can be different when it is read versus when it is being acted out or displayed with illustrations.
3. Consider acting out the script, *Francesca's Request*, with your student.

 ### Demonstrate

1. Now, have your student complete the **Show It** activity. Then, have them read their script aloud.
2. Encourage your student to compare their script to the example in the **Show It AK**. If they are having trouble getting started, allow them to view the example before they begin writing.
3. Finally, have your student use their selected text to complete the Application section of the **Show It**.

• • •

Conflict

 ## Activate

1. Ask your student to describe an instance when they experienced a struggle. Perhaps, they were invited to two parties that occurred at the same time. Maybe they were in a situation where one friend was excluding another friend.
2. Explain to them that these are examples of conflict.
3. Tell your student they will learn about how authors intentionally create conflict between characters in literature.

 ## Engage

1. Direct your student to read through the content of the **Read It**. Pause them to review plot structure.
2. Then, discuss the four main types of conflict in literature, challenging your student to think of examples from stories they have read.

 ## Demonstrate

1. Now, move on to the **Show It** and have your student complete the activity.
2. Working together, review the **Show It AK** to compare your student's paragraph to the sample.
3. To reinforce learning, encourage your student to identify types of conflict in their favorite movie.

Spelling Digraph *gh*

 ## Engage

1. To aid your student in reviewing their spelling words, have them complete the activity in the **Practice It**. Spelling practice activities for this subtopic will span Lessons 168 to 170.

LESSON 170

Topic	Drama

Learning Objectives

The activities in this lesson will help your student meet the following objectives:

- write a poem that illustrates precise emotions
- analyze how a story event affected the outcome
- spell words in which the digraph *gh* is not silent

Materials

- "The Dagda's Harp: A Celtic Myth"
- dry erase board and marker
- highlighter

Precise Emotion Poem

 ## Activate

1. Ask your student what it means to be emotional. (Answer: When someone is emotional, they are expressing a feeling of love, anger, fear, sadness, etc.)
2. Then, have them share a time when they have been emotional. For example, did they ever score a goal during a sporting event where they were elated? Perhaps they were angry when a sibling borrowed something of theirs without asking.
3. Explain that they will learn about poems that evoke certain emotions.

 ## Engage

1. As your student reads the **Read It**, have them share additional adjectives for the words used in the examples.
2. Next, remind them that a thesaurus is a dictionary of synonyms and antonyms. Encourage them to search the Internet for an online thesaurus. This resource can be used to select alternative words that evoke stronger emotions than the original adjectives used in the poem.
3. Write the following words on the dry erase board.
   - happy
   - sad
   - angry
4. Then, ask your student to brainstorm words that can evoke more precise emotion. If necessary, have them use a online thesaurus as a resource. Possible answers have been provided below for your reference.
   - happy (Possible answers: elated or ecstatic)
   - sad (Possible answers: disheartened or disappointed)
   - angry (Possible answer: outraged or appalled)

Demonstrate

1. Now, have your student complete the **Show It** activity. Remind them to write eight lines in their poem and highlight the precise emotion words. Encourage them to read their poem aloud.
2. To help your student understand the expectations of the activity, consider allowing them to read the example in the **Show It AK** before they begin.

Analyze Event

Activate

1. Encourage your student to share a personal story with a positive ending. For instance, a baseball player spent time each day at batting practice and then hit a home run to win the game for the team.
2. Ask them, "Would the outcome change if the player did things differently?" If the player did not practice often, perhaps they would have struck out instead of hitting a home run.

Engage

1. As your student reads the **Read It**, have them write the guiding questions from the Event Analysis section in their journal to use as a reference.
2. Discuss with your student the significance of the pivotal event in a story. Then, have them share the pivotal event in their favorite story or movie.
3. To extend learning, consider taking your student to the library. Ask a librarian to recommend books that have alternative endings. In these books, the reader selects the pivotal event that leads to a specific outcome. Encourage your student to read each of the endings to see how they compare.

Demonstrate

1. Move on to the **Show It** and have your student complete the activity.
   a. Instruct your student to read over the event analysis questions before they begin reading the story "The Dagda's Harp: A Celtic Myth."
   b. Consider printing the story and encouraging your student to highlight the parts that answer any of the questions.
   c. Once they have finished reading, tell them to return to the highlighted sections of the story when answering the event analysis questions.
2. Use the **Show It AK** and work with your student to check their answers.

Spelling Digraph *gh*

Engage

1. To give your student extra practice with their spelling words, have them complete the activity in the **Practice It**. If time permits, allow them to play the game more than once. Spelling practice activities for this subtopic will span Lessons 168 through 170.

LESSON 171

Topic	Drama

Learning Objectives

The activities in this lesson will help your student meet the following objective:

- describe how poetry, drama, and prose are arranged differently

Materials

- "The Fundamental States of Matter," and "Ribbons in the Breeze"
- *The Vision of Gwen*

Arrangement of Text

 ## Activate

1. Ask your student to describe how prose, poetry, and drama are structured. Prose uses paragraphs; poetry uses stanzas; and drama uses scripts.

 ## Engage

1. Have your student read the content of the **Read It**. Prompt them to write the common elements for prose, poetry, and dramas in their journal.
2. Have a discussion with your student about the differences between the three types of text.
3. Then, direct your student to view the **Parts of a Script - Watch It**. When your student is finished watching, ask them to reiterate the structure of a script. Prompt them to explain why the stage directions are important. (Answer: Stage directions can specify the actions of the characters.)
4. Next, have your student open the **Characteristics of Poetry - Watch It**. Ask your student how poets incorporate figurative language into their writing. (Answer: Poets may choose to be descriptive, using figurative language to compare one thing to another. Idioms, similes, and metaphors are types of figurative language.)
5. Finally, have your student engage in the **Plutarch's Library-Literature Vocabulary - Play It**. This game reinforces vocabulary common in literature.

 ## Demonstrate

1. Now, move on to the **Show It** and have your student complete the activity.
2. Review the **Show It AK** with your student, and help them to compare their paragraph to the sample.
3. To extend learning, have your student share their favorite drama or television show, poem, and prose. Why are these their favorite?

LESSON 172

Topic	Drama

Learning Objectives

The activities in this lesson will help your student meet the following objectives:

- research the time period in which a story takes place to determine if the author portrayed it accurately
- write synonyms for unfamiliar words
- spell words in which the digraph *gh* is not silent

Materials

- "Snow-White"
- dry erase board and marker

Time Period

Activate

1. Ask your student to share a story they have read where the setting takes place in the past. If they cannot recall a book they have read, ask them to share a movie instead. For example, in the story *George Washington's Socks*, by Elvira Woodruff, a campout with several young characters turns into an experience during American colonial times.

Engage

1. Begin with the **Read It** and have your student read the content. Ask them to explain the parts of a story that can depict a time period. (Answer: location, language, description of the characters' wardrobes, dates, etc.)
2. Then, have your student identify the elements of the story they shared in the Activate section that indicate it takes place in the past.
3. Your student may not have read *George Washington's Socks*; however, ask them what elements of the story could suggest that it takes place during colonial times. (Answer: George Washington lived during the colonial times.)

Demonstrate

1. Next, have your student read "Snow-White" and complete the activity in the **Show It**.
2. Use the **Show It AK** to make sure your student's work meets the criteria. Allow them to compare their paragraph to the example provided.

• • •

Synonyms for Unfamiliar Words

 **Activate**

1. Ask your student to explain the meaning of a context clue. (Answer: Context clues are hints or clues that an author gives in a sentence that helps the reader define difficult words.)
2. Write the following sentence on a dry erase board. Have your student identify the meaning of the bold word using context clues: Jenn was **lethargic** from staying up late studying.
3. *Lethargic* means having a lack of energy. The clue, **staying up late**, helps the reader to understand the meaning of the word.
4. Tell your student that synonyms can be used as context clues to help define unknown words.

 **Engage**

1. As your student reads the content of the **Read It**, engage them in a discussion about ways to find the meaning of unfamiliar words.
2. Remind them that a thesaurus is a great resource for finding a list of synonyms for an unknown word.
3. Next, have your student engage in the **Carnival Racers-Synonyms - Play It**.

 **Demonstrate**

1. Now, have your student move on to the **Show It** and list at least two synonyms for the words in bold. If they have difficulty completing this activity, suggest that they use an online thesaurus as a resource.
2. Assist your student in checking their work with the **Show It AK**. Encourage your student to add additional synonyms to their list.
3. To extend learning, create a Mad Lib for your student to complete.
   a. Choose a poem or a paragraph from a short story.
   b. Cross out the adjectives.
   c. Ask your student to share a synonym for each adjective that is crossed out. For example, if the word *sad* is crossed out, your student could say *devastated*.
   d. Read the poem the way it was originally written.
   e. Then, read the poem with the adjectives your student suggested.

● ● ●

Spelling Digraph *gh*

 **Engage**

1. Encourage your student to review and practice their spelling words before they complete the **Assess It**.

 **Demonstrate**

1. Now, move on to the **Assess It**. Have your student write, and correctly spell, the words they hear spoken in the assessment. This assessment covers the spelling words presented in Lessons 168 through 170.
2. When they are finished, scan the document or take a photo of it and upload it to the Dropbox. For additional instructions on how to use the Dropbox, click on the paper clip icon in the upper-left corner of the **Assess It**.

LESSON 173

Topic	Drama

Learning Objectives

The activities in this lesson will help your student meet the following objectives:

- explain how structural elements of poetry, drama, and prose affect a reader's experience of events and ideas in a text
- spell words with the digraph *gu*

Materials

- *Different Colors: A Play*
- "Seasons Change"
- dictionary
- index cards

Structural Elements

Activate

1. Have your student open and view the **Text Structure and Genre - Watch It**.
2. Pause the video at 5:07, and have them complete the activity identifying the phrases that describe a poem, a drama, and a book.

Engage

1. Next, have your student complete the **Read It**.
2. Ask them to explain the difference between prose and poetry. Encourage them to refer to the **Read It** for help, if necessary.
3. As your student reads "Seasons Change," consider having them point out the lines and stanzas in the poem. Then, have them point out the parts of the drama while they read *Different Colors: A Play*.

Demonstrate

1. Then, have your student complete the activity in the **Show It**. Remind them to include specific vocabulary terms in their response.
2. Use the **Show It AK** and work with your student to compare their answer to the example provided.

Spelling Digraphs *gu*

Engage

1. Begin with the **Read It** and have your student read the content.
2. Direct your student to listen to the audio clip for the digraph *gu*.
3. Next, have them read the list of spelling words. You may want your student to write each word and its definition in their journal or on an index card.
4. Have your student complete the word search activities to practice using the spelling words.
5. As an opportunity for your student to review their spelling words, have them complete the **Practice It** activity. Encourage them to play multiple rounds of the game so that they can practice all the words. Spelling practice activities for this subtopic will span Lessons 173 through 175.

LESSON 174

| Topic | Drama |

Learning Objectives

The activities in this lesson will help your student meet the following objectives:

- construct sentences that contain antonyms for unfamiliar words
- spell words with the digraph *gu*

Materials

- none required

Antonyms for Unfamiliar Words

Activate

1. Ask your student to explain the meaning of an antonym. (Answer: An antonym is a word that has the opposite meaning of another word.)
2. Then, ask them to state an antonym for each of the following words:
   a. disappointed (Possible answer: excited)
   b. joyful (Possible answer: sorrowful)
   c. nervous (Possible answer: calm)

Engage

1. As your student reads the content of the **Read It**, engage them in a discussion about ways to find the meaning of unknown words.
2. Remind them that a thesaurus is a great resource for finding a list of antonyms.
3. Next, have your student play the **Carnival Racers-Antonyms - Play It**.
4. Then, direct your student to complete the **Practice It** activity to review synonyms, antonyms, and homographs.

Demonstrate

1. Now, have your student move on to the **Show It** and complete the activity. If they are struggling, suggest that they use an online thesaurus as a resource.
2. Then, use the **Show It AK** and work with your student to review their answers.
3. To extend learning, ask your student to provide an antonym for words they observe on billboards they encounter during their travels.

• • •

Spelling Digraphs *gu*

Engage

1. Use the **Practice It** activity to give your student extra practice with their spelling words. If time permits, encourage them to play the game more than once. Spelling practice activities for this subtopic will span Lessons 173 through 175.

LESSON 175

Topic	Drama

Learning Objectives

The activities in this lesson will help your student meet the following objectives:

- examine the supporting reasons an author uses in a text
- use the correct forms of frequently confused words
- spell words with the digraph *gu*

Materials

- "California Gold Rush"
- "John Adams and the Boston Massacre"
- dictionary
- teacher- or student-selected text

Supporting Reasons

Activate

1. Have your student open and view the **Author's Argument - Watch It**.
2. Pause the video at 4:23 to allow your student time to identify the three specific claims that support the argument of why soda should be banned from schools. Have a discussion with your student about how this argument differs from the first.
3. Then, pause the video at 5:37 to allow your student to write the bullet points in their journal. These points are items to keep in mind when evaluating an author's argument.

Engage

1. Now, have your student work through the content of the **Read It**.
2. After they read, ask them to explain why an author's argument should be supported with facts and not opinions. (Answer: Authors who use facts to support their argument show that their work is valid.)

Demonstrate

1. Now move on to the **Show It** and have your student complete the activity.
2. Then, use the **Show It AK** to help your student evaluate their response. Discuss any of the supporting details they did not include.
3. Finally, prompt your student to use their selected text to complete the Application section of the **Show It**.

• • •

Use the Right Word

Activate

1. Ask your student if they remember what word describes words that sound alike, but are spelled differently and have different meanings. (Answer: *homophones*)
2. Then, ask them if they can share an example of words that are homophones.

Engage

1. Start with the **Read It**. Ask your student if they know another homophone for *their* and *there* that is occasionally misused. (Answer: they're)
2. Challenge your student to use the following homophones correctly in a sentence:
   - sore/soar
   - sweet/suite
   - course/coarse
3. Next, instruct your student to open the **Homophones and Homographs - Watch It**.
   a. Pause the video as needed to allow your student time to identify the correct homophone in each sentence.
   b. Then, pause the video again, at various times, to allow your student to select the correct homograph.
   c. Afterward, ask your student to share the mnemonic device mentioned in the video for understanding the difference between a homophone and a homograph. (Answer: The word *homophone* has *phone* in it. Homophones are words that sound the same. *Homograph* includes the word *graph*. A graph is something you draw. These are words that look the same.)

Demonstrate

1. Then, have your student complete the activity in the **Show It**.
2. Finally, instruct your student to use the **Show It AK** to check their answers. Discuss any incorrect answers.

Spelling Digraphs *gu*

Engage

1. To give your student extra practice with their spelling words, have them complete the activity in the **Practice It**. If time permits, encourage them to play the game more than once. Spelling practice activities for this subtopic will span Lessons 173 through 175.

Topic | **Drama**

Learning Objectives

The activities in this lesson will help your student meet the following objectives:

- identify the similarities and differences among prose, poetry, and drama
- explain why an author uses specific facts to support a point of view

Materials

- "Healthful Habits"
- highlighter
- magazine

Compare Types of Texts

Activate

1. Begin by having your student look through a magazine. Tell them to find an advertisement, a nonfiction article, and a fictional text, such as a story or a comic strip. If the magazine does not have all three of these text types of texts, guide your student in finding at least two of the three.
2. Then, ask them to identify the purpose of each type of text.
   - The advertisement is used to persuade the reader to buy the product.
   - The nonfiction article is used to inform the reader.
   - The fictional text is meant to entertain the audience.

Engage

1. As your student reads the **Read It**, prompt them to share their experiences with reading or writing prose, poetry, and drama. Ask them which type of writing they like the most.

Demonstrate

1. Now, have your student move on to the **Show It**. Encourage them to copy the chart below in their journal and use it to complete the activity.
2. Then, help them to compare their answers to the sample in the **Show It AK**.

Prose, Poetry, Drama	
Similarities	**Differences**

• • •

Point of View

 **Engage**

1. Instruct your student to read the content of the **Read It**.
2. Then, prompt them to describe how they might change the purpose of the text about flying fish from informative to persuasive or entertaining. They may explain that they could change the text to persuade the reader to take a boat or virtual tour to see flying fish.

 **Demonstrate**

1. Now, direct your student to complete the activity in the **Show It**. Encourage your student to print the story and use a highlighter to mark the supporting details in the text.
2. Then, work with them to compare their response to the sample in the **Show It AK**.
3. Finally, direct your student to complete the activity in the Application section in the **Show It**.

LESSON 177

Topic | **Drama**

Learning Objectives

The activities in this lesson will help your student meet the following objectives:

- list homophone pairs that may be frequently confused
- words with the digraph *gu*

Materials

- dictionary

Common Homophones

Activate

1. Start by having your student open the **Homophones & Homographs Search - Watch It** to view the video.
2. Then, have them explain the differences between homophones and homographs.
   - Homophones are words that sound the same but are spelled differently and have different meanings.
   - Homographs are words that are spelled the same and sound the same but have different meanings.

Engage

1. Instruct your student to read the content of the **Read It**. Prompt them to choose a set of homophones and use them in two different sentences.
2. Then, direct them to open the **Play Its** titled **Carnival Racers-Homonyms** and **Carnival Racers-Review** to reinforce their knowledge of homonyms.
3. Next, encourage your student to complete the exercise provided in the **Practice It**.

Demonstrate

1. Guide your student to complete the **Show It** activity. Allow them to use the Internet to find a list of homophones, and have them identify sets that are unfamiliar.
2. Then, use the **Show It AK** to see a sample list of homophones.
3. To extend learning, have your student write sentences for each set of homophones they identified in the **Show It**. Their sentences should show the difference in the meanings of each word pair. They may need to use a dictionary to help them write their sentences.

• • •

Spelling Digraph *gu*

Engage

1. Encourage your student to review the list of spelling words from Lesson 173 before they complete the **Assess It**.

Demonstrate

1. Now, move on to the **Assess It**. Have your student write, and correctly spell, the words they hear spoken in the assessment. This assessment covers the spelling words presented in Lessons 173 through 175.

2. When they are finished, scan the document or take a photo of it and upload it to the Dropbox. For additional instructions on how to use the Dropbox, click on the paper clip icon in the upper-left corner of the **Assess It**.

LESSON 178

Topic	Drama

Learning Objectives

The activities in this lesson will help your student meet the following objectives:

- explain whether the characters in a story are authentically or unrealistically portrayed
- write a reflection on the ideas of an influential historical figure

Materials

- "Fingerprints" and "Frederick Douglass: Abolitionist"
- colored pencils
- comic strip
- highlighter

Reflection in Writing

 ## Activate

1. Begin by having your student read a comic strip. Then, discuss if the characters are portrayed using realistic or unrealistic traits. For example, do any characters have superhuman powers, or do animals talk?
2. Ask them, "Why are these traits used for the characters in the comic strip?" They may mention that these traits allow the characters to progress through the story with the abilities they need.

 ## Engage

1. As your student reads the **Read It**, prompt them to reflect on the authenticity of another character from the *Wizard of Oz* such as the scarecrow. If they are not familiar with the *Wizard of Oz*, allow them to choose a character from a story they know well.
2. Then, engage in a conversation with your student about why authors choose to have realistic and unrealistic characters in their stories. If an author wants the reader to have an experience that seems more real, they will portray the characters accurately. However, to have a more fantastical experience, the author must portray the characters as unreal.

 ## Demonstrate

1. Now, instruct your student to complete the **Show It** activity. Allow them to print the text and use a highlighter to mark the supporting details for each character reflection.
2. Then, help them compare their response to the sample in the **Show It AK**.
3. Finally, direct your student to complete the activity in the Application section of the **Show It**.

• • •

Reflection on Historical Figure

Engage

1. While your student reads the **Read It**, ask them if the reflection on Nelson Mandela reminds them of someone else in history. Help them to make the connection between Nelson Mandela and Dr. Martin Luther King, Jr. Both men fought for equal rights.

Demonstrate

1. Now, have your student move on to the **Show It** activity. Consider printing the text for your student so they can mark important details or take notes.
2. Then, work with them to compare their response to the **Show It AK** example.
3. To extend learning, discuss other important rights for which people have had to fight to achieve. Examples include women's right to vote, land rights, or environmental rights.
   a. Then, help your student research more information about one of these topics.
   b. Encourage them to create a display of information, such as a brochure, to share with others.

LESSON 179

Topic	Drama

Learning Objectives

The activities in this lesson will help your student meet the following objectives:

- compare a character's experience to a real-life situation you have experienced
- write sentences that include commonly confused words

Materials

- "Blue Hole"
- art supplies
- dictionary
- index cards

Character's Actions

Activate

1. Start by having your student open the **Making Connections - Watch It** and ask them to make note of the username and password provided on the Discovery Education image. Be sure that they click the link for the video and enter the provided username and password to watch.
2. Then, pause the video at 3:15 for your student to answer the question.

Engage

1. While your student reads the **Read It**, emphasize how the environment, a situation, or another person may cause a character's reaction.
2. Now, ask your student if they ever made plans to do something fun, but the plans had to be canceled at the last minute. Ask them to share how they felt and how they dealt with the situation.

Demonstrate

1. Next, direct your student to complete the **Show It**. Be sure they create a T-chart as directed in the text. You may need to help them brainstorm situations that would compare to the story, "Blue Hole," after they read it.
2. Then, help your student evaluate their work with the **Show It AK**. Encourage them to compare their response to the sample provided.

• • •

Commonly Confused Words

 ## Activate

1. Prompt your student to use the words *here* and *hear* in two difference sentences. For example:
   - I called the dog over *here*.
   - I can *hear* the band practicing from my house.

 ## Engage

1. As your student reads the **Read It**, have them take note of the commonly misused words in their journal. Encourage them to write a sentence using each word.

 ## Demonstrate

1. Now, instruct your student to complete the **Show It** activity.
2. Finally, help them reference the **Show It AK** to compare their sentences to the examples.
3. To extend learning, have your student write the homophone pairs on index cards. Then, play a memory game with the cards.
   a. Place the cards face down and take turns flipping over two cards at a time to find the pairs.
   b. When a pair is found, the player has to use the words in different sentences.
4. The next lesson is a **Mastery Assess It**. Encourage your student to review Lessons 159 through 179 in order to prepare for the assessment.

LESSON 180

Topic | **Drama**

Learning Objectives

The activities in this lesson will help your student meet the following objectives:

- not applicable

Materials

- none required

Mastery Assess It 12

1. **Mastery Assess It 12** will cover what your student has learned in Lessons 159 through 179.
2. Click on the **Mastery Assess It 12** icon to begin the online assessment.
3. Have your student read the instructions before they get started. Remind them to take their time and to do their best work.
4. When they are finished and ready for their assessment to be graded, have them click the **Submit** button.